EXCHANGE-RATE DEVALUATION IN A SEMI-INDUSTRIALIZED COUNTRY

The Experience of Argentina 1955-1961

M.I.T. MONOGRAPHS IN ECONOMICS

1 *The Natural Resource Content of
   United States Foreign Trade 1870–1955*
   JAROSLAV VANEK

2 *Iron and Steel in Nineteenth-Century America:
   An Economic Inquiry*
   PETER TEMIN

3 *Labor Migration and Economic Growth:
   A Case Study of Puerto Rico*
   STANLEY L. FRIEDLANDER

4 *The Theory of Oil Tankship Rates:
   An Economic Analysis of Tankship Operations*
   ZENON S. ZANNETOS

5 *Exchange-Rate Devaluation in a
   Semi-Industrialized Country:
   The Experience of Argentina 1955–1961*
   CARLOS F. DIAZ ALEJANDRO

6 *Urban Migration and Economic Development in Chile*
   BRUCE H. HERRICK

7 *Unemployment, Money Wage Rates, and Inflation*
   GEORGE L. PERRY

EXCHANGE-RATE DEVALUATION IN A SEMI-INDUSTRIALIZED COUNTRY

The Experience of Argentina 1955-1961

CARLOS F. DIAZ ALEJANDRO

THE M.I.T. PRESS
Massachusetts Institute of Technology
Cambridge, Massachusetts, and London, England

Copyright © 1965
The Massachusetts Institute of Technology

All Rights Reserved. This book may not be reproduced, in whole or in part, in any form (except by reviewers for the public press), without written permission from the publishers.

Library of Congress Catalog Card Number: 66-17553
Printed in the United States of America

ISBN 0-262-51149-5 (paperback)

A M., P., R., B., E., y M.

Preface

This monograph is a revised version of my Ph.D. thesis submitted in September 1961 to the Department of Economics at the Massachusetts Institute of Technology. The revision has left the basic argument and structure of the thesis unchanged, but new data have been incorporated and several sections have been modified and expanded, taking advantage of the recent revision of the Argentine National Accounts as well as of other research with which I became acquainted after completing my doctoral dissertation.

Many persons and institutions helped me during the writing and revision of this work. My greatest debt is to Professor Charles P. Kindleberger, who first suggested to me the topic of the role of income distribution in the analysis of devaluation and who throughout the last five years provided steadfast encouragement and advice. But my debt of gratitude to Professor Kindleberger goes beyond his help on this work and includes the many insights on international trade and methodology obtained from his lectures at M.I.T.

While in Cambridge I benefited from comments, both constructive and destructive, of my friends and colleagues, especially George L. Perry, Albert Ando, Harry Grubert, Thomas Rothenberg, and Edward Foster. I am especially grateful to George L. Perry for his many attempts to raise the theoretical level of, and to give some semblance of rigor to, the arguments presented in this book.

After leaving M.I.T., I had the opportunity to discuss various aspects of the thesis with several Argentine economists. I am especially grateful to Roberto Alemann, Aldo Ferrer, Alberto Fracchia, Benjamin Hopenhayn, Ernesto Malaccorto, and Javier Villanueva for useful and stimulating conversations, from which I was able to obtain several Argentine points of view on devaluation and the stabilization plans. Seminars at the Di Tella Institute in Buenos

Aires were also very helpful in clarifying some of my ideas on this subject.

In New Haven, I had the benefit of detailed and thoughtful comments from Gerald K. Helleiner and of stimulating conversations with my colleagues of the Growth Center, especially Stephen Hymer. While I was in Washington, I profited from the insights of Felipe Pazos. Professor W. M. Corden read a final draft of this work and made very useful comments.

I am grateful to the Ford Foundation for financing my first year of research on this topic; to the Centro de Investigaciones Económicas of the Instituto Torcuato Di Tella in Buenos Aires for its hospitality during 1963/1964 and the stimulating atmosphere it provided; to the Economic Growth Center at Yale University where this monograph was completed; and to the United Nations Economic Commission for Latin America for allowing me to look through its files on Argentina in Santiago de Chile. The Department of Economics at M.I.T. is naturally the institution to which I owe the greatest debt of gratitude for four years of joyous intellectual stimulation.

I wish to acknowledge the prior publication of excerpts from Chapter 2 in an article in *Kyklos*, Vol. 18, No. 3 (1965). Some of the ideas in Chapter 2 have also previously appeared in an article in *The Journal of Political Economy*, Vol. LXXI, No. 6 (December 1963).

The expert typing and editing of Mrs. Lillian Dayos were an invaluable help in 1961; the same talents of Mrs. Margaret Oscanyan also proved a blessing in 1964/1965.

CARLOS F. DIAZ ALEJANDRO

November 1965

Survey

The purpose of this study is to analyze the impact of devaluation of the exchange rate on the Argentine economy and the balance of payments. It contains a study of the short-run mechanism of adjustment of the balance of payments of that country during the nineteen-fifties and early sixties, concentrating especially on an analysis of the effects of the December 1958 devaluation of the peso.

Chapter 1 presents what is considered to be the basic structure of the traditional theory of the impact of devaluation as well as some issues raised in the devaluation literature that are of special interest to this study. No attempt will be made to deal exhaustively with the massive amount of books and journal articles that discuss devaluation and related topics.

Chapter 2 will argue that the established theory needs to be amended in several ways before it can serve as a useful guide to the study of Argentine devaluations. In particular, it will stress the importance of taking explicitly into account the impact of devaluation on income distribution. Chapter 2 will thus provide the analytical framework that will be used to examine the devaluation of December 1958, as well as other devaluations in Argentina.

To study the impact of devaluation on the economy of a country, it would be ideal to have a system of equations describing the whole economy in as much detail as possible. Data and time limitations, however, make such an approach impractical. This book will thus rely on independent estimates of several key relationships in the Argentine economy, as well as on other data that reveal the structure and evolution of that economy. In spite of its limitation, this information will be sufficient for a satisfactory study of the impact of devaluation and for judging whether the analytical framework developed in Chapter 2 represents a fruitful approach for this study.

Chapters 3, 4, and 5 will examine the main features and structural relationships of Argentine foreign trade, and will also explore some key mechanisms of the domestic economy that are relevant to the study of the process of adjustment of the balance of payments. Chapter 6 deals with several attempts at solving balance-of-payments difficulties in Argentina, most of which included a devaluation of the exchange rate. This chapter will concentrate on the devaluation and stabilization plan announced on December 1958. Finally, Chapter 7 will present some conclusions.

Contents

Preface   vii

Survey   ix

1 The Theory of Devaluation   1

An Interpretation of the Theory   1
Final Remarks   16

2 Some Extensions of the Theory of Devaluation   19

The Pure Redistributive Effect   20
Wealth Effects   30
A Digression. The Manufacturing Sector: Import-Competing or Home Industry?   32
Demand and Supply Rigidities in the Long Run   35
A Final Comment   40

3 The Balance of Payments, Tradable Goods, and the Import Function of Argentina   41

The Argentine Balance of Payments, 1950–1963   41
Importables and Exportables in the Argentine Economy   44
The Nature of the Demand for Imports in Argentina   47
Statistical Appendix to Chapter 3   64

4 The Supply and Demand for Exportables   68

The Structure of Argentine Exports   68
World Demand for Argentine Exports   70
The Domestic Supply of Exportables   72
The Domestic Demand for Exportables   87
Statistical Appendix to Chapter 4   94

5 Savings, Investment, and the Inflationary Process in Argentina   100

The Structure and Nature of Domestic Savings   101
The Structure and Nature of Domestic Gross Capital Formation   103
A Digression: A Rough Calculation of the Impact of Devaluation on Domestic Output in the Short Run   108
The Inflationary Process, Devaluation and Income Distribution   109
The Dynamics of the Argentine Inflation   115
Statistical Appendix to Chapter 5   125

6 The Impact of Devaluation, 1955-1961   131

Pre-1955 Stabilization Efforts   133
The Prebisch Plan and the Cycle 1955–1958   134
The Frondizi-International Monetary Fund Stabilization Plan and the Cycle 1959–1961   145
The Economic Impact of Devaluation   149
Epilogue to the 1959–1961 Cycle   182

7 Conclusions   184

On the Fruitfulness of the Model of Chapter 2   184
Observations on the 1959–1961 Stabilization Efforts   186
The Price Mechanism, Devaluation and Stabilization: Some Final Comments   189

Selected Bibliography   196

Index   205

Tables

3.1	The Balance of Payments of Argentina, 1951–1963	42
3.2	Indices of Export and Import Prices and the Terms of Trade of Argentina	40
3.3	Structure of Merchandise Imports of Argentina According to Uses	48
3.4	Structure of Merchandise Imports of Argentina According to Industrial Origin	49
3.5	Imported Raw Materials and Intermediate Products as Percentages of the Gross Value of Production of Argentine Commodity-Producing Sectors in 1953	51
S.1	Data Used in the Estimation of the Import Function of Argentina: Independent Variables	64
S.2	Data Used in the Estimation of the Import Function of Argentina: Dependent Variables	65
4.1	Structure of Merchandise Exports of Argentina	69
4.2	Share of Argentine Exports in World Exports of Selected Commodities	70
4.3	Structure of the Total Value of Gross Output of the Argentine Agricultural and Livestock Sector	72
4.4	Output Indices for Agriculture and Livestock in Argentina	74
4.5	Indices of Wholesale Prices of Rural Products Relative to Wholesale Prices of Manufactured Goods	75
4.6	Share of Output of Selected Exportable Commodities Absorbed Domestically, 1950–1961	88
4.7	Structure of the Basic Budget of a Typical Working-Class Family in Buenos Aires in 1960	89
S.1	Basic Data Used to Estimate the Supply Response of Cereals and Linseed	95
S.2	Data Used to Estimate the Short-Run Supply Response of Beef	97
S.3	Data Used to Estimate the Domestic Demand Schedule for Exportable-Type and Importable-Type Commodities	98
S.4	Data Used to Estimate the Domestic Demand Schedule for Beef	99
5.1	Structure of Gross Domestic Saving in Argentina, 1950–1961	101
5.2	Structure of Gross Domestic Investment in Argentina, 1950–1961	105
5.3	Income Distribution According to Factor Shares in Argentina, 1950–1961	112

5.4	Implicit Prices of Value Added by Sectors of the Argentine Economy Relative to Implicit Prices of Gross Domestic Product	113
5.5	Net Borrowing of the Public Sector from the Banking System as a Percentage of Gross National Product	117
5.6	Changes in the Consolidated Balance Sheet of the Banking System in Argentina	118
S.1	Data Used to Estimate Private Saving Responses	126
S.2	Basic Data Used to Estimate Private Investment Responses	127
S.3	Data Used to Analyze the Dynamics of Inflation: Independent Variables	128
S.4	Data Used to Analyze the Dynamics of Inflation: Dependent Variables	129
6.1	Percentage Changes of Key Exchange Rates, Price and Wage Variables in Argentina, 1955–1958	138
6.2	Percentage Changes of Implicit Prices in the National Accounts, 1955–1958	139
6.3	Percentage Changes of Exchange Rates and Prices in Argentina, 1958–1961	150
6.4	Percentage Changes of Implicit Prices in the National Accounts, 1958–1961	152
6.5	Percentage Changes of Money and Real Industrial Wages in Argentina, 1958–1961	155
6.6	Percentage Changes in Real Wages per Employed Wage Earner, 1958–1961	155
6.7	Percentage Changes in Real Total Gross Nonwage Income, 1958–1961	156
6.8	Percentage Changes in Monetary Variables in Argentina, 1958–1961	160
6.9	Structure of Sources of Monetary Expansion in Argentina, 1958–1961	161
6.10	Revenues and Expenditures of the Public Sector in Argentina, 1958–1961	163
6.11	Percentage Changes in Real Domestic Absorption in Argentina, 1958–1961	167
6.12	Percentage Changes in Total and Sectorial Output in Argentina, 1958–1961	170
6.13	The Argentine Balance of Payments, 1958–1961	173
6.14	Structure of Merchandise Imports of Argentina, 1957–1961	177
6.15	Export Performance Relative to Output of Exportables, 1957–1961	179
6.16	Monthly Averages and Range of Daily Closing of Selling Spot Exchange Rates in Buenos Aires, 1959	181

1

The Theory of Devaluation

An Interpretation of the Theory

The topic of devaluation[1] has exerted a strong attraction for both theoretical and applied economists. The complexities inherent in any analysis of a devaluation have come to light one by one, leaving behind them innumerable controversies and absolete formulas. Why is it that after many years of studies on this topic, starting with Marshall in the nineteenth century, economists have found it so difficult to give a complete and unanimous theoretical answer to the question of devaluation and exchange rate stability? The answer must be found in the peculiar blend of relative price and real income effects produced by a devaluation. From considering devaluation as just a device affecting relative prices, economists swung to regarding it simply from the point of view of its impact on real expenditure, or "absorption." Only recently have both aspects of a devaluation been brought together into cumbersome marriages involving fearsome formulas and embracing concepts developed in microeconomics, defined holding income constant (for example, price elasticities), as well as concepts developed in macroeconomics and defined holding all prices constant (for example, the marginal propensity to save). And now we deal not with just one country but with at least a pair of countries.

One way to handle a purely theoretical analysis of the effects of devaluation would be to construct a complete general equilibrium model.[2] But such a model would inevitably get us lost in a "sea of

[1] Resulting from either a movement of an adjustable peg or a change in a freely fluctuating exchange rate.
[2] But the use of a general equilibrium model assuming full employment at all times, flexible prices, and Walras' Law presents some difficulties. It clearly becomes useless for the analysis of devaluation under conditions of unemployment. Furthermore, Walras' Law and deficits or surpluses in the balance of

coefficients." To get manageable results, simplifying assumptions are then in order. The history of the devaluation literature may be characterized as the continuous process of accusing one more simplifying assumption of destroying or at least limiting the validity or usefulness of previous results. More specifically, the theory has advanced by dropping some of the early assumptions regarding constancy of expenditures out of a given money income, and constancy of income itself. Such evolution provides a simple way of dividing the effects of devaluation on the trade balance into (a) the initial effect, associated mainly with the effects of the devaluation on relative prices; and (b) the reversal effect, associated mainly with real income changes. Although we shall discuss later the possibility of certain income effects occurring before the initial relative price effect, the traditional two stages will be examined first.

The Initial Effect

Until 1950, all discussion regarding the impact of devaluation on the trade balance[3] could be summarized by the well-known partial-equilibrium formula involving the price elasticities of the somehow defined aggregate supply of exports and the equally aggregated demand for imports of each country[4] (usually two: "our" country and

---

trade cannot be reconciled without some special and artificial assumptions. While in Keynesian models deficits or surpluses in the balance of trade are compatible with equilibrium in the national income, such is of course not the case with a general equilibrium model using Walras' Law.

[3] Most discussions have ignored capital movements that may be regarded as autonomous. The most important contributions to the devaluation literature up to 1950 are A. Marshall, *Money, Credit and Commerce* (London: Macmillan, 1924), Appendix J; C. F. Bickerdike, "The Instability of Foreign Exchange," *Economic Journal*, Vol. XXX, No. 1 (March 1920), pp. 118–122; Joan Robinson, "The Foreign Exchanges," *Essays in the Theory of Employment* (London: Macmillan, 1937); A. P. Lerner, *The Economics of Control* (New York: Macmillan, 1944), Chapter XXVIII.

The conditions for improvement in the balance of trade when devaluation takes place with a deficit or surplus, in either foreign or domestic currency, were worked out by A. O. Hirschman in "Devaluation and the Trade Balance," *Review of Economics and Statistics*, Vol. XXXI, No. 1 (February 1949), pp. 50–53.

[4] It was recognized, however, that these elasticities depend on the more fundamental elasticities of domestic demand and supply for importables and exportables within each country. The partial equilibrium formula may be found in L. A. Metzler, "The Theory of International Trade," in *A Survey of Contemporary Economics*, Vol. I, Howard S. Ellis, ed. (Homewood, Ill.: Richard D. Irwin, Inc., 1948).

The use of models involving only two goods avoids the index-number difficulties of defining aggregate demand and supply schedules for imports and exports.

the rest of the world). By assuming perfectly elastic supplies and a balanced trade before the devaluation, the formula reduces to the classic condition that a devaluation will improve the trade balance if the sum of the elasticities of the demand for imports and exports has an absolute value of more than one. If supply schedules are less than perfectly elastic, the requirements for a successful devaluation are less demanding. As a matter of fact, if the supply schedule of our exports has a zero elasticity, a devaluation can never worsen the trade balance in terms of foreign currency; but, of course, neither can it improve it by very much, unless there is an extraordinary elasticity in the demand for imports.

Whether because of the pleasing simplifications allowed by it or because the large amount of unemployed resources during the nineteen-thirties made it sound plausible, the assumption regarding perfectly elastic supply schedules for imports and exports soon was taken for granted, and economists divided into warring camps depending on their optimism or pessimism regarding the sum of the demand elasticities.

Much of the discussion[5] between optimists and pessimists centered around the precise meaning of elasticities. Confusion existed as to whether they should include only the initial price effect or the total impact of the devaluation, allowing income and other variables to change. Pessimists were mainly concerned with short-run price elasticities, which they deemed not high enough to meet the requirement for a successful devaluation. Optimists pointed out that one should look at both the elasticities of the goods already being traded and all the exports that would become feasible after a devaluation. Attempts by econometricians to settle the issue by empirical studies opened up fresh areas for debate and research, but settled nothing regarding the size of the elasticities.[6]

[5] For a sample of the discussion see A. J. Brown, "Trade Balance and Exchange Stability," *Oxford Economic Papers*, No. 6 (April 1942), pp. 57–75; P. T. Ellsworth, "Exchange Rates and Exchange Stability," *Review of Economics and Statistics*, Vol. XXII, No. 1 (February 1950), pp. 1–12; G. Haberler, "The Market for Foreign Exchange and the Stability of the Balance of Payments," *Kyklos*, Vol. III, No. 3 (1949), pp. 193–218; P. Streeten, "Elasticity Optimism and Pessimism in International Trade." *Economia Internazionale*, Vol. VII, No. 1 (February 1954), pp. 85–112; J. E. Meade, *The Balance of Payments* (London: Oxford University Press, 1951), and P. A. Samuelson, "Disparity in Postwar Exchange Rates," in *Foreign Economic Policy for the United States*, S. E. Harris, ed. (Cambridge, Mass.: Harvard University Press, 1948).

[6] Although early studies resulted in low price elasticities, more recent econometric research on United States and Canadian imports has yielded

Some optimists have based their opinion on purely theoretical grounds. It is pointed out that in a general-equilibrium setting, which assumes Walras' Law, static instability in the foreign-exchange market is not compatible with domestic stable markets.[7] Furthermore, it has been observed that even if a certain range exists at which the foreign-exchange market is unstable, movements from the unstable region must eventually find stable equilibrium points at *either* direction.[8]

The previous arguments, buttressed by the residual nature of foreign-trade demand and supply schedules, yield a strong theoretical presumption in favor of a high sum of the partial and static price elasticities, and thus for a favorable first effect. However, their potency in reassuring us of a substantial favorable total effect of the domestic devaluation on a trade balance is considerably reduced by their failure to take fully into account, along Keynesian lines, the income and price changes induced by a successful first effect.

It should be observed that the recovery of European economies and the removal of bottlenecks in production, which gave rise to price inelasticity in the immediate postwar period, suggest that the number of elasticity pessimists has diminished considerably since the 1945–1950 years. But as we now shall see, elasticity optimism assures us only of a successful first effect, not of a successful devaluation.

Other authors have pointed out that the lack of perfect competition in export industries will tend to assure us that a devaluation will not result in a deteriorating trade balance. Devaluation can at

---

fairly high price elasticities of demand. The research on Canadian and United States imports has been done by M. C. Kemp and R. R. Rhomberg, respectively. It will be remembered that devastating criticism was levied against the initial estimates of price elasticities in foreign trade by G. Orcutt and others. For a bibliography on empirical studies on foreign trade elasticities, see Hang Sheng Cheng, "Statistical Estimates of Elasticities and Propensities in International Trade: A Survey of Published Studies," *Staff Papers*, Vol. VII, No. 1 (April 1958), pp. 107–158.

[7] E. V. Morgan, "The Theory of Flexible Exchange Rates," *American Economic Review*, Vol. XLV, No. 3 (June 1955), pp. 279–295.

[8] Egon Sohmen, *Flexible Exchange Rates* (Chicago: University of Chicago Press, 1961, pp. 5–17). Sohmen works with total elasticities in a general equilibrium context, which also assumes Walras' Law. Keynesian difficulties and complications are absent from such formulation. Minor theoretical objections to the necessity of finding stable equilibrium points in *either* direction have been raised within the framework of Sohmen's analysis by J. Bhagwati and H. G. Johnson, "Notes on Some Controversies in the Theory of International Trade," *Economic Journal*, Vol. LXX, No. 277 (March 1960), pp. 74–93. See also P. A. Samuelson, *op. cit.*, pp. 409–410.

worst leave unchanged the total expenditure of our country in terms of foreign currency on imports, and our monopolistic exporters will assure us that they will never work on the inelastic range of the foreigners' demand schedule for our exports.[9]

The widespread use of the assumption of perfectly elastic supply schedules in models considering only two goods, importables and exportables, has led to some unfortunate consequences. As we have seen, it has led to an exaggerated emphasis on the importance of demand elasticities for exports and imports, in the sense that it neglected to explore further the conditions in the domestic economy giving rise to such elasticities. When it is assumed that each country specializes in the production of only one good while consuming two, the further assumption of a perfectly elastic supply makes it difficult to introduce considerations of domestic income redistribution arising from the devaluation. The simple models assume constant costs and thus a constant domestic price for the good produced locally; constant wages, implicitly or explicitly; and, in general, constant rewards to other factors of production.

But perhaps the worst consequence of the use of two-good models in devaluation analysis, with or without perfectly elastic supplies, has been the misleading emphasis placed on changing the terms of trade to alter the balance of trade. Indeed, in a two-good model, a change in the terms of trade is imperative if devaluation is going to have any impact at all. And given the assumption of perfectly elastic supplies, the terms of trade to the devaluing country will grow worse in proportion to the extent of the devaluation. Although it is well known that no necessary link exists between a successful devaluation and a change, either way, in the terms of trade, the use of two-good models has obscured the basic fact that any change at all in the terms of trade is really an incidental by-product of the devaluation.

The best way to expose the weakness of two-good models with regard to devaluation is to consider the impact of devaluation on a country too small to have the terms of its trade affected.[10] In such a

---

[9] See A. Smithies, "Devaluation with Imperfect Markets and Economic Controls," *Review of Economics and Statistics*, Vol. XXXII, No. 1 (February 1950), pp. 21–23. Also H. Brems, "Foreign Exchange Rates and Monopolistic Competition," *Economic Journal*, Vol. LXIII (1953), pp. 289–298. Export taxes may also be used temporarily after a devaluation by a country that is not quite sure about the elasticity of the foreign demand for its exports.

[10] This special case has the advantage of permitting fairly simple representations of several issues in the literature in general equilibrium diagrams, as we

case a two-good model of importables and exportables becomes very ambiguous as the relative prices of imports and exports are left unchanged by the devaluation, leaving us with no mechanism to trigger off the desired reallocation of resources. Yet it should be obvious that an international price taker can use devaluation to correct a disequilibrium in its balance of payments just as well as a country that has some influence over its terms of trade (indeed, with more certainty of a successful outcome!). The neglected good in the analysis is of course the home-good or the nontraded good, whose

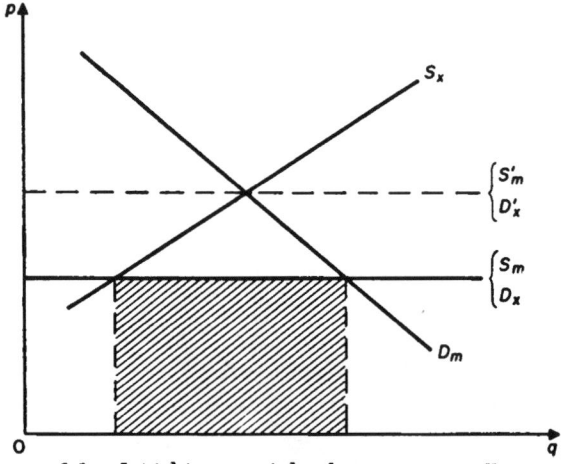

FIGURE 1.1. *Initial impact of devaluation in a small country.*

price is not directly linked to the exchange rate and whose relative price vis-à-vis imports and exports is affected by the devaluation, thus providing the mechanism for the desired reallocation of resources. The two-good models with perfectly elastic supply schedules provided only for a special type of resource reallocation, that is, from unemployment to the production of exportables. The more interesting reallocation problems were thus neglected.

---

shall see later. Furthermore, the initial impact of a devaluation can be shown in a single diagram as in Figure 1.1. The vertical price axis is in terms of domestic currency. By appropriate choice of units, we combine in the same horizontal schedule the foreign supply of imports and demand for exports. A devaluation will shift the horizontal schedule upward. The original trade deficit (in domestic currency) is shown by the shaded area. In the diagram, D_m represents the domestic demand for imports; S_x, the domestic supply of exports. A similar criticism of two-good models including only importables and exportables is made in W. M. Corden, *Recent Developments in the Theory of International Trade*, Special Papers in International Economics, No. 7, Princeton University, March 1965, p. 22.

It could be argued, however, that the neglect of the case of the small country is justified on the grounds that devaluation will inevitably work in improving the balance of trade of a price taker (or at worst, leave it unchanged) as such a country faces a perfectly elastic demand for its exports. Yet, despite this, it seems that the key to a successful devaluation in long-term perspective (that is, reallocation of resources between the foreign and domestic sector) is neglected by the use of only two goods, whether or not they are produced at constant costs. The obsession with the sign of dB/dk, where B represents the balance of trade and k the exchange rate defined as units of domestic currency per unit of foreign currency, left little room to examine the different factors in a domestic economy that would assure us of not only a positive dB/dk but also of a large one. A devaluation in a country with a perfectly elastic foreign demand for its exports may achieve small results because of the failure of such country to reallocate resources internally and put more of them into the production of exportables and importables. By exportables here we mean not only those already in trade but also those which a country with fluid internal resources could develop after a devaluation. In studying the impact of a devaluation on the trade balance of many countries, it may be of greater importance to concentrate on the elasticities of supply of exportables and importables than on the elasticities of the foreign demand for exports and the net domestic demand for imports (which, of course, depends on the elasticity of the domestic supply of importables).[11]

Another objection to the use of two-good models in devaluation has been made on narrower technical grounds. It has been pointed out that a third nontraded good, money, must be assumed if a disequilibrium in the balance of trade is to exist. If we do not explicitly assume a *numéraire*, certain ambiguities will appear in the analysis. Such a third good is, however, usually assumed implicitly and need not cause us great concern.[12]

[11] It is regrettable that devaluation theorists have not paid more attention to the general position of the late F. Graham, who emphasized the dangers of rely exclusively on two-good models in international trade. An article by I. F. Pearce also puts emphasis on the role of devaluation in changing the relative prices between traded and nontraded goods rather than on the terms of trade. See I. F. Pearce, "The Problem of the Balance of Payments," *International Economic Review*, Vol. II, No. 1 (January 1961), pp. 1–28. See also R. Hinshaw, "Further Comment," *Quarterly Journal of Economics*, Vol. LXXII, No. 4 (November 1958), pp. 616–625.

[12] This point has been made in connection with the slightly different stability conditions that emerge depending on whether a general-equilibrium model is used, assuming full employment and Walras' Law, or whether the partial-

Whether based on models with two or more goods, some other features of the initial impact of a devaluation have been discussed in the literature, giving rise to an amendment of the classical requirement for exchange stability. Laursen and Metzler[13] pointed out that if a devaluation or appreciation of the exchange rate does alter the terms of trade, the real income implied by a fixed physical output and a fixed level of money spending would be changed. Assuming an average propensity to spend which is higher at lower levels of real income than at higher levels, it follows that as the terms of trade become worse money spending would tend to increase in the devaluing country for a given level of employment and output. In other words, while we would move down along the real-spending schedule, the money-spending schedule would shift upward. The result of such an effect was to make the conditions for exchange stability more difficult to meet, as devaluation would lead to a worsening of the terms of trade and thus to an immediate upward shift in the money-spending schedule.[14]

It should be observed that even granting the original presumption regarding the sign of the effect, it does not follow that the chances of success of devaluation in models with more than two goods will be reduced by it, as we have seen that there is no necessary link between a devaluation and a given change in the terms of trade. A devaluation resulting in an improvement of the terms of trade will have this effect working in its favor.

---

equilibrium model of, for example, Robinson is employed. The role of supply elasticities emerges as the main source of ambiguity. For a careful reconciliation of the different formulas (including J. E. Meade's formulation) see R. W. Jones, "Stability Conditions in International Trade: A General Equilibrium Analysis," *International Economic Review*, Vol. II, No. 2 (May 1961), pp. 199–209. See also footnote 2.

[13] L. Metzler and S. Laursen, "Flexible Exchange Rates and the Theory of Employment," *Review of Economics and Statistics*, Vol. XXXII, No. 4 (November 1950), pp. 281–299. In their model a devaluation had to adversely affect the terms of trade, because they used two goods with perfectly elastic supplies. See also A. C. Harberger, "Currency Depreciation, Income and the Balance of Trade," *Journal of Political Economy*, Vol. LVIII, No. 1 (February 1950), pp. 47–60.

[14] This effect was elaborated further by John Spraos in "Consumers' Behaviour and the Conditions for Exchange Stability," *Economica*, Vol. XXII, No. 86 (May 1955), pp. 137–151. Spraos points out that depending on what assumptions we make regarding consumer behavior, this effect may have different magnitudes and may even be changed in sign if a strong cash-balance effect exists. The importance of the effect was challenged on more empirical grounds by William H. White, "The Employment-insulating Advantages of Flexible Exchanges: A Comment on Professors Laursen and Metzler," *Review of Economics and Statistics*, Vol. XXXVI, No. 2 (May 1954), pp. 225–228.

It has already been noticed that this refinement of the criteria for exchange stability is not only ambiguous in sign but it is also considered to have small empirical importance.[15] Thus the classical condition for exchange stability may be used at least as a fairly accurate first approximation to the criteria for a successful first effect of a devaluation. This completes the examination of the first effect of a devaluation. During the analysis of the first effect, output and employment were assumed constant. We now turn to the repercussions of the initial effect on the economy.

Reversal and Total Effects of the Devaluation

One way to handle the impact on the domestic economy of changes in the balance of trade is to assume that any increases or decreases in total domestic expenditure arising from the devaluation are swiftly offset by internal fiscal and monetary measures. In such a case, there will be no reversal effects, and the total effect of a devaluation will be the same as the immediate result.[16] But if no offsetting official policies are assumed, there will be further repercussions within the economies affected that will tend to cancel the initial effect of a devaluation, whether positive or negative. Total expenditure has changed after the first effect (unless the sum of the elasticities is exactly equal to one, in the simpler models) as a result of the change in the balance of trade and the possible shift in the money-expenditure schedule due to any change in the terms of trade. A successful devaluation will increase both domestic prices and income. Such increases will cancel part of the favorable initial effect, by stimulating expenditures on importables and exportables and by tending to increase the domestic price level; but, barring foreign-trade accelerators, the reversal factors can never on balance, change the direction of the initial effect of the devaluation.

The reversal (and thus the total) effects have also been analyzed using simple models, often using two goods and assuming perfectly elastic supplies.[17] The reversal term is a slightly more complex for-

---

[15] See for example C. P. Kindleberger, "Flexible Exchange Rates," essay in *Monetary Management*, prepared for the Commission on Money and Credit (Englewood Cliffs, N.J.: Prentice-Hall, Inc., 1963), p. 415.

[16] This approach has been followed by J. Meade, *The Balance of Payments* (London: Oxford University Press, 1951).

[17] The fundamental contributions of A. C. Harberger, *op. cit.*, and S. S. Alexander, "Effects of a Devaluation: A Simplified Synthesis of Elasticities and Absorption Approaches," *American Economic Review*, Vol. XLIX, No. 1 (March 1959), pp. 22–42, contain the relevant formulas. For nonalgebraic presentations of the total impact of a devaluation, see J. Black, "A Savings and

mulation of the familiar income multiplier, having as key parameters each country's marginal propensity to save and to import. The initial effect times the reversal multiplier will give us the net increase in hoarding arising from the devaluation, that is, the net improvement in the trade balance. If the marginal propensity to save is zero in either country, the total effect of a devaluation will be zero (although its first effect may be very large and positive). In other words, and as it has been observed by several authors, elasticity optimism does not necessarily lead to devaluation optimism. Not only must the relative price elasticities be high but the marginal propensities to save must also be large. If the marginal propensities to import in both countries were zero (with positive marginal propensities to save) the total effect of devaluation would be reduced to the initial effect. Obviously, if the initial effect is zero, the total effect will also be zero, regardless of the nature of the marginal propensities.

This presentation of the total effects of devaluation avoided many of the difficulties of the pure absorption approach, introduced in the published literature by S. S. Alexander.[18] The pure absorption approach could be summarized by the statement that dB/dk will yield an improvement in the trade balance if and only if both of the marginal propensities to save (for each country) are positive. Such a statement is not true. The positive marginal propensities to save are necessary but not sufficient conditions for a successful devaluation. It may be argued that the pure absorption approach could be better summarized by saying that devaluation will work, say under full employment, if and only if domestic absorption is decreased relative to domestic output. Note that the first condition is of an *ex ante* nature, while the latter is of an *ex post* nature. The latter statement, as a matter of fact, is simply a truism. What was needed, and was provided by Alexander in his more recent article, was a

---

Investment Approach to Devaluation," *Economic Journal*, Vol. LXIX, No. 274 (June 1959), pp. 267–274; H. G. Johnson, "Toward a General Theory of the Balance of Payments," in *International Trade and Economic Growth* (London: George Allen and Unwin, 1958), pp. 153–169; and E. M. Bernstein, "Strategic Factors in Balance of Payments Adjustment," *Review of Economics and Statistics*, Vol. XL, No. 1, Part 2 (February 1958), pp. 133–142. This chapter is particularly indebted to Professor Alexander's article, which originated the generalized distinction between the initial and the reversal effects.

[18] S. S. Alexander, "Effects of a Devaluation on a Trade Balance," *International Monetary Fund Staff Papers*, Vol. II, No. 2 (April 1952), pp. 263–278. It will be seen later that a similar approach was developed in 1948 by J. Polak of the International Monetary Fund.

description of the precise mechanism that induces a decrease in absorption, while giving full recognition to the initial effect of devaluation.

Was the development of the pure absorption approach useless? Far from it. It will be remembered that models such as Harberger's assumed inter alia constant costs all around, thus implying that we deal with conditions of less than full employment. Such models lose much of their significance when full employment is reached. One of the great virtues of the simple models, their precision in establishing functional relationships in a simple fashion, becomes the cause of their failure in explaining the effect of a devaluation at or near full employment. In such homogeneous models, which do not take into account income redistribution, money illusion, or the importance of asset holding in the demand functions, the real marginal propensities to save will have to equal zero when full employment is reached. Thus, for a devaluation undertaken at full employment, these models would yield a zero total effect, regardless of the size of the first effect. The stage is thus set for the pure absorption approach of Alexander. The main contribution of the pure absorption approach is then in the field of devaluation under full employment conditions. The emphasis is now properly placed on the ways and means by which total absorption can be cut. None of Alexander's "direct effects" can be revealed by the simple model of, for example, Harberger.

But even if we are at full employment, complete reliance on the pure absorption approach can be very misleading. Figure 1.2 presents the production-possibility frontier of a small, price-taking country which cannot by its own actions affect the terms of trade. In such a case, it is legitimate to lump exportables and importables into one Hicksian composite good,[19] which we may call the foreign (F) good. All other goods within the economy whose prices will not be affected directly by the exchange rate variations may be lumped into a composite home (H) good. If the exchange rate and the terms of trade are given and there are no tariffs or quantitative controls, the price ratio to consumers for F and H will be determinate and will yield an income-consumption line, such as IC, in Figure 1.2. There

---

[19] See J. R. Hicks, *Value and Capital* (2nd ed.; Oxford: Clarendon Press, 1946), pp. 33 and 312. "A collection of physical things can always be treated as if they were divisible into units of a single commodity so long as their relative prices can be assumed to be unchanged, in the particular problem in hand." (p. 33)

will be, of course, one income-consumption line for each exchange rate; the more devalued the exchange rate becomes, the more the *IC* line will shift toward the *H* axis. Given a certain percentage of devaluation, the precise degree of such a shift will depend on the shape of the indifference curves of all consumers. For the sake of simplicity, let us assume that the economy is made up of individuals having identical linear homogeneous utility functions. Under these circumstances, there will only be one *IC* line that will yield both internal and external equilibrium with full employment.

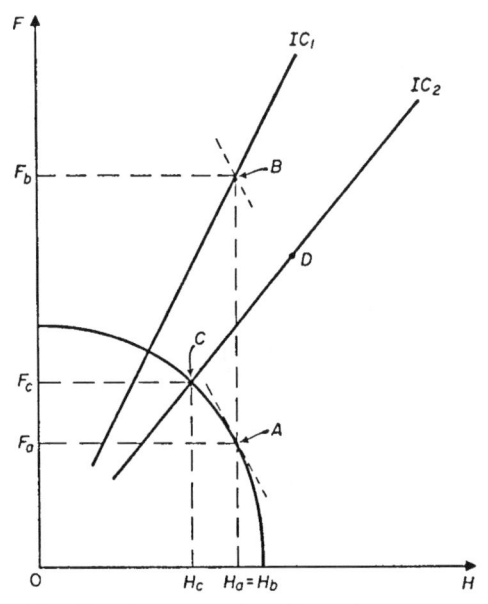

FIGURE 1.2. *Devaluation under full employment conditions.*

A disequilibrium in the balance of trade under conditions of full employment may be represented by two points. The country is producing at *A* and consuming at *B*, on *IC*, and is using an exchange rate that can never yield full-employment equilibrium in all markets. The price lines tangent to points *A* and *B* are, of course, parallel to each other. The deficit in the balance of trade is represented by the difference between F_b and F_a. It is assumed that the inflationary pressure has been released on foreign goods, that is, no excess demand exists for the *H* good and $H_a = H_b$. The *H* industry can only produce in equilibrium that amount of output which domestic real spending will absorb. The point along the *IC* line at which the society will find itself will depend on the spending decisions of consumers, investors, and the government. While in a closed economy the inflationary gap implied by point B can never be observed ex post, in an open economy such a gap is very likely to result in a balance-of-trade deficit.

Suppose now that the authorities devalue the currency to precisely that exchange rate which is compatible with full employment and balance of trade equilibrium. The new income consumption line will be IC_2 and C will be the only point at which both full employment and external balance are possible. To reach such a point, we need not only to cut absorption from F_b to F_c and from H_b to H_c *but to reallocate resources from the H industry to the F industry;* in other words, we must move along the production-possibilities frontier from A to C. A successful devaluation under conditions of full employment must, in general, cut down absorption *and* give rise to resource reallocation. Only in very special cases may a straightforward policy of deflation be enough. For example, if after a while we find ourselves producing at C and consuming at D, no devaluation is required; we would need only a deflationary fiscal and monetary policy to cut absorption. The pure absorption approach came dangerously close to regarding devaluation as just another deflationary policy, that is, by emphasizing movements along the IC lines it tended to neglect movements along the production-possibilities frontier. Such emphasis provides the justification to some of F. Machlup's criticism of S. Alexander.[20]

Figure 1.2 also shows that different combinations of exchange-rate and income policies may be required to achieve full employment and balance-of-trade equilibrium, depending on which region of the diagram we are at originally. The typical situation given by points A and B has been depicted, calling for both deflationary policies and devaluation.[21]

[20] F. Machlup, "Relative Prices and Aggregate Spending in the Analysis of Devaluation," *American Economic Review*, Vol. XLV, No. 3 (June 1955), pp. 255–278. We will see in the next chapter, however, that it may be useful to concentrate on the deflationary aspects of devaluation in the short run, while leaving the reallocation of resources for the long run.

[21] The alternative policy combinations which may be required have been examined in detail by W. M. Corden in "The Geometric Representation of Policies to Attain Internal and External Balance," *The Review of Economic Studies*, Vol. XXVIII(1), No. 75 (October 1960), pp. 1–19. This article employed geometrical techniques similar to those used here, and which seem to have been originally developed by W. E. G. Salter, "Internal and External Balance—The Role of Price and Expenditure Effects," *Economic Record*, Vol. XXXV, No. 70 (April 1959), pp. 47–66. This type of analysis has recently been

The foregoing analysis does not go into the details of how a society moves up and down along the *IC* lines. Such movements would be associated with changes in real aggregate demand. The Alexander "direct effects" of devaluation (cash balance, redistribution, money illusion, and so forth) would tend to push us down along the *IC* curve.[22] Fiscal and monetary policies have an obvious importance in determining our position along the *IC* lines. Thus, the reversal effect of a devaluation will also be greatly influenced by the types of policies assumed.[23]

We have now completed the review of the standard two-stage analysis of the impact of devaluation on the trade balance. Before we turn to a preview of the ways in which the next chapter will modify this standard analysis, some other issues related to devaluation will be discussed.

Devaluation and the Price Level

In most of the theoretical literature on devaluation, it has been assumed that a devaluation will increase the domestic prices of importables and exportables not only relative to other prices in the economy but also in absolute amounts. Indeed, this is the fundamental mechanism that triggers off the first effect of devaluation. Thus, a price index that includes importable and exportable commodities as well as nontraded goods is bound to show an increase.

While such a result is self-evident in the case of a devaluation taking place without any other changes in trade policy, it has been argued that the joint effect of devaluation *and* a removal of quantitative controls over trade may well be a fall in the general level of prices.[24] The argument is based on the following key assumptions:

   a. An unchanged balance of trade, although presumably both exports

---

extended by R. A. Mundell, "The Appropriate Use of Monetary and Fiscal Policy for Internal and External Stability," International Monetary Fund *Staff Papers*, Vol. IX (March 1962), pp. 70–79.

[22] Although as we will see later, income redistribution will also shift the *IC* line if different groups in the society have different tastes.

[23] It has been argued by F. Machlup, *op. cit.*, that (even assuming plentiful exchange reserves) a balance-of-trade disequilibrium will eventually come to an end simply by the refusal of the monetary authorities to replenish the money loss implied by the deficit in the balance of trade. Presumably high interest rates will push us down along a given *IC* line, cutting absorption in a purely deflationary way. But while we can always get balance-of-trade equilibrium by deflationary means, a devaluation is required if the goal of full employment is also to be reached.

[24] The main exponent of this point of view is Egon Sohmen, *op. cit.*, pp. 102–111.

and imports will increase after the adoption of both policy measures.
b. An unchanged money value of total domestic absorption. Although not necessary for the argument, full employment is assumed.
c. Completely flexible prices (this is implicitly assumed).

After removal of quantitative controls and devaluation, we shall reallocate resources so as to specialize more along the lines of our comparative advantage. Less home and import-competing goods and more export goods will be produced. Since such a reallocation of resources must presumably make us better off (that is, in some quantitative or qualitative sense it must increase the quantity Q produced with the same amount of resources as before) and by assumption the total money value of domestic absorption is fixed ($\Sigma PQ =$ constant), it clearly follows that the price level P must fall.[25] Once again it is shown that autarky is less desirable than specialization along the lines of comparative advantage.

While the conclusions follow from the assumptions, the latter may strike most people as unrealistic when applied to actual cases of devaluation. The reallocation of resources from home goods to export goods must take place under full-employment conditions in such a smooth manner that the current value of domestic absorption is unchanged. Presumably resources are bid away from home and import-competing industries, whose prices must fall, by the expanding export industries, whose prices have risen. No asymmetry in price responses is allowed. The increases in investment necessary for the process of reallocation will be forthcoming from a reduction in consumption, brought about without general price increases. The realism of such implications may be questioned.

The argument, furthermore, can be applied strictly only in the case of an unchanged balance of trade. As a matter of fact, the argument implies that in spite of devaluation, the level of imports will increase following the removal of import restrictions. It is perhaps more interesting to consider what will happen to the price level when we want to cut down real domestic absorption relative to output, that is, reduce the trade-balance deficit. In attacking the exaggerated fears that devaluation will set off an inflationary spiral, Sohmen is willing to give away a potent tool in bringing about a cut in real absorption, that is, devaluation-induced increases in the general price level.[26]

[25] For simplicity, assume constant terms of trade.
[26] R. Hinshaw, "Further Comment," *Quarterly Journal of Economics*, Vol. LXV, No. 4 (November 1951), pp. 447–462.

It should be observed, however, that Sohmen is quite willing to admit that resource reallocation may take time, and therefore, prices may rise in the short run after a devaluation. Even in the short run, the removal of quantitative restrictions on imports will offset the impact on domestic import prices of the changes in the exchange rate. But if in the short run the quantity of exports is fixed and we postulate a fixed balance of trade, we must not allow the domestic price of importables to fall, as this would encourage larger imports. Thus, given the increase in the domestic price of exports, the price level must rise in the short run.

In a recent paper,[27] Professor Harberger has given powerful support to the standard view that a devaluation can be expected to have a strong impact on the domestic price level. On the basis of assumptions that are influenced by Argentine and other Latin American conditions, he concludes that a devaluation of about 50 per cent (an increase by 50 per cent of the domestic price of one unit of foreign currency) will probably result in increases of the price level of between 24 and 30 per cent, depending on the values of some key parameters. Besides the direct impact of devaluation on the prices of exportables and importables, he also takes into account price increases forthcoming from attempts to switch expenditures from these to other goods.

Final Remarks

The next chapter will differ from most other analyses of devaluation by its emphasis on the short-run impact of devaluation and on the income redistribution arising from a devaluation.

The emphasis on the short run should not be taken as an attempt to diminish the importance of resource reallocation for the long-run success of devaluation. While it is recognized that the essence of devaluation is the inducement it provides for a reallocation of resources, we must also analyze its short-run impact, which may be quite potent in improving the balance of trade before any resources are reallocated.

A discussion of income redistribution arising from devaluation could be introduced in several ways. For example and still well within neoclassical equilibrium analysis, we could postulate (*a*)

[27] Arnold C. Harberger, "Some Notes on Inflation," in *Inflation and Growth in Latin America*, edited by Werner Baer and Isaac Kerstenetzky (Homewood, Ill.: R. D. Irwin, Inc., 1964).

different factor intensities in the home-good and foreign-good industries and (*b*) different tastes for different groups within the economy. A devaluation by changing relative prices would create a different pattern of output, thereby affecting returns of the factors of production. Furthermore, we may make different assumptions (with or without postulate *a*) regarding the expenditure patterns on home and foreign goods of different groups in society, either because of different indifference maps or because of different positions in the same map of indifference curves.[28]

Chapter 2 will introduce an assumption that, although not in the neoclassical spirit of marginalism, will nevertheless present a more accurate picture of reality in the short run. This assumption, when coupled with assumptions regarding the expenditure patterns of different social groups, suggests that a redistributive effect will occur prior to the classical initial effect of devaluation. It should be observed that under such assumptions the income redistribution will be characterized not only as a real-income transfer from the sector of the economy producing home goods to those sectors producing importables and exportables but also, more accurately, as a real-income transfer from wage earners, wherever they may be employed, to non-wage earners of the import-competing and export industries.

Although several authors have made passing remarks about the impact of a devaluation on income distribution,[29] only two other attempts to analyze the full implications of the redistributive effect could be found in the devaluation literature.

An early, incomplete attempt can be found in an unpublished paper of J. J. Polak.[30] Polak discusses the implications of a wage lag,

---

[28] For illustrations on how these assumptions can be introduced in a geometric general equilibrium presentation, see P. B. Kenen, "Distribution, Demand and Equilibrium in International Trade," *Kyklos*, Vol. XII (1959), pp. 629–638, and H. G. Johnson, "International Trade, Income Distribution and the Offer Curve," *The Manchester School of Economic and Social Studies*, Vol. XXVII, No. 5 (September 1959), pp. 241–260. Professor W. M. Corden has suggested to me that the factor intensity argument could be generalized to say that devaluation raises real incomes of those factors which are predominant in *producing* tradables relative to those factors which are dominant in *consuming* tradables.

[29] It will be remembered that one of Alexander's "direct effects" was a redistributive effect. But Alexander does not explore it fully, particularly neglecting its relation in time to the first effect of devaluation.

[30] J. J. Polak, "Depreciation to meet a situation of overinvestment," Document of the Research Department of the International Monetary Fund, September 1948 (prepared in consultations with I. S. Friedman, W. R. Gardner, J. Marquez,

but his failure to specify a complete model leaves a number of ambiguities in the analysis. A second effort can be found in a paper by J. Spraos,[31] whose main interest is the possibility that a devaluation-induced shift in income distribution may present a new source of instability in the foreign-exchange market.

Pertinent contributions of the literature on the impact of devaluation on the economy and the trade balance of the devaluing country have been critically discussed in this chapter. Chapter 2 will now explore several amendments and extensions to the established theory of devaluation, which are deemed to be necessary before such a theory is utilized to analyze the effects of devaluation in a semi-industrialized economy.

---

and F. Pazos). This paper also presented the basic outlines of what later came to be called the "absorption approach" to devaluation. The models that will be presented in the next chapter contain ideas similar to those of the Polak paper which, incidentally, was motivated by a study of the Mexican devaluation of 1948/1949. E. M. Bernstein refers to the Polak paper in his article "Strategic Factors in Balance of Payments Adjustment," *International Monetary Fund Staff Papers*, Vol. V (1956/1957), p. 159, where he states: "A devaluation will, for a time, bring about a shift in the distribution of income, so that if wages lag, the proportion of income going to receivers of profits will rise."

[31] J. Spraos, "Stability in a Closed Economy and in the Foreign Exchange Market, and the Redistributive Effect of Price Changes," *Review of Economic Studies*, Vol. XXIV(3), No. 65 (June 1957), pp. 161–176.

2

Some Extensions of the Theory of Devaluation

A central theme will dominate this chapter: the search for explanations to the paradox of devaluations that succeed in improving the balance of trade, but which are accompanied by a drop in the real output of the economy. As shown in Chapter 1, existing devaluation theory distinguishes two stages of the impact of devaluation on the trade balance: the initial effect, whose size and sign will be determined primarily by the price elasticities of demand and supply of imports and exports, and the reversal effect, which always works against the first effect mainly through the income mechanism, and which tends to offset the original impact of the devaluation on the trade balance. Thus, according to this theory, a first effect that is successful in improving the balance of trade will also result in an increase in real domestic output by stimulating the production of exports and import-competing goods. Through the income multiplier, such expansionary stimulus will spread to other sectors of the economy. On the other hand, a devaluation yielding a negative initial effect will cause domestic output to decrease.

If the devaluation takes place under conditions of full employment, the absorption approach would indicate the need to cut down total real expenditures to bring them into line with the full-employment output; but such an approach would not predict a drop in aggregate production.[1]

---

[1] However, as the devaluation is likely to induce a reallocation of resources, frictions may appear in such a process, producing unemployment and excess capacity in some sectors. In principle such unemployment could be offset by expansion in other sectors, but asymmetries may prevent a smooth adjustment in reality.

Later chapters will show that during the postwar period Argentine devaluations, which improved the balance of trade in the short run, were generally accompanied by decreases in the level of total output. It could be argued that output decreased simply as a result of deflationary fiscal and monetary measures adopted simultaneously with the devaluation. Although the importance of such autonomous fiscal and monetary measures is not denied and such policies will be discussed in later chapters, this chapter will investigate how decreases in output may arise as a direct result of the devaluation. Later chapters will demonstrate that the direct effects explored here were indeed at work in Argentine devaluations.

The Pure Redistributive Effect

It is well known that a devaluation by increasing the over-all level of prices may cause some redistribution of income among different social groups in much the same way as would inflation in a closed economy. Such a redistribution will be inevitable so long as all prices of outputs and inputs do not change proportionally.

In the case of Argentina, the redistributive effect arising from devaluation has long been recognized, although it has not been analyzed systematically. Several authors have pointed out that throughout Argentine history rural producers, who supplied most of the exported commodities, traditionally advocated a policy of devaluation, expecting that the peso prices for their outputs would rise faster than the peso prices for their inputs, including in the latter the wage rates expressed in current pesos.[2]

Thus, it seems important to investigate with care any systematic pattern of redistribution that may result from devaluation. It will be shown that the redistributive effect helps to resolve the apparent paradox of a devaluation leading to an improvement in the trade balance *and* a decrease in domestic output. Furthermore, it is very likely that the redistributive effect will have a quicker impact than the so-called initial, or relative, price effect. Even elasticity optimists

---

[2] Among the authors who have recognized this effect in Argentina are Aldo Ferrer, *La Economía Argentina* (México: Fondo de Cultura Económica, 1963), pp. 136–138; J. H. Williams, *Argentine International Trade under Inconvertible Paper Money 1880–1900* (Cambridge, Mass.: Harvard University Press, 1920), pp. 157–162; A. G. Ford, *The Gold Standard 1880–1914, Britain and Argentina* (London: Oxford University Press, 1962), pp. 95 and 122; Virgil Salera, *Exchange Control and the Argentine Market* (New York: Columbia University Press, 1941), p. 16.

do not expect price elasticities to be very high in the short run and rely on such devices as short-term capital movements to fill the gap between the time a devaluation takes place and the time when the balance of trade will respond favorably to the change in relative prices induced by the devaluation. In the case of Argentina, it will be observed that the redistributive effect is a more powerful and speedy way of filling this gap.

An algebraic model will now be presented to analyze the redistributive effect. A key assumption in this model is that money-wage rates are constant in the short run, or that at least they increase less than the devaluation-induced increase in the price level. The precise length of such a wage lag will of course change from situation to situation and will be affected at any point of time by such factors as the level of unemployment and the power of trade unions. To explore the theoretical implications of such a lag in this chapter, it will be sufficient to assume that the wage lag exists for an arbitrarily defined short run.

Three goods may be originally considered: importables, exportables, and the home good (H), which because of prohibitive transport costs does not enter into international trade. In Chapter 1, it was argued that there has been in the literature an exaggerated emphasis on the analysis of the impact of devaluation on the terms of trade, while the fundamental relationship between the price of the home good and the domestic prices of imports and exports has been neglected. To focus attention on this fundamental relationship and to simplify the analysis, it will be assumed that we are dealing with a country that faces a perfectly elastic demand for its exports and a perfectly elastic supply of its imports, both expressed in terms of foreign currency. Because it has been assumed that the terms of trade for our country are set exogenously, it is legitimate to lump exportables and importables into a single Hicksian composite good, which is called the foreign good (F). Given the domestic demand and supply schedules, the small country will use the world market to sell its surplus of exportables and to purchase its deficit of importables at the current international prices. It will also be assumed that the rest of the world adjusts passively to the changes in the balance of trade of our small country.

Our country can be divided into two social classes: "wage earners" and "capitalists."[3] Each class is assumed to be composed of individ-

---

[3] It will be seen in later chapters that a threefold distinction of "wage earners," "landlords," and "urban capitalists" may be more useful to study

uals of identical tastes, who consume both H and F, although only "capitalists" are assumed to save. The domestic demand equations for the F good are

$$F_d^w = f_1(P_f, P_h, W) \tag{2.1}$$

$$F_d^t = f_2(P_f, P_h, T) \tag{2.2}$$

$$F_d^w + F_d^t = F_d \tag{2.3}$$

Equations 2.1 and 2.2 reflect the demand for F of "wage earners" and "capitalists" respectively, where the P's are the absolute domestic prices of the goods represented by the subscripts (f for the F good and h for the H good). Total money wages and nonwage income are denoted by W and T, respectively. The subscript d attached to F in Equations 2.1 through 2.3 denotes that we are referring to domestic demand; the supercripts w and t denote that we are referring to the demand of "wage earners" and "capitalists," respectively.

It is assumed that "wage earners" spend all of their income on both F and H, while "capitalists" save a fraction of their money income equal to a. Thus, the demand equations for the H good are as follows:

$$H_d^w = \frac{1}{P_h}(W - P_f \cdot F_d^w) \tag{2.4}$$

$$H_d^t = \frac{1}{P_h}(T - P_f \cdot F_d^t - aT) \tag{2.5}$$

$$H_d^w + H_d^t = H_d \tag{2.6}$$

The assumptions regarding the spending propensities of the different social classes are, of course, of critical importance to the results presented later in this chapter. If both social classes had the same pattern of expenditures at the margin, income redistribution would not be of any interest for us.

The domestic supply functions present the more difficult conceptual problems in this type of model. Here is where the choice must be made between the full employment, general-equilibrium assumption and the assumption of a Keynesian world. The common assumption of perfectly elastic supply curves implies unutilized resources in the economy, as more can be produced of one good with-

---

Argentine reality. However, the basic points of this chapter can be made without introducing these complications.

out curtailing the output of any other. It will be assumed that the supply schedule of the H industry is perfectly elastic, while the supply schedule of the F industry is upward sloping. These supply conditions may be expressed as follows (where subscript u refers to quantity supplied):

$$H_u = H_d \tag{2.7}$$

$$F_u = f_3(P_f, P_h) \tag{2.8}$$

Equation 2.7 denotes the fact that the supply of H will adjust to the demand at the current domestic price. Thus, decreases in the demand for H will result in a lower level of output and higher unemployment, but no change in the price of H. The assumed positive slope for Equation 2.8 $\left(\dfrac{\partial f_3}{\partial P_f} > 0\right)$ may be explained by the presence of a specific, non-wage receiving, input to this industry, which is in fixed supply (that is, land). The domestic price of F will be solely determined by its foreign price and the exchange rate so that Equation 2.8 will only help to determine the amount of good F produced internally for any given foreign price and exchange rate.

Thus, Equations 2.7 and 2.8 imply that there are idle resources which can be put to work productively in the H and F industries, although it is assumed that the F industry under the law of diminishing returns works under conditions of increasing costs. The implications of the assumption of a perfectly inelastic supply for F in the short run will also be examined.

Total money wages and the income of "capitalists" will be determined by the total output produced domestically and by the money-wage rate, assumed to be the same in both H and F industries and constant, at least in the short run. If we let s represent the money-wage rate, that is, the units of domestic currency received during a given time period by wage earners per unit of output of F and H currently produced,[4] we can write

---

[4] This definition of the wage rate is made for convenience of exposition. By assuming a constant labor-output ratio for each industry, s can be made proportional to the more usual definition of the money-wage rate, that is, units of domestic currency received by each wage earner. It is assumed that money-wage rates are given exogenously, and that until full employment is reached, there is a perfectly elastic supply of labor at such money-wage rate. This theory of wage determination is, of course, not as satisfactory as the neoclassical approach for long-run problems, but it seems more relevant for the short run. The implied assumption that money wages represent the same proportion of the value of the output *before* devaluation in each of the sectors of the economy

$$W = s \cdot F_u + s \cdot H_u \tag{2.9}$$

$$T = (P_f - s)F_u + (P_h - s)H_u \tag{2.10}$$

Although this model implicitly assumes the existence of a fourth good which is used as a *numéraire*, the implications of monetary policies other than exchange-rate policy will be ignored. Thus, the cash-balance effect, interest rates, and so forth will not appear in the model. This neglect does not imply that monetary policy is unimportant. Indeed, it will be seen that changes in the real stock of money have played a central role in stabilization efforts of Argentina. But the impact of different monetary policies on the economy are fairly well known and may be considered independently of exchange-rate devaluations at the level of abstraction of this chapter.

Using the composite good the balance of trade in terms of foreign currency may be expressed as follows:

$$B = \frac{P_f}{k}(F_u - F_d) \tag{2.11}$$

To examine the impact of a devaluation ($dk > 0$) Equation 2.11 will be differentiated totally with respect to k to obtain dB/dk. It will be assumed that units are chosen such that the original prices and the initial exchange rate are equal to one.

As a first step, we obtain

$$\frac{dB}{dk} = \frac{dF_u}{dk} - \frac{dF_d{}^w}{dk} - \frac{dF_d{}^t}{dk} \tag{2.12}$$

The impact of devaluation on the supply of F will be given by Equation 2.8, while its impact on the demand of "wage earners" and "capitalists" for F will be obtained from Equations 2.1 and 2.2. However, the change in demand for F will depend on what happens to wage and nonwage income, which according to Equations 2.9 and 2.10 depend not only on the domestic price and output of F but also on the output of H (the price of H being assumed constant). As the output of H is fully demand determined (its supply being assumed perfectly elastic in the relevant range) and as the demand for good H depends also on the level of wage and nonwage income according to Equations 2.4 and 2.5, it is clear

---

could be relaxed without great difficulty. As a matter of fact the wage share in the sector producing exportables in Argentina is lower than in the rest of the economy.

that the whole system of equations must be solved simultaneously to yield the desired goal: dB/dk. The system can be similarly solved to obtain the impact of devaluation on wage and nonwage income or on the level of output of H.

After some tedious algebra, and breaking down all price slopes of demand into income and substitution effects, we obtain

$$\frac{dB}{dk} = \frac{1}{D}\left\{a(1-s)\left[\frac{\partial f_3}{\partial P_f} - \left(\frac{\partial f_1}{\partial P_f}\right)_{\bar{o}} - \left(\frac{\partial f_2}{\partial P_f}\right)_{\bar{o}}\right]\right.$$

$$+ a(1-s)\left(F_{d}{}^{w}\frac{\partial f_1}{\partial W} + F_{d}{}^{t}\frac{\partial f_2}{\partial T}\right)$$

$$+ s\frac{\partial f_1}{\partial W}\left(F_{d}{}^{w} + F_{d}{}^{t} - F_{u}(1-a)\right)$$

$$\left. + (1-s)\frac{\partial f_2}{\partial T}\left(F_{d}{}^{w} + F_{d}{}^{t} - F_{u}\right)\right\} \qquad (2.12a)$$

where

$$D = (1-s)\left(a + \frac{\partial f_2}{\partial T}\right) + s\frac{\partial f_1}{\partial W}$$

The expressions $(\partial f_1/\partial P_f)_{\bar{o}}$ and $(\partial f_2/\partial P_f)_{\bar{o}}$ represent the pure substitution effects of the change in the price of F on the demand for F of "wage earners" and "capitalists." They could also be expressed as pure substitution elasticities.

When the devaluation occurs in a situation of deficit or equilibrium in the balance of trade $(F_{d}{}^{w} + F_{d}{}^{t} \geqslant F_{u})$, the sign of dB/dk in Equation 2.12a will be unambiguously positive. Thus, in spite of the introduction of the redistributive effect we still obtain the result that a devaluation can never worsen the trade balance of a small country that is a price taker in international trade.

Equation 2.12a may be taken as a starting point for the analysis of a short run defined as a situation for which pure substitution effects are absent for consumption and for which the supply elasticities for the F good are zero, although it is assumed that the supply of H is perfectly elastic. Thus, in that short run $(\partial f_1/\partial P_f)_{\bar{o}} = (\partial f_2/\partial P_f)_{\bar{o}} = \partial f_3/\partial P_f = 0$. The extreme inelasticity of the supply of the F good in the short run (for *upward* movements of P_f) could, for example, be caused by exportables from crops planted and harvested once a year and importables for which increases in production require fresh investments with long gestation periods. On the other hand, the perfect elasticity in the supply of H (for *decreases* in production) is consistent with the Keynesian assumption of rigid money wages in the short run.

If for simplicity we also assume an original situation of balanced trade, Equation 2.12a becomes

$$\frac{dB}{dk} = \frac{a}{D} \left\{ \frac{\partial f_1}{\partial W} F_d^w + \frac{\partial f_2}{\partial T} F_d^t \left[1 + s \left(\frac{\frac{\partial f_1}{\partial W}}{\frac{\partial f_2}{\partial T}} - 1 \right) \right] \right\} \quad (2.13)$$

Thus, even in a short run characterized by a zero supply elasticity for the F good and zero substitution effects, the pure redistributive effect will unambiguously result in an improvement in the balance of trade. The improvement will be greater, the larger the magnitudes of: a (the marginal propensity to save); the over-all marginal propensity of the society to spend on F (the weighted sum of the corresponding propensities of "workers" and "capitalists"); and the marginal propensity of "workers" to spend on F relative to that of "capitalists."[5]

[5] It is interesting to note that in this model no value for $\partial f_2/\partial T$ that is $\leqslant 1$ can yield a worsening of the trade balance as a result of the redistributive effect that favors "capitalists." Even if it had been assumed that "capitalists" do not spend anything at all on the H good, so that they either spend on F or save, the equation equivalent to 2.13 would be

$$\frac{dB}{dk} = \frac{1}{C} \left\{ F_d^w \frac{\partial f_1}{\partial W} \left(1 - \frac{\partial f_2}{\partial T} \right) \right\} \quad (2.13a)$$

where

$$C = 1 - s \left(1 - \frac{\partial f_1}{\partial W} \right)$$

Thus, even with this extreme assumption regarding the propensity to spend of "capitalists," the trade balance would not worsen in the short run. If only the impact effect of devaluation on wage and nonwage income is taken into account other results become possible. See C. F. Díaz Alejandro, "A Note on the Impact of Devaluation and the Redistributive Effect," *The Journal of Political Economy*, Vol. LXXI, No. 6 (December 1963), pp. 577–580. In that paper, the *real* income gain of "capitalists" following a devaluation was expressed as what they gained as producers of F minus what they lost as consumers of F, or

$$(F_u - F_d^t) \cdot dk$$

In the more complete model presented above, the impact of devaluation on the output of H and thus on profits earned in the H industry is also taken into account, so that the change in real profits is now written:

We can now turn to the impact of devaluation on the level of domestic output, which will be given by the sum of dF_u/dk and dH_u/dk. As for dB/dk, we can first obtain a general expression for dY/dk (denoting by Y the level of total real output), and from that expression derive the short run one. The general expression is

$$\frac{dY}{dk} = \frac{1}{D}\left[\frac{\partial f_3}{\partial P_f} - \left(\frac{\partial f_1}{\partial P_f}\right)_{\bar{o}} - \left(\frac{\partial f_2}{\partial P_f}\right)_{\bar{o}} - F_d{}^w\left(1 - \frac{\partial f_1}{\partial W}\right) \right.$$
$$\left. - F_d{}^t\left(1 - \frac{\partial f_2}{\partial T}\right) + F_u\left(1 - a - \frac{\partial f_2}{\partial T}\right)\right] \quad (2.14)$$

For the short run and assuming initially balanced trade, we obtain:

$$\frac{dY}{dk} = \frac{1}{D}\left[F_d{}^w\left(\frac{\partial f_1}{\partial W} - \frac{\partial f_2}{\partial T}\right) - F_u \cdot a\right] \quad (2.15)$$

In contrast to Equation 2.13, the sign of dY/dk can be either positive or negative, depending on the relative size of the parameters. If $\partial f_2/\partial T > \partial f_1/\partial W$, the sign of dY/dk will be unambiguously negative, that is, domestic output will fall following the devaluation.[6] Even if $\partial f_1/\partial W > \partial f_2/\partial T$, if $F_u \cdot a > F_d{}^w(\partial f_1/\partial W - \partial f_2/\partial T)$ domestic output will also fall. It may be noticed that the condition $\partial f_2/\partial T > \partial f_1/\partial W$ is likely to be met in many countries, as the "capitalists" will tend to have an expenditure pattern (consumption plus investment) more biased toward imports than "workers." Even when that is not the case, it may be noticed that

---

$$(F_u - F_d{}^t) \cdot dk + (1-s) \cdot dH_u$$

Given a value for a, the marginal propensity to save (or hoard), a higher value for the import propensity means a lower value for the propensity to spend on H, and thus a lower level of domestic activity, which depresses wages and profits enough to offset from the point of view of the balance of payments the higher propensities to spend on F. See also the next footnote.

[6] Using the relations $1 = \partial f_1/\partial W + \partial H_d{}^w/\partial W$ and $1 = a + \partial f_2/\partial T + \partial H_d{}^t/\partial T$ the conditions for an *increase* in output in the short run following a devaluation undertaken with an initially balanced trade becomes

$$\partial f_1/\partial W + \partial f_2/\partial T > 1 + a(F_d{}^t/F_d{}^w)$$

or

$$\partial H_d{}^t/\partial T - \partial H_d{}^w/\partial W > a(F_d{}^t/F_d{}^w)$$

If it had been assumed that "capitalists" either save their income or spend it on good F the increase in domestic output in the short run would be impossible. From Equations 2.15 and 2.13 it can be seen that, *given a value for a, the higher $\partial f_2/\partial T$* (and thus the lower $\partial H_d{}^t/\partial T$), the greater the improvement in the trade balance in the short run and the greater the short-run fall of domestic output.

$F_u > F_d^w$, making a drop in output in the short run extremely likely, even if $\partial f_1/\partial W > \partial f_2/\partial T$ and $a < (\partial f_1/\partial W - \partial f_2/\partial T)$.

Thus, the introduction of a redistributive effect solves the apparent paradox of a devaluation that leads in the short run to *both* an improvement in the balance of trade and a drop in the level of domestic output. From Equations 2.14 and 2.12, it is easily seen that when the short-run assumptions of $\partial f_3/\partial P_f = (\partial f_1/\partial P_f)_{\bar{o}} = (\partial f_2/\partial P_f)_{\bar{o}} = 0$ are lifted, both a greater improvement in the balance of trade and a greater expansion (or a smaller drop) of domestic output will follow a devaluation. But even in the long run a simultaneous improvement in the balance of trade and a drop in domestic output remain possible after a devaluation because of the redistributive effect. But, of course, the greater the ability of a country to substitute one good for another in its consumption and investment and the greater its capacity to expand and transform in production, the more likely will be an improvement in both the balance of trade and in home production following a devaluation.

From Equations 2.14 and 2.12, it can also be easily seen that the greater the original deficit in the balance of trade (that is, the greater $F_d^w + F_d^t$ relative to F_u), the greater will be the improvement in the balance of trade and the drop in domestic production following a devaluation, for in such a case the negative income effects of the change in P_f will have a larger bite.

The short-run impact of devaluation on total money wages and profits is easily obtained by combining Equations 2.9 and 2.10 with Equation 2.15. In the likely case of a fall in domestic output after a devaluation, total real wages, as well as the real wage rate, will drop. Total absolute money profits will increase in the F industry as well as profits per unit of output. Profits in the production of the nontraded good H will remain the same in per unit money terms, but will fall as output contracts. The change in real profits (total and per unit of output) will of course depend on the expenditure pattern of "capitalists." Taking into account these factors, a short-run rate of exchange that optimizes real profits could be computed. Such a rate would only by coincidence be compatible with either full employment or balance-of-trade equilibrium. Regardless of the effect of devaluation on total profits, it is clear that the profit share in the national income will necessarily improve after devaluation.

In the model just presented, devaluation changed the ratio of P_f to P_h, leaving the terms of trade between imports and exports unchanged. The over-all price level of the country will rise according to the importance of importables and exportables in the economy, but the elasticity of the price level with respect to changes in the exchange rate will be less than one. It may be noticed that in the model just presented, the domestic prices of both importables and exportables will rise, in contrast to the standard devaluation models that assume perfectly elastic supply schedules for exportables. It is such a price increase that yields the cut in real-wage rates and the increase in the profit rate in the F industry, triggering off the redistributive effect. As income is redistributed in favor of the saving class, the trade balance will improve even in the short run, and the greater the simultaneous drop in domestic output, the more it will improve. The contraction of real-wage rates leading to the fall of real output will result in a decrease in demand for both importables and exportables. Because foreign demand has been assumed to be perfectly elastic, an immediate increase in exports is possible even though the total output of exportables is frozen in the short run, for the previously domestically consumed exportables will now be shipped abroad.

The process of price inflation coupled with real-income deflation, which has been described, has a great number of similarities with the theory of inflation in a closed economy. It can be objected that this process is nothing more than deflationary policy under a different costume. Yet if devaluation is used for this purpose in the short run, an examination of its impact falls well within the province of the study of devaluation.

As it has been mentioned, the length of the short run when money-wage rates are fixed and $\partial f_3/\partial P_f = (\partial f_1/\partial P_f)_{\bar{o}} = (\partial f_2/\partial P_f)_{\bar{o}} = 0$ will vary from country to country and in the same country for different time periods. If the devaluation took place under conditions of less than full employment, real-wage rates may regain part or all of their losses in the long run when output of F expands. In other words, absorption may increase without endangering the improvement in the balance of trade as long as total output expands. On the other hand, if devaluation was undertaken under full-employment conditions and with a deficit in the balance of trade, part of the short-run drop in real-wage rates will have to be maintained even in the long run, when the resources freed by the drop in the ouput of H flow into the F industry and total domestic output regains a full-employment level with a product mix different from the predevaluation situation. Such a permanent cut in real-wage rates would be required to decrease total absorption at the full-employment position, given the spending propensities assumed for the two social classes. Devaluation under conditions of full employment and balance-of-trade deficit requires *both* a cut in total absorption and a reallocation of resources from industry H to industry F to achieve an equilibrium in the balance of trade and maintain full employment. As such a reallocation is to be carried out by entrepreneurs responding to profit incentives, it is extremely likely that the main burden of the cut in absorption will be thrust on the shoulders of nonentrepreneurs, which is also assumed to be the class with a zero saving propensity.[7]

Finally, it should be stressed that the model which has been presented and the discussion flowing from it represent neither an attempt to put forth a general theory of devaluation nor an effort to cover all the relevant variables and relationships which in the Argentine economy influence the outcome of a devaluation. Rather, the model had the modest aim of exploring fully the implications of certain special assumptions which are deemed to be relevant to Argentina. The following chapters will attempt to show that the discussion of this chapter is quite useful in guiding the analysis of Argentine devaluations, especially that of December 1958, although the simple scheme presented has to be expanded and modified to take into account relevant complexities of the real world, such as the circumstances under which devaluation is undertaken, the existence of a government sector with an autonomous fiscal and monetary policy, and foreign demands that are less than perfectly elastic. The following chapters will also try to justify the emphasis that has been given to the speed of pure income effects as compared with pure substitution effects in consumption and production.

Wealth Effects

The pure redistributive effect has dealt with the impact of devaluation on income flows. It is likely that devaluation will also have wealth effects which will affect social classes in different ways. This

[7] Of course, it remains possible to achieve the cut in absorption by attempting to increase the share of income saved by "capitalists," while sustaining real-wage rates after a devaluation. The rate of profit per unit of output produced would still improve in industry F *relative* to industry H after the devaluation, but the absolute level of profits would be lower than in the model that assumes a drop in real-wage rates after devaluation.

section will examine two of these effects deemed relevant to the Argentine situation.

When the production of exportables requires inputs that have a perfectly inelastic supply in the long run, such as land, or in the short run, such as cattle stocks, the change in relative prices brought about by devaluation will not only increase the real income of the producers of exportables but will also increase the real wealth of the owners of these inputs by increasing the real value of these assets (land and cattle herds). It is not uncommon that the owners of these inputs are also the producers of exportables.

If it is assumed that devaluation does not change the aggregate real net wealth of the country, the gain in real wealth by owners of, say, land and cattle herds must be offset by a loss of real wealth from the rest of society, such a transfer being realized through a change in relative prices of the different types of assets. The effect of such a redistribution of wealth on expenditure will depend, of course, on the spending propensities of each class and the relative weight which each of them gives to the real wealth variable in its expenditure function. The fact that the same sectors whose income flows, including pure rents, are increased by devaluation benefit from an increase in their real wealth would seem to reinforce the presumption that such a shift will increase the over-all savings of the economy, thus tending to improve the trade balance. On the other hand, the existence of inputs that even in the long run have a fixed supply indicates that the price stimulus of a devaluation will to some extent be dissipated by increased pure rents. Thus the potential supply response will be less elastic than in situations when all inputs can be increased in the long run.

Devaluation may produce another type of wealth effect when some groups of the country have debts to foreigners expressed in terms of foreign currencies. A devaluation will then increase the value of the debt expressed in domestic currencies and will exert a depressing influence on the expenditures of these groups, especially when the domestic prices they receive for the sale of their products or services do not increase proportionally with the devaluation. When a country has a net foreign debt, this effect will make more likely both an improvement in the trade balance and a drop in domestic output following devaluation, especially when the debt is held by the private sector and is concentrated in short-term maturities.

A Digression. The Manufacturing Sector: Import-Competing or Home Industry?

The model presented earlier in this chapter relied heavily on the distinction between home goods, and importables and exportables. Although such a distinction is easily made in a theoretical model without intermediate products, it may be harder to apply it neatly to a real economy. In particular, the question may be raised as to whether the manufacturing sector is catalogued as producing home goods or importables. When dealing with semi-industrialized economies, one is tempted to put all of the manufacturing sector into the category of import-competing industries and to leave services as the only home good.

It is well known that a devaluation has a symmetrically stimulating effect on both export- and import-competing *activities*.[8] Yet in many semi-industrialized countries, the *existing* manufacturing sector generally takes a dim view of exchange-rate devaluations and fears such policy as much as it fears tight monetary policies. This suggests that at least part of the manufacturing sector falls in a category more nearly like that of the H than of the import-competing industry.

Two simple partial-equilibrium situations will be presented to clarify (1) the conditions under which the *impact effect* of devaluation provides symmetrical stimuli to the export and manufacturing sectors and (2) conditions in which devaluation is harmful to the existing firms in the manufacturing sector. In the first case, the manufacturing sector could be called import competing, while in the latter a more appropriate label would be home industry. The introduction of intermediate products complicates the integration of the analysis of this section with that of earlier sections, but the basic point arising from it is relevant to our previous discussion.

Figure 2.1 considers a situation in which there are two types of imports: M_c (imports of consumer goods) and M_t (imports of intermediate products). There is no domestic production that can compete with M_t, although there is domestic production of good P that competes with M_c. At a given exchange rate (and a level of ad valorem tariff duties, transport costs, and so forth), the domestic price of good P is 0A, while the schedules for total domestic de-

---

[8] The existence of intermediate products requires a distinction between an "importable" (a final good) and an import-competing activity (value added that may represent a small proportion of the value of the final good).

mand and world and domestic supply are given by D_p, S_{wp}, and S_{dp}, respectively. Domestic production of amount OB will generate a demand schedule for imported raw materials, D_t, which because there are no substitutes is assumed to be perfectly inelastic in the range OA of prices, falling to zero for higher prices. The world-supply schedule for M_t is denoted by S_{wt}. Net import substitution valued in domestic currency will be equal to $OAEB$ minus $OGFD$. A devaluation of the exchange rate, which raises the domestic price of foreign exchange, will raise S_{wp} and S_{wt} to S'_{wp} and S'_{wt}, respectively. It will also raise S_{dp} by the same amount to S'_{dp}, because of

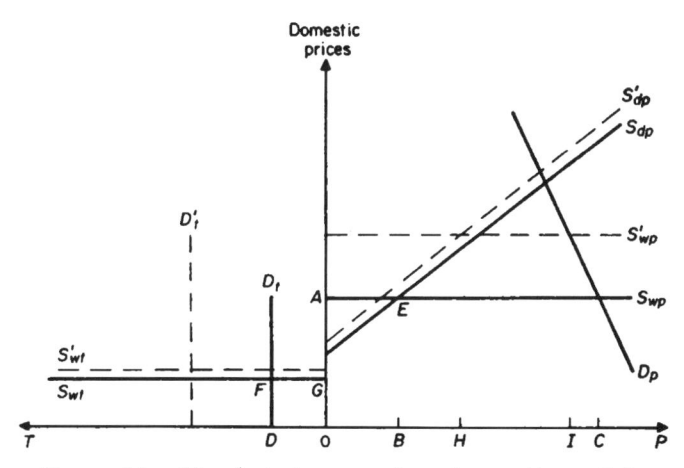

FIGURE 2.1. *Manufacturing as an import-competing activity.*

the increased cost of the imported raw material. In spite of this, gross domestic production of good P will increase by BH, while imports of good P will fall (in addition to BH) by the quantity IC because of the negative slope of D_p. Although demand for imported raw materials will shift to D'_t, net import substitution will expand, as a diagram expressing prices in terms of foreign currency would reveal more clearly.

The definition of net import substitution as the value added domestically, not as the gross domestic production of good P, makes it clear under the conditions of Figure 2.1 that the stimulus of devaluation will be symmetrical, regardless of the imported raw material needs of the import-competing and export sectors.

Figure 2.2 presents a situation in which prohibitive ad valorem tariffs on imports of finished good P have shifted S_{wp} upward in such a way that all goods P are domestically produced, under domestic competitive conditions, at price $0A$ and in quantity $0B$. Imports are exclusively raw materials in quantity $0C$, which enter duty free, and for which domestic manufacture is very difficult, as shown by supply schedule S_{dt}. Under these circumstances a devaluation similar in magnitude to that shown in Figure 2.1 will fail to stimulate domestic production of raw materials and will result in an upward shift in the domestic supply of good P from S_{dp} to S'_{dp}. Thus, domestic production of P will fall by amount DB, bringing about a fall of raw ma-

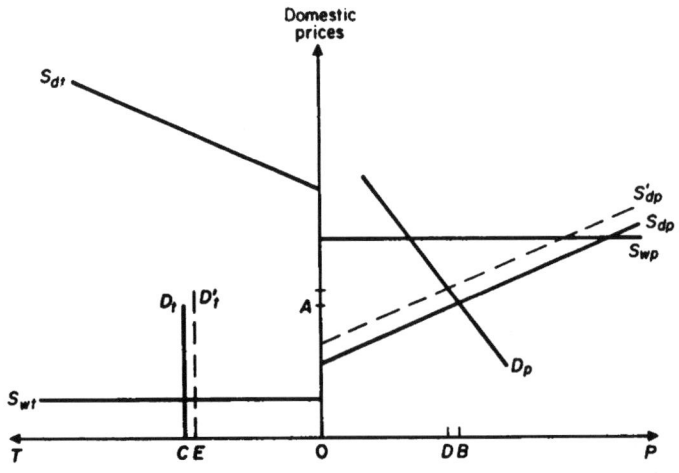

FIGURE 2.2. *Manufacturing as an activity producing home goods.*

terial imports in the amount CE. In this case, the manufacturing sector will be adversely affected by the impact of devaluation, and the fall in imports will result from a fall in domestic production, and not from an expansion of output as in the case of Figure 2.1. It may be noted that under the circumstances described in Figure 2.2 a devaluation tends to produce both an improvement in the balance of trade and a drop in the internal output of the nontradable goods which are complementary with tradable goods (the imported raw material).[9]

The two cases represent extreme situations, and combinations of

---

[9] As W. M. Corden has pointed out to me, in this case the switching of expenditures resulting from devaluation is not only a switch from tradables to nontradables but also from those nontradables that are complementary with tradables toward nontradables that are substitutes for tradables.

the two could yield more complex cases. By lowering S_{dt} in Figure 2.2, one could create cases in which the fall in output of the sector producing P could be less or more than offset by an increase in the domestic production of previously imported raw materials. Further situations would be presented changing the nature of the restrictions imposed against imports in Figure 2.2, as well as the assumptions regarding internal competition, but with little gain in insight into the problem.

Several semi-industrialized countries seem to be passing through conditions similar to those described in Figure 2.2. A devaluation will then be painful to the existing manufacturing sector, as it will not be able to reduce imports without also reducing the output of existing firms. Under these circumstances, existing firms will tend to oppose further import substitution, unless they can be assured that it will not increase the prices of their inputs. Clearly the best of all possible worlds for firms producing good P in Figure 2.2 is one with prohibitive duties or restrictions against imports of good P, coupled with an overvalued exchange rate, or other types of subsidies, for the importation of raw materials. This snag in "backward linkage" could become fairly important in slowing down the growth of the more sophisticated branches of manufacturing in semi-industrialized countries.

In summary, it is clear that great care should be exercised when trying to subdivide the manufacturing sector and manufactured products into home industry and import-competing categories and into home goods and importables. A given product may embody value added in home as well as in import-competing industries, besides having components directly imported. In principle one could decompose each product into its home-good and importable components and label each manufacturing firm according to the link between its *net* prices and international prices. But in practice the line between importables and home goods will necessarily remain slightly fuzzy, and the manufacturing sector in semi-industrialized countries is likely to have elements both of home and import-competing industries.

Demand and Supply Rigidities in the Long Run

The model presented earlier in this chapter emphasized demand and supply rigidities in the analysis of the short run. This section will explore the implications of the permanence of the demand and supply rigidities in the long run for the impact of devaluation on a small price-taking country.

Let us suppose that to produce the nontraded good H only homogeneous labor is necessary, while the production of the composite good F requires fixed proportions of labor and capital. These production functions, which may be assumed to be linear and homogeneous, will produce an aggregate production-possibilities curve of the type shown in Figure 2.3, providing that each input constrains production, although not at all times. If we assume that this is a small price-taking country, it will never produce within the production-possibilities curve, as foreign demand always gives it the

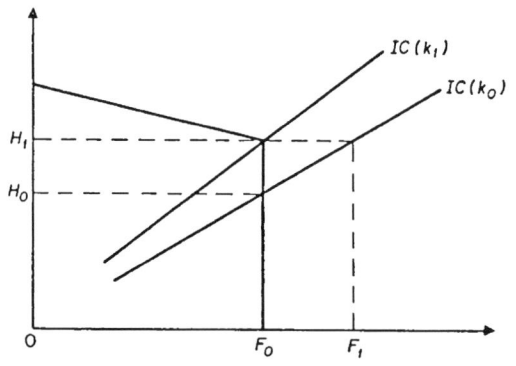

FIGURE 2.3. *Rigid supply and flexible demand conditions.*

alternative of producing along the vertical section of the production frontier. However, full employment of both capital and labor will not occur unless production takes place at the vertex of the frontier. Beyond the vertex, it is fruitless to compress the output of H in the hope of increasing the output of F.

On the basis of individual preferences and propensities and a given income distribution, we can obtain for different exchange rates and prices of H and F different income-consumption lines relating the amounts of H and F demanded for different levels of the national product.[10] At the rate of exchange k_o implicit in the income consumption line $IC\ (k_o)$ of Figure 2.3, only domestic production of H_o will be compatible with equilibrium in the balance of trade, as then $F_u = F_d$. For example, a policy of maintaining full employment

[10] As F_u is always at its full employment point, the national product will change as H_u changes.

of labor, requiring an output of H_1, will result in a deficit of $P_f(F_1 - F_o)$ at the given rate of exchange k_o.

If pure substitution effects in consumption were high enough, an exchange rate such as k_1 (which would be devalued relative to k_0) would result in an income consumption line IC (k_1) through the vertex of the production frontier, allowing the achievement of both full employment of labor and balance-of-trade equilibrium. On the other hand, if the domestic preference maps between F and H are L-shaped (or close to L-shaped), a devaluation would not raise the income-consumption lines significantly. The term bottleneck would appear to be warranted for describing such a situation of incompatibility of full employment of labor with equilibrium in the trade

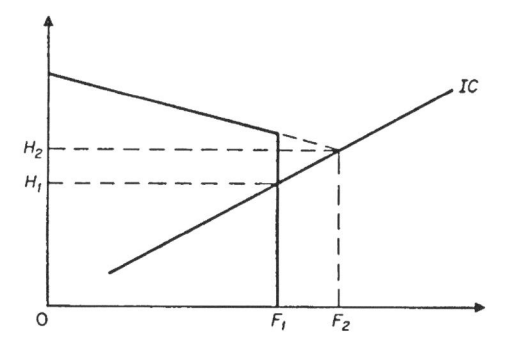

FIGURE 2.4. *Rigid supply and demand conditions.*

balance at "any" exchange rate.[11] Yet in a longer run, a new possibility appears for obtaining both desired goals. Based on the (unshiftable) income-consumption line, the output of F could be expanded in the long run by capital formation so that the production frontier would expand from the solid line to the broken line in Figure 2.4. From outputs of H_1 and F_1, the increase in capital formation would allow us to go to H_2 and F_2, a full employment point.

Yet bottlenecks are not so easily eliminated. The suggested increase in capital formation is likely to require *in advance* special imports beyond those implicit in the IC line of Figure 2.4, thus shifting this curve downward and to the right before the expansion of

[11] The rationale for such extreme lack of substitutability between H and F will be discussed in the next chapter insofar as it affects the substitutability between importables and home goods. In general, such rationale involves arguments which are hard to squeeze into the simple diagrams presented here, although they lead to bottleneck-type situations such as the ones just described.

the production is realized. If no foreign loans are available to finance the special imports of capital goods, a policy of internal deflation could free the foreign exchange needed by depressing the output of the home good. A devaluation that resulted in a redistributive effect such as the one earlier described would also achieve such an objective. The devaluation would reduce the absorption of F and the production of H and would induce a shift in income distribution in favor of "capitalists," as a result of their windfall gains in the production of F, which is the sector whose output we are trying to encourage. To the extent that the increased profits in industry F lead to capital accumulation in this sector and thus to future increases in the output of F, the policy of devaluation will be more beneficial than that of pure deflation. This is so in spite of the fact that the long-run increase in the output of F will not come about by withdrawing resources from H. Only in the roundabout sense that a lower output in industry H leads to lower income and thus to a lower internal demand for F for non-capital formation purposes, can it be said that the lower output of H frees resources for use in industry F.

Finally, an increase in capital formation requiring foreign exchange may be financed by increases in the saving propensities of each social class. The ease with which these marginal domestic savings can be turned into additional foreign exchange will depend on the nature of the goods released from domestic absorption by the higher level of savings and the elasticity of substitution among different goods. At one extreme we have a situation in which the goods freed from domestic absorption are exportables or importables. At the other extreme, the marginal savings may be realized at the expense of absorption of home goods. In the first case, the increase in savings will be fully converted into foreign exchange without depressing the domestic level of output or requiring a change in relative prices. In the second case, the efficiency with which savings can be translated into foreign exchange will be considerably reduced, especially in cases where there are low elasticities of substitution in consumption. Under these adverse circumstances, to earn a given amount of foreign exchange, the drop in domestic output accompanying the increase in savings will be much larger than when part of the marginal savings is realized at the expense of importables or exportables and there are higher elasticities of substitution.

These relationships may be illustrated with a very simple Keynesian model for our small country. Ignoring the redistribution effect and setting all prices equal to one, we can write

$$C = Y(f+h) \qquad (2.16)$$

$$Y = H_u + \overline{F}_u = \overline{F}_u + h \cdot Y \qquad (2.17)$$

$$B = \overline{F}_u - F_d = \overline{F}_u - f \cdot Y \qquad (2.18)$$

Equation 2.16 expresses total consumption, where f and h are the marginal propensities to spend on good F and good H, respectively. Equation 2.17 indicates total national income, assuming that total production of F is fixed in the short run and that the supply of H will equal its demand. Finally, Equation 2.18 presents the balance of trade. The equilibrium values for national income and the balance of trade will then be

$$Y_e = \frac{\overline{F}_u}{1-h} \qquad (2.17a)$$

$$B_e = \frac{\overline{F}_u(1-h-f)}{1-h} \qquad (2.18a)$$

The impact of a change in h or f on the equilibrium values can now be compared. For a change in f, we have

$$\frac{dY_e}{df} = 0 \qquad (2.17b)$$

$$\frac{dB_e}{df} = -\frac{\overline{F}_u}{1-h} = -Y_e \qquad (2.18b)$$

For a change in h, we will get

$$\frac{dY_e}{dh} = \frac{\overline{F}_u}{(1-h)^2} = \frac{Y_e}{(1-h)} \qquad (2.17c)$$

$$\frac{dB_e}{dh} = -f\frac{\overline{F}_u}{(1-h)^2} = -\frac{f \cdot Y_e}{(1-h)} \qquad (2.18c)$$

Thus, a change in f, say a negative shift corresponding to an autonomous increase in savings at the expense of F absorption, will leave the equilibrium value for Y unchanged, but will result in an improvement in the balance of trade equal to the increase in savings. On the other hand, a negative shift in h will result in a drop in the equilibrium level of income, while the improvement in the balance of trade is smaller than in Equation 2.18b. This is so because $f <$

$1 - h$ as long as there is a positive marginal propensity to save; this improvement in the balance of trade will also be smaller than the original increase in savings.

If there is a high elasticity of substitution in the consumption of goods H and F and changes in relative prices are considered, the ease with which increased domestic savings can be turned into foreign exchange would be increased even if at first the marginal increase in savings takes place wholly at the expense of absorption of H.

A Final Comment

This chapter has given great emphasis to all sorts of rigidities hampering the workings of the mechanism of relative prices, especially in the short run. The relevance of this analysis will depend, of course, on the realism of the assumptions made, either for the short run or the long run. The next few chapters will describe some of the key relationships influencing balance of payments in the Argentine economy. It will be shown then that the rigidities examined in this chapter represent fairly realistic assumptions, especially for the short run. Nothing in these arguments should be interpreted to suggest that such rigidities are inevitable in semi-industrialized countries. Indeed, in the Argentine case, it appears that "structural" difficulties arose primarily as a result of neglecting marginal adjustments for several years. While continuous marginal adjustments appear to be the best prevention against structural rigidities, once such rigidities appear for whatever reason, economic analysis must take them into account.

3

The Balance of Payments, Tradable Goods, and the Import Function of Argentina

This and the next two chapters will examine the key characteristics of the foreign trade and the internal economy of Argentina during the post-Second World War period. The balance of payments will be presented in this chapter, and a discussion of the weight of F goods (or tradable goods) in the Argentine economy will follow, taking into account not only actual exports and imports but also all importables and exportables. Finally, the results of attempts to measure the import function will be presented.

The Argentine Balance of Payments, 1950–1963

Table 3.1 summarizes the Argentine balance of payments. Since 1948, there has been a tendency toward deficits in the current account, which has acted as the principal brake on the economic growth of Argentina. The large gold and foreign-exchange reserves accumulated during the Second World War and the immediate postwar years were rapidly drawn down, so that from a level of net reserves of $1,687 million at the end of 1946, they fell to $357 million at the end of 1951.[1] Chapter 6 will discuss some of the features of

[1] See *Memoria Anual*, 1958, Banco Central de la República Argentina,

the "stop-go" fiscal, monetary, and exchange policies that emerged from the foreign exchange difficulties of the nineteen-fifties.

For the period under discussion, "invisible" items have played a rather minor role in the determination of the balance on current

TABLE 3.1
THE BALANCE OF PAYMENTS OF ARGENTINA, 1951–1963
(*Yearly averages in millions of current U.S. dollars*)

	1951/ 1952	1953– 1955	1956– 1958	1959– 1961	1962/ 1963
Merchandise Exports	929	1027	971	1017	1291
Merchandise Imports	—1330	— 982	—1224	—1234	—1169
Balance of Merchandise Trade	— 401	45	— 253	— 217	122
Real Service Exports	92	88	82	124	140
Real Service Imports	— 71	— 73	— 55	— 108	— 130
Net Profits and Interests	— 22	— 16	— 20	— 66	— 70
Net Other Services	17	8	17	15	— 79
Net services	17	7	24	— 35	— 139
Balance in Current Account	— 385	52	— 229	— 252	— 17
Net Unilateral Transfers	— 17	— 6	— 2	— 8	— 3
Private Long-Term Capital	93	52	75	195	229
Private Short-Term Capital	42	— 53	7	34	— 286
Official and Banking Long-Term Capital	47	— 9	— 49	68	— 48
Official and Banking Short-Term Capital and Monetary Gold	227	— 43	207	— 36	125
Net Capital and Monetary Gold	409	— 52	241	— 261	20
Errors and Omissions	— 8	5	— 10	— 2	0

Sources: Data elaborated from *Balances de Pagos de la República Argentina, Años 1951–1958*, Suplemento del Boletín Estadístico No. 1, January 1960, Banco Central de la República Argentina, Buenos Aires; and *Boletín Estadístico*, Banco Central de la República Argentina, several issues.
A negative sign indicates a debit entry.

account, which has been dominated by fluctuations in merchandise exports and imports. Only in recent years with the renewal of large-scale private foreign investment in Argentina has the service account shown interesting and significant changes. New activities by foreign companies in Argentina have resulted not only in larger profit and

---

pp. 1–5. The net reserves were used mostly to finance the purchase of assets held by foreigners in Argentina during 1947–1949.

interest remittances but also in a greater flow of license agreements, business trips, and so on. This chapter and the next two will neglect the service account, which shall be discussed briefly in connection with foreign investment in Chapter 6. It will also neglect private and long-term official capital flows, which may be taken as either autonomous or induced by developments in the current account. Thus, the analysis of the external sector of Argentina and of the endogenous short-term mechanism of adjustment of the balance of payments will be limited to merchandise trade, a simplification that seems warranted by the relative magnitudes of the figures presented in Table 3.1 and by the presumption that errors of observation are likely to be higher for the individual invisible items than for merchandise trade.

The remaining chapters of this study will analyze the internal causes for the pressure on foreign exchange reserves and will discuss the jerky nature of the short-run mechanism of adjustment of the balance of payments. At this point, however, it should be pointed out that besides internal pressures, the Argentine balance of payments was subjected to external pressures as the terms of trade worsened throughout the nineteen-fifties relative not only to the very favorable levels of the immediate postwar period but also to the levels of 1935–1938 as shown in Table 3.2. This adverse long-run exogenous factor tended to put additional pressure on the short-term mechanism of adjustment of the balance of payments, but it would

TABLE 3.2
INDICES OF EXPORT AND IMPORT PRICES AND
THE TERMS OF TRADE OF ARGENTINA
(1946–1949 = 100)

	Export Prices	Import Prices	Terms of Trade
1935–1939	32	39	82
1950–1952	99	132	75
1953–1955	87	120	73
1956–1958	75	120	63
1959–1961	73	106	69

Sources: Elaborated from price indices found in: *Análisis y Proyecciones del Desarrollo Económico: V, El Desarrollo Económico de la Argentina,* Naciones Unidas, México, 1959, Part 1, p. 110; *Comercio Exterior,* Informe C48, Dirección Nacional de Estadística y Censos, Buenos Aires, April 1958, and the *Boletín Mensual de Estadística* of the same institution. Data from the two basic sources were linked in 1951. It should be noted that these indices may not fully take into account quality changes in imported goods.

be a gross exaggeration to blame Argentina's balance-of-payments difficulties solely on the deteriorating terms of trade. The internal conditions that accounted for the inefficient response to the unfavorable external conditions will provide the fundamental explanation for such difficulties.

Importables and Exportables in the Argentine Economy

Chapter 2 put emphasis on the distinction between home goods (nontradable), whose prices were independent of foreign prices and the exchange rate, and foreign or F goods (tradable), which include both importables and exportables and whose domestic prices were tied to the exchange rate and foreign prices. In practice, the line between these two categories is likely to be blurred, as in the case of manufactured goods discussed in Chapter 2, as cross-elasticities of substitution and supply conditions are not likely to show large breaks and discontinuities in the real world, thus providing a continuum of "tradability" rather than neat isolated categories, especially in the long run. The issue is further complicated by the fact that the basic causes for the distinction between home and tradable goods may be "natural" (for example, very large transport costs) or "artificial" (for example, government actions which forbid or practically forbid the importation or exportation of some commodities or services). While the former cause is likely to change slowly through time, the latter may change overnight, so that a good whose price is today closely linked to foreign prices and the exchange rate may tomorrow find its price determined independently of such factors. Finally, the existence of intermediate goods blurs distinctions further, as even items that seem to fall obviously in the home-good category (for example, urban transportation services) may have their prices linked to the foreign sector through inputs that are either importables or exportables (for example, fuel).

In spite of these conceptual difficulties, it may be useful to obtain an over-all idea of the weight of importable and exportable goods in Argentina, roughly defined given the transport costs and the protectionist policies that prevailed during most of the period under discussion.

Exportable goods seem to provide the clearest picture. The main exports of Argentina (grains, meat, wool, and so on) are also consumed internally in very substantial amounts. Although a small share of the value added in agriculture and livestock corresponds to goods that are not close to the exportable category for Argentina (for example, flowers), the whole of value added in these rural activities, which represented 15 per cent of the gross domestic product during the period 1950–1961, may be taken to belong to the exportable category.[2] Argentina has failed to develop significant and sustained nonrural exports, and it is doubtful that any serious error is made by assuming that no manufactured and mined goods or services could be placed in the category of exportables, beyond those actually exported during this period, which amount to around 1 per cent of the gross domestic product.

There is another minor snag in the transition from the analysis of Chapter 2 to the realities of exportables in Argentina. It was assumed in the previous chapter that we were dealing with a country so small that it could not influence the international prices of importables and exportables. It will be seen that, although Argentina's share in world commerce has been declining for most of its exportables, for some goods, such as chilled beef, its share is rather high. Thus, even assuming no other frictions and imperfections it cannot be expected that the internal prices of exportables will move in exactly the same proportion as the exchange rate. But for the bulk of exportables, such close correspondence can be expected in the absence of frictions. The next chapter will return to this issue.

During 1950 to 1961, imports of goods and services amounted to 9 per cent of the gross domestic product. In the same period, the domestic manufacturing and mining sectors, which accounted for 33 per cent of the gross domestic product, were given a high degree of protection from foreign competition, either through quantitative restrictions on imports or through nearly prohibitive exchange surcharges and similar devices. The degree of protection was sufficiently high to break the direct links that may have existed among the domestic prices of most of these goods, world prices, and the exchange rate, although the indirect link provided by imported intermediate products and raw materials remained. For some products, such as oil, a direct link may have remained, but it is doubtful that such importable products amounted to more than 5 per cent of the gross domestic product, including in that percentage services that may be candidates for the importable category (for example, shipping services).

[2] Data on the national accounts have been obtained from *Cuentas Nacionales de la República Argentina*, Consejo Nacional de Desarrollo, Presidencia de la Nación, República Argentina, Buenos Aires, April 1964. Percentages are obtained from figures expressed in current prices.

In summary, it may be roughly estimated that exportables plus importables amount to between 25 and 30 per cent of the gross domestic product of Argentina. What will be the expected direct and immediate impact of an increase in the domestic price of foreign exchange of 10 per cent on the domestic price level under these circumstances, assuming downward rigidity of prices? The answer depends, of course, on the precise definition used for the domestic price level.[3] If the general price level refers to all goods consumed and invested within the country, the direct impact will take into account only the weight of importables plus exportables *not sent abroad* in total domestic absorption. Since between one third and one fourth of the agricultural and livestock production of Argentina is sent abroad as exports, the general price level that refers to total absorption could be expected to increase between 2.0 per cent and 2.6 per cent solely as a direct and immediate result of a devaluation. If the price level refers to all goods and services produced in the country (a concept approximated by the implicit gross domestic product deflator), the prices of actual imports would be given zero weight, but all exportables and importables produced domestically would be taken into account. Such a price level could be expected to increase by between 1.6 and 2.1 per cent as a direct and immediate result of a devaluation of 10 per cent.

Other price levels could be defined for the "absorption baskets" of wage earners and other members of society. Attempts will be made when the demand and supply conditions for importables and exportables are discussed to isolate or at least obtain some information regarding the shares of demand arising from wage earners and other members of society for each of these categories of goods.

Chapter 2 demonstrated that the larger the total absorption and production of the F good, or of importables and exportables, the greater the leverage of the pure redistributive effect, other things being equal. This conclusion follows from the assumption of constant money-wage rates in the short run. On the other hand, it may be argued that the assumption of constant money-wage rates becomes less and less realistic the larger the weight of the F good, or the greater the ratio of tradable to nontradable goods, for in such cases the elasticity of the price level with respect to the exchange rate will be greater and so will the resulting cut in real-wage rates.

[3] See Arnold C. Harberger, "Some Notes on Inflation," in *Inflation and Growth in Latin America*, Werner Baer and Isaac Kerstenetsky, eds. (Homewood, Ill.: R. D. Irwin, Inc., 1964), p. 337.

If the F good has a greater than average weight in the budgets of wage earners, as exportables have in Argentina, such considerations will be strengthened. Thus, the optimum level of F-good consumption, from the point of view of maximizing the redistributive effect, will depend on the existence and precise nature of the trade unions' "threshold" of perception for movements in real-wage rates; these "thresholds" may change from year to year, just as the bargaining power of such unions is likely to change from time to time.[4] The relative weight of exportables and importables in the Argentine economy seems to be large enough to stimulate trade union pressures following a devaluation, but it also makes the redistributive effect potentially significant. Chapter 6 will deal with the net results of the clash of these conflicting forces in specific historical circumstances.

The Nature of the Demand for Imports in Argentina

The demand for imports reflects the difference at any point in time between the domestic demand for all importable goods and the domestic supply of such goods. It was implied in Chapter 2 that the main hope for a favorable short-run improvement in the balance of trade would be a drop in the demand for importables (or exportables) rather than an expansion of the supply of importables (or exportables). The conceptual and practical difficulties involved in measuring independently the demand and supply of all importables make it advisable to concentrate on discussing and measuring directly actual merchandise imports. This will be done in this section, which will also discuss some features of the domestic supply of importables in Argentina.

Structure and Significance of Merchandise Imports in Argentina

The average propensity to import goods has been declining in Argentina throughout the twentieth century, dropping from around

[4] It has been argued that when the ratio of tradable to nontradable goods is high in an economy, money illusion will not be much help in getting labor to accept a cut in real wages. This view seems one-sided in that it does not take into account the greater leverage that the high ratio of tradable to nontradable goods gives to the redistributive effect. As such a ratio approaches zero it becomes harder to notice any change in real wages simply because either such changes do not occur in reality or they become smaller and smaller, and insignificant. See Ronald I. McKinnon, "Optimum Currency Areas," *The American Economic Review*, Vol. LIII, No. 1, Part 1 (March 1963), pp. 717–725, and Robert A. Mundell, "A Theory of Optimum Currency Areas," *The American Economic Review*, Vol. LI, No. 4 (September 1961), pp. 657–665.

0.30 (measured with respect to the gross domestic product) at the beginning of the century to less than 0.09 for 1950–1961. Yet the Argentine economy continues to depend very heavily on imports for its smooth functioning. Indeed, it is often suggested that the secular decrease in the average propensity to import may have been accompanied by an increased vulnerability of the domestic economy to

TABLE 3.3
STRUCTURE OF MERCHANDISE IMPORTS OF
ARGENTINA ACCORDING TO USES
(*In percentages of all merchandise imports c.i.f.*)

	1948–1952	1953–1955	1956–1958	1959–1961
Consumer Goods	12.6	8.5	9.9	8.9
Nondurable	7.6	6.1	5.0	3.6
Durable	5.0	2.4	4.9	5.3
Intermediate Products and Raw Materials	58.0	67.1	65.9	53.8
Fuels	14.6	20.0	22.7	14.4
Metallic products	12.8	15.2	17.7	16.5
Other intermediate products and raw material	30.6	31.9	25.5	22.9
Capital Goods	28.8	24.1	24.2	36.4
Construction materials	6.5	4.0	2.0	4.7
Agricultural machinery and equipment	2.5	3.8	3.1	3.1
Transport and communication machinery and equipment	7.0	6.8	9.0	10.7
Other machinery and equipment	12.8	9.5	10.1	17.9
Miscellaneous	0.5	0.3	0.3	0.8

Sources: Basic data obtained from the *Boletín Económico de América Latina*, Comisión Económica para América Latina, Naciones Unidas, several issues of the *Suplemento Estadístico* and regular numbers. For an explanation of the categories employed, see the *Suplemento Estadístico* of November 1960, pp. 93–96. Percentages were computed from figures in current dollars.

adverse external circumstances, for the remaining imports are of such strategic nature in the process of production that a failure to maintain them at appropriate levels would cause severe dislocations in the economy.

Tables 3.3 and 3.4 present the structure of merchandise imports according to uses and industrial origin, respectively. During the period under discussion around 60 per cent of all imports was composed of a large variety of raw materials and intermediate products, such as oil, iron and steel, chemicals, paper pulp, and rubber, on a steady flow of which the industry and economy of Argentina depend for their smooth functioning. During the same period about 30 per cent of all imports represented capital goods, a large fraction of which was destined to replace and repair the existing capital stock. These imports of capital goods represent perhaps the most important single channel for transferring to Argentina technological advances

TABLE 3.4
STRUCTURE OF MERCHANDISE IMPORTS OF ARGENTINA
ACCORDING TO INDUSTRIAL ORIGIN
(*In percentages of all merchandise, imports, c.i.f.*)

	1951/ 1952	1953– 1955	1956– 1958	1959– 1961
Foodstuffs and Tobacco	5.6	8.6	6.4	3.3
Textiles and their Manufactures	9.1	6.1	3.0	3.0
Chemicals and Drugs	6.5	7.8	6.8	6.1
Paper and Paperboard	4.9	1.7	2.6	2.7
Wood and its Manufactures	8.2	9.5	7.6	4.7
Stones, Glass, and Earth	2.9	1.6	0.9	0.9
Iron and its Manufactures	13.8	13.6	14.7	16.6
Machinery and Vehicles	14.8	20.2	26.4	39.3
Noniron Metals and their Manufactures	5.7	5.7	5.5	5.2
Fuels and Lubricants	17.6	19.6	22.3	13.4
Rubber and its Manufactures	1.9	1.9	1.9	2.7
Miscellaneous	8.9	3.7	1.9	2.1

Sources: *Comercio Exterior, op. cit.*, and *Boletín Mensual de Estadística, op. cit.*, several issues. Percentages were computed from figures in current dollars. Totals may not add to 100.0 due to rounding errors.

taking place in the rest of the world. Only about 10 per cent of all imports was composed of consumer goods, a high fraction of which is made up of tropical products such as coffee, cocoa, and bananas.

A Priori Reasons for a Presumption of Price Inelasticity in the Argentine Demand for Imports

Tables 3.3 and 3.4 show that most of the demand for imports in Argentina is in the nature of derived demand. It will be argued now that such derived demand has characteristics that create a powerful presumption against high price elasticities in the total demand for imports, especially in the short run.

First of all, most of the raw materials and intermediate products imported during the period under study are of such a nature that they may not be easily substituted for other inputs, some of which could be available domestically. Thus, it would be hard to substitute imported oil for domestic charcoal in most domestic industries, and similar arguments could be made for imported rubber, newsprint, aluminum, iron and steel, some chemicals and petrochemicals, and so on.

Second, the domestic manufacture of many imported raw materials and intermediate products is difficult and possible only after substantial investments with long gestation periods have been carried out. For many industrial lines competing with imports during 1950–1961, special government policies and decisions were of greater importance than changes in the relative prices of their outputs, and for some of such industries government control was almost complete. The most dramatic example is the Argentine petroleum industry, although the steel, petrochemical, and motor vehicle industries are also good examples of industries for which changes in the relative prices of their output arising from exchange-rate variations are unlikely to influence their decision to expand output even in the long run, unless such changes are part of more comprehensive official policies of promotion.

Third, the imported raw materials and intermediate products represent on the whole small percentages of the final gross value or price of the goods which they contribute to produce, as shown in Table 3.5. Thus, a given increase in the price of imported inputs will result in a less than proportional direct increase in the prices of the final goods. Whatever the price elasticity in the demand for the final goods, this consideration would imply a much lower price elasticity in the derived demand for imported inputs.

These considerations refer primarily to the 60 per cent of Argentine imports composed of raw materials and intermediate products, although the large fraction of the imports of capital goods representing replacements and repairs to the existing capital stock shares many of the properties discussed and may be lumped with the category of raw materials and intermediate products. For that share of capital-goods imports that is destined to the expansion of capacity of the export or the import-competing sector, a further consideration must be borne in mind when discussing the price elasticity of the demand for imports and the role of exchange-rate variations in choking off that demand via changes in relative prices. This consideration is based on the fact that other things being equal, a change in the exchange rate that makes imported capital goods relatively more expensive also tends to increase the relative profitability of investment in the import-competing and export industries. Thus, with a weak domestic capital goods industry, the net result of the change

TABLE 3.5
IMPORTED RAW MATERIALS AND INTERMEDIATE PRODUCTS AS PERCENTAGES OF THE GROSS VALUE OF PRODUCTION OF ARGENTINE COMMODITY-PRODUCING SECTORS IN 1953

Agriculture	0.2
Cattle Raising	*
Mining	0.5
Foodstuffs (manufacturing)	1.7
Tobacco (manufacturing)	0.7
Textiles	2.0
Clothing	6.3
Wood Products	12.9
Paper, Printing, and Publishing	8.2
Chemical Products	7.5
Petroleum Derivatives	24.2
Rubber Products	11.0
Leather Products	0.9
Stones, Glass, and Ceramics	3.8
Metals and their Manufacture	8.8
Vehicles and Machinery (excluding electrical)	6.7
Electric Machinery and Appliances	14.8
Other Manufactures	7.8

Sources: Obtained from data found in Banco Central de la República Argentina, *Transacciones Intersectoriales de la Economía Argentina,* Suplemento del Boletín Estadístico No. 4, April 1964, Buenos Aires, pp. 47 and 48.
Sign * implies that number is less than 0.1 per cent. The calculations are based on data expressed in 1962 pesos, to avoid the bias that would be present if 1953 prices reflecting the overvalued 1953 peso had been used. The prices used refer to prices to the buyers.

in relative prices could well be a greater demand for imported capital goods, unless there is a compensating fall in investment in other sectors of the economy.[5]

[5] If, as is likely to be the case, the imported capital-output ratio is higher in expanding import substituting industries than in the rest of the economy the required compensating fall of investment in other sectors of the economy would have to be the greater. During the transition period, during which increased net investment is taking place but the capacity it is creating has not yet started to produce, the level of imports may increase. Thus, attempts to step up the rate of growth of import-substituting sectors or of exports may lead to an increase in the level of imports during such transition periods, and a worsening of the balance of trade.

Estimation of Import Functions for Argentina

Any study of the mechanism of adjustment of the balance of payments must make an effort to measure and evaluate the coefficients that determine the weight which income and price effects have on the determination of the demand for imports. The previous section has advanced on a priori grounds the presumption that income, rather than relative price effects, has been the dominant influence in determining the level of imports in the short run. Unfortunately, in the case of Argentina, it does not seem possible to test such a presumption in a foolproof way. To the well-known difficulties and pitfalls involved in estimating import functions for any country,[6] one must add further complications in estimating the Argentine import function. During most of the period under study, exchange control and other quantitative restrictions were used to reduce the level of imports. The presence of such policies, combined with some weakness in the available data, makes it very difficult to obtain a "true" measure of the price elasticity of the demand for imports. In spite of these difficulties, an attempt will be made to obtain some idea of the nature of the import function, including the different propensities to import of wage earners and non-wage earners.

The method we have used to estimate the different import functions is that of least squares applied to single equations. The marginal role of Argentina as a consumer of most imported commodities suggests that Argentina faces a perfectly elastic world supply of importables; this assumption is consistent with my method of estimating the import function.[7]

The low average propensity to import in Argentina seems to

---

[6] See for example G. Orcutt, "Measurement of Elasticity in International Trade," *Review of Economics and Statistics*, Vol. XXXII, No. 2 (May 1950), pp. 117–132. Also, Ta-Chung Liu, "The Elasticity of U. S. Import Demand: A Theoretical and Empirical Reappraisal," International Monetary Fund *Staff Papers*, Vol. III, No. 3 (February 1954), pp. 416–441.

[7] See Ta-Chung Liu, *ibid.*, especially pp. 421–427. It may be noticed that the five largest suppliers of imports to Argentina during 1956–1960 (United States, West Germany, United Kingdom, Brazil, and Venezuela) accounted for only around 55 per cent of all Argentine merchandise imports. The annual import bill of Argentina (slightly more than $1 billion) represents a small fraction of world trade taken as a whole or broken down by individual commodities or countries. For example, crude petroleum, which before 1960 was one of Argentina's most important imports, represented in 1956–1958 1.3 per cent of total world imports of petroleum. The Argentine share for natural rubber was 2.0 per cent in 1956–1958 and that for machine tools was 2.6 per cent in 1955–1958. Data obtained from United Nations *Yearbook of International Trade* and United States Department of Commerce, *World Trade in Machine Tools, 1955–1958*.

justify the use of single equations, as compared with a system of simultaneous equations describing the economy, for estimating the import function. On the other hand, it has been suggested that most of the imports are so strategic to the Argentine economy that they represent very critical inputs into the aggregate production function of the country, so that an autonomous change in imports has a significant effect on output and other variables, which in the single equation model are used as independent variables. If imports represent a significant input into the aggregate production function, then the estimation of the import function should involve the simultaneous estimation of both the production and the import function. It can be shown that a failure to do so would lead to a bias that tends to yield an estimated marginal propensity to import (estimated using a single equation) which is larger than the "true" propensity (estimated on the basis of the two equations). Unfortunately, available data are not sufficiently reliable to enter into the refinements involved in techniques beyond single-equation least squares, but the existence of the bias resulting from the use of the simpler technique should be borne in mind when the results of the following pages are examined.

In the estimation of the import function of Argentina, a crude attempt has been made to allow for the existence of exchange control and other quantitative restrictions on imports until 1959. It has been assumed that a country's level of net foreign exchange reserves was the main variable Central Bank authorities took into account when determining the harshness of the quantitative controls over imports at a given point in time. It will be assumed that the greater the decline of net reserves below the level reached at the end of 1947, the harsher the degree of restrictions became. This measure could be refined in several ways: for example, by taking into account the rate of change of reserves and the state of bilateral accounts, by redefining the ideal level of reserves every few years with respect to the level of imports, and so on. Yet considering the roughness of this index, such elaborations seem somewhat artificial. For any given year, the level of net reserves at the end of the *previous* year is taken as the basis for the index of quantitative restrictions, thus making such index independent of the level of imports one is trying to explain. In spite of its roughness, the index has the advantage of providing a simple objective criteria for quantifying the degree of control over imports, in contrast with ad hoc subjective estimates often used to estimate the harshness of quantitative restrictions.

To use an index of quantitative controls alongside an index of the relative price of imports calls for some explanation. Depending on the type of policy we assume the exchange authorities followed during this period, we may expect that our procedure will give, at the extremes, either (*a*) an unbiased estimate of the price slope of the demand-for-imports schedule, or (*b*) a zero price elasticity of demand for imports. Suppose we assume that the exchange authorities followed a policy of granting a given percentage of the requests for import licenses, the percentage depending on the level of net reserves at the end of the previous year. Under such circumstances and assuming there are no other sources of bias, we can obtain the "true" price elasticity of demand in spite of the existence of exchange controls. If, on the other hand, the exchange authorities set an absolute level of the quantity of imports allowed to enter the country during a given period, then the observed price elasticity will be zero for at least a range of the postrestriction demand-for-imports schedule. The price used in this argument is that paid by importers, with no import-license auctioning by the government. If import licenses have been auctioned off by the government or the internal price of imports is determined by domestic supply and demand conditions, we would observe points on the true-demand schedule; but least squares, which uses the quantum of imports as the dependent variable, would give estimates of price elasticities biased toward zero.[8] Beyond noticing that no auctioning system was used in the granting of import licenses, it is hard to establish precisely the general policy followed by the authorities in Argentina toward exchange and price control. Indeed, such general policy was probably never explicit even in the minds of the authorities, and changing circumstances and policies probably led to shifting rules of thumb during the period under study. Unfortunately, these considerations cast further doubt on the reliability of any estimates of price elasticities obtained empirically.

To estimate the import functions, yearly data for the period 1947–1962 and for 1939 have been used, with a total of 17 observations.[9]

---

[8] However, in the case where exchange-control authorities limit the quantity of imports and then let domestic market conditions determine the prices of those goods, an unbiased estimate of the price elasticity of demand could be obtained by making price the *dependent* variable. An attempt will be made to get to the "true" price elasticity of demand using this technique.

[9] The sources and methods used to obtain and elaborate these data, together with the time series employed in the regressions, are presented in the statistical appendix to this chapter.

Besides price and quantitative-restriction indices, several import and income variables have been employed, all of which are expressed in pesos, in per capita terms, and in constant 1960 prices. Altogether, the dependent and independent variables include

$M =$ total imports
$M_k =$ imports of capital goods
$M_o =$ non-capital-goods imports (consumer goods, raw materials, and intermediate products)
$W =$ wage income per wage earner
$T =$ nonwage income per non-wage earner
$Y =$ gross domestic product
$C =$ total private and public consumption
$I =$ gross fixed capital formation, private and public.
$P =$ index of prices of imported goods divided by prices of industrial goods produced domestically
$Q =$ index of quantitative restrictions
$S =$ level of value added which industries whose production directly replaces imported goods are capable of reaching

The last variable attempts to measure the long-run growth of capacity of domestic industries whose value added tends to reduce the import bill. Thus, it is a measure of potential domestic supply of importable goods.[10] To obtain this variable, the sum of several potentially import-competing industries was used, with the restriction that if the total value added in any given year was smaller than that reached in any previous year, then the largest level reached in the past would be used as the variable for that year. Thus, a true measure of capacity is approximated and we avoid the danger of having variable S "steal" some of the explanatory power of other independent variables, such as P. The use of variable S also allows us to isolate the short-run income marginal propensities, defined holding import-substituting capacity constant. The industries whose value added make up variable S are mining (mainly composed of petroleum), textiles, paper and cardboard, chemical products, petroleum derivatives, rubber manufacturing, metals (excluding ma-

---

[10] The term "importable goods" is here used in a different sense from that employed earlier in this chapter and in Chapter 2. Industries making up the S variable do not necessarily have their prices directly linked to foreign prices and the exchange rate. Due to the nature of protectionist policies, it is likely that goods previously imported rapidly passed into a quasi-home-good category after they began to be produced domestically.

chinery), vehicles and machinery (excluding electrical), and electrical machinery and appliances.

The estimates of the type of import function most often found in the literature will be presented first. The standard errors of the coefficients are shown in parentheses under their respective coefficients. The multiple-correlation coefficient is represented by R, while d stands for the Durbin-Watson statistic.

$$M = -2{,}553 + 0.42\,Y - 0.02\,P - 3.30\,Q - 1.40\,S$$
$$\qquad\qquad\;\;(0.18)\;\;\;\;(2.75)\;\;\;\;(0.84)\;\;\;\;(0.41)$$
$$R = 0.82$$
$$d = 1.04$$
$$\tag{3.1}$$

$$M_k = -1{,}824 + 0.18\,Y + 0.04\,P - 1.79\,Q - 0.57\,S$$
$$\qquad\qquad\;\;(0.07)\;\;\;\;(1.11)\;\;\;\;(0.34)\;\;\;\;(0.16)$$
$$R = 0.87$$
$$d = 1.65$$
$$\tag{3.2}$$

$$M_o = -907 + 0.25\,Y - 0.04\,P - 1.46\,Q - 0.82\,S$$
$$\qquad\qquad\;\;(0.14)\;\;\;\;(2.08)\;\;\;\;(0.64)\;\;\;\;(0.31)$$
$$R = 0.70$$
$$d = 0.99$$
$$\tag{3.3}$$

The correlation coefficients obtained imply reasonable fits, especially for Equations 3.1 and 3.2. The Durbin-Watson statistics obtained do not allow us either to accept or reject the hypothesis regarding the existence of serial correlation in the error terms, at the 5 per cent level of significance.

The marginal propensities to import obtained, which may be read directly from the coefficients of Y, are quite high and are significant in Equations 3.1 and 3.2.[11] The mean over-all average propensity to import implied in the observations used in the regressions is 13.6 per cent (with Y and M measured in 1960 prices). Thus, the estimated over-all marginal propensity to import of 42.2 per cent implies a mean income elasticity in the aggregate demand for imports of 3.1. The implied income elasticity in the demand for imported capital goods is even higher, as with an implied average

---

[11] All tests as to whether the estimated coefficients are significantly different from zero will be carried out at the 5 per cent level, using the t distribution.

propensity of 4.0 per cent and an estimated marginal propensity of 17.8 per cent, an income elasticity of 4.5 is obtained.

While the price coefficients are insignificant, and in the case of Equation 3.2 of the incorrect a priori sign, the coefficients of the index of quantitative restrictions are significant for all equations. In Equations 3.1 and 3.2, the Q coefficients are significant even at the 1 per cent level. To judge the quantitative importance of this coefficient, we can obtain the elasticity of the demand for imports with respect to the changes in net reserves, which induce changes in quantitative restrictions.[12] For the years for which the Q index was not set equal to zero and assuming the mean values to be the relevant variables, we infer from the Q coefficient in Equation 3.1 that a 1.00 per cent change in the level of net reserves (which averaged U.S. $316 million) induced a change in quantitative restrictions in turn changing imports (which averaged U.S. $1,069) by about 0.09 per cent in the same direction as the change in net reserves (other things being equal). For imports of capital goods, the implied elasticity is higher (0.17 per cent); while for non-capital-goods imports, it is lower (0.06 per cent), implying that the first type of imports were considered to be the marginal ones by the exchange authorities.

If the industries chosen to represent the capacity of production of the import-competing sector do indeed measure perfectly such concept, one would expect the coefficient of variable S in Equation 3.1 to have a value of -1.00. The estimated coefficient is not significantly different from the a priori expectation, while it is significantly different from zero. The S coefficients are also significant in Equa-

---

[12] Denoting by R_{t-1} the level of net reserves at the end of year $t-1$ and by R° the level of net reserves at the end of 1947, the definition of the index of quantitative restrictions used for a given year t may be written as

$$Q_t = \left(\frac{R^\circ - R_{t-1}}{R^\circ}\right) \times 1,000$$

Therefore, the elasticity of the demand for imports with respect to the level of net reserves becomes

$$\frac{\partial M_t}{\partial R_{t-1}} \cdot \frac{R_{t-1}}{M_t} = \left(\frac{\partial M_t}{\partial Q_t} \cdot \frac{Q_t}{M_t}\right)\left(\frac{\partial Q_t}{\partial R_{t-1}} \cdot \frac{R_{t-1}}{Q_t}\right)$$

It may be noted that the elasticity of the Q index with respect to the level of net reserves can be written

$$\frac{\partial Q_t}{\partial R_{t-1}} \cdot \frac{R_{t-1}}{Q_t} = -\frac{R_{t-1}}{R^\circ - R_{t-1}}$$

tions 3.2 and 3.3, implying that an increase of 100 pesos in the value added by the industries making up the S variable will reduce imports of capital goods by 57 pesos and other imports by 82 pesos, other things being equal.

Equations 3.1 to 3.3 yield some insights into the nature of the demand for imports in Argentina, but leave unanswered several questions posed in Chapter 2. In particular, they tell nothing regarding the propensities to import of different social classes. Equations 3.4 to 3.6 provide additional information:

$$M = 1{,}007 + \underset{(0.118)}{0.001\,W} + \underset{(0.05)}{0.18\,T} - \underset{(2.38)}{1.98\,P} - \underset{(0.81)}{1.50\,Q} - \underset{(0.21)}{0.84\,S}$$
$$R = 0.90$$
$$d = 1.47$$
$$(3.4)$$

$$M_k = -727 + \underset{(0.06)}{0.08\,W} + \underset{(0.02)}{0.05\,T} - \underset{(1.15)}{0.08\,P} - \underset{(0.39)}{1.36\,Q} - \underset{(0.10)}{0.36\,S}$$
$$R = 0.89$$
$$d = 1.65$$
$$(3.5)$$

$$M_o = 1{,}598 - \underset{(0.08)}{0.08\,W} + \underset{(0.03)}{0.13\,T} - \underset{(1.67)}{1.89\,P} - \underset{(0.57)}{0.08\,Q} - \underset{(0.15)}{0.47\,S}$$
$$R = 0.86$$
$$d = 1.71$$
$$(3.6)$$

The correlation coefficients show an improvement when compared with those of Equations 3.1 to 3.3, especially for the third equation explaining M_o. The Durbin-Watson statistic is also increased for Equations 3.1 and 3.3, although it still falls in the ambiguous zone where we can neither accept nor reject hypotheses regarding serial correlation at the 5 per cent level of significance.

Equations 3.4 to 3.6 imply a marginal propensity to import for wage earners which is not significantly different from zero. On the other hand, all coefficients of T are significant and imply a total marginal propensity to import of approximately 0.60, once the coefficient of Equation 3.4 is weighted by the ratio of total population to the population of non-wage earners (which amounts to 3.3 for the period under study). This rather high estimated direct and indirect marginal propensity of non-wage earners to import is composed of a marginal propensity to import capital goods of 0.18 and other goods of 0.42. The size and significance of this latter propensity raises a question on the true nature of at least part of the imports of raw materials and intermediate goods going to domestic industries whose output (automobiles, electric appliances, and so on) could be considered luxury consumption. Such apparently "indispensable" imports (steel, rubber, and so on) could hide substantial disguised indirect luxury imports. On the other hand, a sizable part of those imports do go into domestic industries producing capital goods purchased by non-wage earners.

During the period under study, Argentina's wage earners and other groups engaged in a tug of war over income distribution, and this helped us to isolate the marginal propensities of the two groups. Thus, the correlation coefficient between W and T for the years studied is only $+0.11$.

As before, the price coefficients are insignificant, although of the right sign, while only one Q coefficient, that for imported capital goods, remains significant. The S coefficients are all significant (even at the 1 per cent level), and of the right order of magnitude.

A third type of import function may now be explored. This type has a different nature from the previous functions, which may be characterized as attempts to measure ex-ante or behavioral schedules. The estimates shown in Equations 3.7, 3.8, and 3.9 are *ex post*, as they relate imports to absorption, where absorption is broken down into consumption (C) and investment (I). The estimates are

$$M = 848 + \underset{(0.13)}{0.09\,C} + \underset{(0.30)}{1.08\,I} + \underset{(2.20)}{1.52\,P} - \underset{(0.99)}{1.05\,Q} - \underset{(0.29)}{1.42\,S}$$
$$R = 0.90$$
$$d = 1.12$$
$$(3.7)$$

$$M_k = -335 + \underset{(0.04)}{0.02\,C} + \underset{(0.10)}{0.52\,I} + \underset{(0.70)}{0.76\,P} - \underset{(0.32)}{0.66\,Q} - \underset{(0.09)}{0.60\,S}$$
$$R = 0.95$$
$$d = 1.91$$
$$(3.8)$$

$$M_o = 1{,}061 + \underset{(0.11)}{0.08\,C} + \underset{(0.27)}{0.55\,I} + \underset{(1.98)}{0.77\,P} - \underset{(0.89)}{0.37\,Q} - \underset{(0.26)}{0.81\,S}$$
$$R = 0.75$$
$$d = 1.10$$
$$(3.9)$$

Equations of the type 3.7 to 3.9 could be helpful in answering the question: How large a drop in imports could we expect if we cut one of the main components of domestic absorption, either consumption or investment, by 1.00 peso, holding constant the productive capacity of the import competing sector? The low insignificant coefficients obtained for C imply that such a cut in domestic consumption would have little effect on imports. However, the use of more disaggregated consumption variables (for instance, durables, nondurables, and so on) would probably show that a cut in the consumption of durable goods would have a significant effect on imports, while a cut in consumption of nondurables would have a negligible effect. Unfortunately, available data do not permit a test of these hypotheses. The coefficients for I are high and significant in Equations 3.7 and 3.8. The coefficient in Equation 3.9 barely fails the test of significance at the 5 per cent level. Yet these equations seem to show that a change in domestic investment will be powerfully reflected not only in the level of imports of capital goods but also in the level of imports of intermediate goods and raw materials, suggesting that a fair proportion of the latter commodities go into domestic industries producing capital goods.[13]

For Equations 3.7 to 3.9 the coefficients for P and Q have little significance, either on empirical or a priori grounds. The S coefficients are significant, although they appear to be slightly larger than one would expect on a priori grounds.

Further Comments and Summary of the Statistical Results

In spite of the limitations of the methods and data employed to obtain the statistical results presented, some general conclusions

---

[13] Table 3.5 indicated the relatively high average import components for the three branches of manufacturing which account for most of the domestic production of nonconstruction capital goods: electric machinery and appliances, vehicles and machinery, and metals. These industries also account for most of the output of durable consumer goods. The development of the motor vehicle industry since 1953 may have raised the average import component of these three branches.

The *ex post* nature of Equation 3.8 permits us to interpret it in the following fashion. Ignoring the insignificant coefficients for C, P, and Q, it can be used as a rough way to estimate the level of gross fixed investment from the knowledge of data on capital-good imports and value added in domestic industries producing capital goods. Thus, 3.8 may be written

$$I = 644 + 1.92\,M_k + 1.15\,S$$

The coefficients for M_k and S are greater than 1.00 due to commercialization margins, installation costs, and so on. Better results could of course be obtained by narrowing down the definition of S.

regarding the nature of the demand for imports in Argentina for the period under study may be obtained from them. Perhaps the single most striking fact which has emerged is that the short-run over-all marginal propensity to import is much higher than the over-all average propensity to import, yielding income elasticities significantly above one. This fact has made it especially difficult for Argentina to achieve simultaneously high growth rates and balance-of-payments equilibrium.

The results suggest that the propensities of non-wage earners to spend are the main cause of the high over-all marginal propensity to import. Non-wage earners carry out practically all of the private investment expenditure done in Argentina and account for the larger share of the expenditure on consumer durable goods, both of which have a high import component.[14] While it is not possible to obtain an accurate measure of the average values of such propensities, the estimated equations have established a strong presumption that non-wage earners have a much higher *marginal* propensity to import than wage earners.

The results obtained suggest a tempting simplification for the analysis of the Argentine economy: to link wage income with consumption expenditures of zero import content and nonwage income with gross capital formation of high import content. Although such links clearly exist,[15] the existence of consumer durable goods of relatively high import content, mostly but not exclusively consumed by high income groups, plus the presence of a large public sector preclude such neat simplification.

The estimated price coefficients are not significantly different from zero, although for the reasons just discussed such evidence cannot be considered conclusive proof of price inelasticity in the demand for imports in Argentina.[16] But these results coupled with the a priori

[14] An unpublished survey study carried out in 1963 by a team jointly sponsored by the Organization of American States, the Interamerican Development Bank, and the Consejo Nacional de Desarrollo shows that 80 per cent of all automobiles and 68 per cent of all radio-phonograph combinations and air conditioning units purchased are accounted for by families in the upper 28 per cent range of the income scale. Purchases of refrigerators and washing machines seem to be more evenly distributed among different income groups, however, suggesting that in spite of the results obtained in Equations 3.4 through 3.6, wage earners are likely to have a positive and significant average and marginal propensity to import, when derived demand is taken into account.

[15] The correlation coefficient between W and C is $+0.75$, exactly the same as the correlation coefficient between T and I. The corresponding coefficients for W and I, and T and C, are much lower: $+0.21$ and $+0.43$, respectively.

[16] Another attempt was made to estimate the price elasticity of demand

presumption previously discussed make it reasonable to assume that the true price elasticity of the demand for imports is very low in Argentina.

The estimated coefficients for the Q variable imply not only that exchange control was successful in reducing the demand for imports below its "normal" levels, but also that the authorities considered imports of capital goods as the marginal or expendable category, the first to be compressed in case of exchange difficulties. Indeed, the simple correlation coefficient between variables I and Q yields a value of -0.66, while the same coefficient for C and Q is practically zero.

The introduction of the S variable was found to be helpful in isolating the short-run values for the various coefficients. The introduction of this or a similar variable seems to be indispensable in the estimation of import functions of countries engaged in a rapid process of secular import substitution. It may be noted that when this variable was not used in the regressions, the coefficients of the remaining income terms lost some significance and the estimated price coefficients continued to be not significantly different from zero.

Given these findings, what can we expect the impact of devaluation to be on imports? Little can be expected in the short run from a substitution from imports to other goods arising from the change in relative prices, unless very substantial excess capacity exists in the true import-competing industries, a situation not typical of the period under study according to the statistical results obtained. At first sight it may appear that a devaluation-induced income redistribution in favor of non-wage earners could actually increase the level of imports. However, it may be remembered from Chapter 2 that with the existence of a money-wage lag, a higher marginal propensity to import on the part of non-wage earners will be more than offset, from the point of view of imports, by a drop in the level of domestic output — a conclusion based on the implied fact that the

---

for the exchange control years, by putting the price variable as *dependent* variable, and M, Y, and S as independent variables in one case, and M, W, T, and S in another. If exchange control authorities allowed internal market conditions to determine the domestic prices of imported goods once they had decided on the quantity of imports to admit, this procedure would yield the true price elasticity of demand as the inverse of the estimated coefficient for M (all variables having been transformed into logarithms). The results of this experiment also yielded an estimated elasticity not significantly different from zero.

marginal propensity to spend domestically is higher for wage than non-wage earners. It remains true, however, that the estimated propensities to import of the different social groups, taken by themselves, tend to hinder the drop in imports caused by devaluation-induced domestic real deflation, as the redistribution of income will raise the average propensity to import. Taking a longer-run view, we observe that to the extent that the greater level of imports purchased directly or indirectly out of nonwage income go to capital formation in import-competing or export industries, the balance of trade, after a transition period, will tend to improve. It will be seen in the next chapter that while importables weigh little in the market basket of wage earners, this is not the case for exportables, which provide the key leverage in the devaluation-induced redistribution of income from wage earners to non-wage earners.

The combination of a low price elasticity in the demand for imports and a high over-all marginal propensity to import makes the simultaneous achievement of high rates of growth and balance-of-payments equilibrium (not to mention a stable price level, including the exchange rate as a price) a very difficult task. With the sluggish resource mobility implied by a low price elasticity, attempts to expand output rapidly in the short run will spill inordinately into higher imports, unless careful long-run government planning precedes the expansion, especially in fostering steady growth of the type of industries making up variable S.

If the achievement of high growth rates and full employment is neglected, the high marginal propensities to import suggest an easy way to correct balance-of-payments disequilibrium, that is, fiscal and monetary deflationary policies. Specifically, a reduction in the level of investment, which may be brought about by government policies, will yield a quick reduction of imports in the short run, although perhaps at the expense of the long-run expansion of the import-competing and export sectors.[17]

---

[17] The speed with which changes in the income variables are reflected on the level of imports was also tested using quarterly data for the years 1950–1960, with all imports as the dependent variable and the index of industrial production as the independent variable. The results yielded a lag structure which implies that a change during quarter t in the independent variable will have 88 per cent of its very substantial total final impact on the dependent variable during quarters t and $t + 1$. Although the index of industrial production used as independent variable has some notorious weaknesses, the lag structure derived from this experiment is not likely to change much by using a more accurate income index.

Statistical Appendix to Chapter 3

Tables S.1 and S.2 present the time series used in the estimation of the import function of Argentina. The variables have been obtained as indicated in the summary that follows.

1. Gross domestic product (GDP) per capita, in 1960 pesos (Y). For 1950–1962 the source for the total GDP in 1960 prices is *Cuentas Nacionales de la República Argentina, op. cit.*, pp. 192 and 193. For

TABLE S.1
Data Used in the Estimation of the Import Function of Argentina: Independent Variables

Year	Y	C	I	W	T	P	Q	S
1939	35,930	28,822	6,435	16,931	64,538	917	591	3,345
1947	44,016	33,987	9,991	22,374	84,629	1,174	0	5,276
1948	45,443	36,370	10,120	25,221	83,513	1,147	0	5,276
1949	43,800	38,104	8,451	26,027	68,937	1,070	421	5,276
1950	43,238	36,118	8,064	25,196	65,655	1,000	550	5,276
1951	43,800	36,659	8,596	23,457	69,331	1,117	406	5,276
1952	40,514	34,275	7,483	23,734	59,220	1,052	693	5,276
1953	42,200	33,156	7,612	23,659	64,538	999	842	5,276
1954	43,410	35,503	7,185	24,767	65,523	946	676	5,601
1955	45,745	38,610	7,862	24,868	73,336	961	681	6,252
1956	45,918	38,393	8,120	23,759	71,104	1,331	898	6,345
1957	47,215	38,862	9,055	23,558	74,649	1,183	914	7,025
1958	48,902	40,163	9,152	26,934	78,851	1,109	970	7,592
1959	45,832	36,623	8,160	21,996	80,493	1,387	0	7,592
1960	47,691	36,948	10,991	22,500	81,149	1,323	0	7,853
1961	49,680	39,982	11,805	24,314	80,099	1,162	0	8,859
1962	47,215	36,406	11,402	23,029	76,028	1,212	0	8,859
Mean Values	44,738	36,411	8,852	23,666	73,035	1,123	450	6,250

earlier years, total GDP in 1950 prices is obtained from *Producto e Ingreso de la República Argentina en el Período 1935–1954*, Secretaría de Asuntos Económicos, Poder Ejecutivo Nacional, Buenos Aires, 1955, p. 133. These two series are linked in 1950 using indices with $1950 = 100$ for both, from which the series at 1960 prices is then obtained for pre-1950 years. The total GDP has been deflated by the revised population figures elaborated at the Consejo Nacional de Desarrollo (to be published).

2. Private and public consumption per capita, in 1960 pesos (C). Obtained from the same sources and using the same methods shown for Y.

3. Private and public gross fixed investment per capita, in 1960 pesos (I). Obtained from the same sources and using the same methods shown for Y.

4. Wage income per capita, in 1960 pesos (W). Data in current prices obtained from the same basic sources shown for Y. Wage income excludes social security contributions made by both employers and employees. For pre-1950 years, employees' social

TABLE 5.2

Data Used in the Estimation of the Import Function of Argentina: Dependent Variables

Year	M	M_k	M_o
1939	7,472	1,672	5,774
1947	10,118	3,604	6,543
1948	9,577	3,646	5,855
1949	6,494	2,130	4,349
1950	5,752	1,703	4,049
1951	6,793	1,802	5,009
1952	5,033	1,568	3,458
1953	3,888	1,241	2,640
1954	4,435	1,075	3,381
1955	5,073	1,098	4,009
1956	4,768	1,051	3,749
1957	5,729	1,413	4,336
1958	5,545	1,066	4,523
1959	4,866	1,282	3,596
1960	6,045	2,088	3,936
1961	6,471	1,843	4,636
1962	5,487	2,066	3,385
Mean Values	6,091	1,785	4,308

Note: Columns 2 and 3 do not add up to Column 1 because of the rounding errors involved in the indices utilized to estimate these series.

security contributions have been obtained from unpublished worksheets of the U.N. Economic Commission for Latin America. Data in current prices have been deflated by the implicit price deflator of the gross national product. Data in per capita terms are based on 1960 figures for the total number of wage earners in the economy, on the assumption that this number increased in the same proportion as total population and that wage earners' families had the same average size as those of non-wage earners. Figures for the total number of wage earners in 1960 were obtained from the Consejo Nacional de Desarrollo. For that year, it was estimated that out of a total employed population of 8.11 million, 5.67 million were wage earners and 2.44 million were employers and the self-employed. Working members of employers' families were also included in the latter group. Total population in 1960 is estimated at 20.67 million.

5. Nonwage income per capita, in 1960 pesos (T). Basic data in current prices as for Y. For post-1950 years, nonwage income includes profits from unincorporated enterprises; interests, rents and dividends; net savings of private corporations (excluding government enterprises); and depreciation allowances. Data on net profits of government enterprises were obtained from worksheets of the Consejo Nacional de Desarrollo. For pre-1950 years all nonwage income as shown in the national accounts was used as a base for an index that was linked in 1950 with the post-1950 data. The figures in current prices were deflated in the same way as for W. Data in per capita terms were obtained by starting from 1960 figures for non-wage earners (total employed population minus wage earners) and proceeding as for W. It was not possible to remove direct taxes from W and T, although indirect taxes have been excluded.

6. Index of wholesale import prices deflated by an index of wholesale prices of domestically produced nonrural goods with $1950 = 1,000$ (P). Data for 1939–1956 were obtained from *Boletín Estadístico,* Banco Central de la República Argentina, Buenos Aires, September 1962. Post-1956 prices were obtained from the *Boletín Mensual de Estadística,* Dirección Nacional de Estadística y Censos, several issues. This index reflects at least in part the efforts of authorities in controlling prices directly.

7. Index of quantitative restrictions (Q). Elaborated as described in the text from data on net reserves of gold and foreign exchange found in the *Memoria Anual,* 1958, Banco Central de la República Argentina for 1943–1958. Reserves for 1938 and 1939 obtained from earlier *Memorias* of the same institution.

8. Value added (capacity) of import competing industries (S). Elaborated as described in the text on the basis of data obtained in the two basic sources mentioned for Y for manufacturing and mining production, and on the basis of unpublished data obtained from the Consejo Nacional de Desarrollo (for absolute figures of value added by branches of manufacturing).

9. Total imports per capita, in 1960 pesos (M). Obtained from the same source and basic data on total imports used for Table 3.3 in the text, but originally expressed in 1955 dollars. Those figures were converted into indices with $1960 = 100$, which were then

linked with the actual value of imports in 1960 in pesos. Per capita figures obtained as in previous variables.

10. Imports of capital goods (M_k) and other imports (M_o) per capita, in 1960 pesos. Data obtained as for M. The definition of capital goods is the same used in Table 3.3.

4

The Supply and Demand for Exportables

In the model developed in Chapter 2, it was implicitly stated that the level of exports was determined by the difference between the domestic production and absorption of exportable goods, very much in the same way as the level of imports is determined by the difference between the domestic absorption and supply of importable goods. It was then assumed that we were dealing with a country so small that it faced a perfectly elastic world demand for its exports. This chapter will first examine the structure of Argentine exports and the validity of the small-country assumption and then proceed to study the nature of the domestic supply of and demand for exportable goods.

The Structure of Argentine Exports

The structure of Argentine exports is more diversified in both products and markets than that of most Latin American countries. Table 4.1 shows that although around 95 per cent of all merchandise exports are primary products that in most cases are shipped abroad without much processing, such high percentage is made up of a great variety of goods, such as beef, wool, wheat, corn, hides, linseed and sunflower oils and cakes, and so on. In recent years, the six most important foreign purchasers accounted for only 66 per cent of all Argentine exports.[1]

---

[1] During 1959–1963 the six major importers of Argentine products were: United Kingdom (18 per cent), Netherlands (13 per cent), Italy (12 per cent),

A detailed study of the domestic supply and demand for each of the exportable commodities is beyond the scope of this book. Rather, this chapter will concentrate on the three most important groups of exportables: meat (mainly beef), wool, and cereals and linseed, which in 1959–1961 accounted for 63 per cent of all merchandise exports. The similarities among the production functions for most exportable commodities and the obvious links between the

TABLE 4.1
STRUCTURE OF MERCHANDISE EXPORTS OF ARGENTINA
(*In percentages of all merchandise exports*)

	1951–1952	1953–1955	1956–1958	1959–1961
All Livestock Products	48.9	43.7	52.1	51.0
Meat	14.9	16.7	27.3	22.8
Hides	10.3	6.2	6.3	7.2
Wool	15.9	14.0	11.7	13.4
Other	7.7	6.7	6.8	7.6
All Agricultural Products	44.5	50.9	42.1	44.0
Cereals and linseed	22.9	36.6	28.0	26.6
Oilseeds (excluding linseed) and their products	14.5	7.3	9.7	11.5
Other	7.1	7.0	4.4	5.9
Products from Mining, Manufacturing, and Other Industries	6.7	5.4	5.8	5.1

Sources: *Comercio Exterior*, Informe C48, Buenos Aires, April 1958, *Anuario de Comercio Exterior*, several issues, and *Boletín Mensual de Estadística*, several issues. All of these publications are the responsibility of the Dirección Nacional de Estadística y Censos. Percentages were computed from figures in current dollars. Totals may not add to 100.0 because of rounding errors.

three most important groups of exportables and other exportables (for instance, meat with hides and other cattle by-products; cereals, especially maize, with sunflower) indicate that the results obtained for wool, meat, and cereals and linseed will provide an adequate description of the nature of the over-all domestic supply and demand for exportables.

United States (9 per cent), West Germany (8 per cent) and Brazil (6 per cent). The figures in parentheses refer to the share of the different countries in total Argentine exports. These figures and Table 4.1 may overstate the degree of diversification of Argentine exports, as in many cases individual countries take very high proportions of individual commodity exports (for example, United Kingdom for chilled beef and Brazil for wheat).

World Demand for Argentine Exports

Table 4.2 presents the share which Argentine exports represented of total world exports for some of the most important exportable products during two periods: 1934–1938 and 1959–1962. This table illustrates the downward trend of the Argentine share of the world market for primary products. It also suggests that for some commodities, such as beef, Argentina apparently has a substantial

TABLE 4.2
Share of Argentine Exports in World Exports
of Selected Commodities
(*In percentages*)

	1934–1938	1959–1962
Wheat and Wheat Flour	19.3	5.5
Maize	64.0	18.5
Greasy Wool	11.7	9.9
Degreased Wool		13.9
Linseed and Linseed Oil	67.6	49.3
Sunflower Seed and its Oil	n.a.	14.1
All Meat (fresh, chilled, or frozen)	39.7	17.5
Meat of Bovine Animals (fresh, chilled, or frozen)	n.a.	30.5
All Meat (dried, salted, smoked), or Meat Preparations	n.a.	8.0

Sources: *Trade Yearbook, 1963*, Food and Agriculture Organization of the United Nations, Rome, and *Análisis y Proyecciones del Desarrollo Económico*, V, *op. cit.*, Part 2, p. 48. It has been assumed that three tons of linseed and sunflower seed are equivalent to one ton of linseed oil and sunflower seed oil.

Data not available are designated by n.a.

amount of market power, so that the small-country assumption must be reconsidered with care.

The decline in the Argentine share of world exports of primary products suggests a prima facie presumption that internal supply difficulties, rather than world demand conditions, account for the secular decline of the quantum of exports.[2] Even after taking into

---

[2] The absolute quantum of exports for the period 1935–1939 has not been reached since. The quantum for 1935–1939 was 7 per cent below the level for 1925–1929. See *Análisis y Proyecciones del Desarrollo Económico: V, El Desarrollo Económico de la Argentina*, Naciones Unidas, México, 1959, Part 1, p. 110. The considerations regarding the Argentine position in world markets apply for the period under study, but not necessarily for the future, which can be drastically influenced by exogenous events such as the evolution

account exogenous influences, such as the British Commonwealth preferences and the United States Public Law 480, which have tended to reduce foreign markets for Argentina, the prima facie presumption provides the most likely basic explanation for the decline in the Argentine share in world markets in recent years. Indeed, during the postwar years it has not been uncommon for the Argentine government to limit by decree the exports of certain commodities to assure an adequate level of domestic absorption of exportables at "reasonable" prices, even at the expense of cutting back deliveries to traditional overseas markets.

The decline of the Argentine share in world markets has taken the market shares for some commodities, such as wheat, to such low levels that for them the small-country assumption appears justified. Furthermore, for most exportables not individually listed in Tables 4.1 and 4.2 this assumption also appears to be warranted. Yet, the world market shares shown in Table 4.2 for maize, meat, and linseed and linseed oil are fairly high. The extent to which these percentages accurately reflect market power may be open to discussion. For some commodities, the share of total Argentine production in total world production may be a more meaningful measure, and such a measure will yield smaller percentages. So long as there are a significant number of new potential buyers and sellers ready to enter the world market if prices drop or increase, high figures for the share of existing world trade do not give a country much market power, as Argentina found out in the case of linseed in the postwar period.[3] Even without taking into account the entry of potential buyers and sellers into the world market, a yearly change of plus or minus 10 per cent in the quantity of Argentine exports would change total world supply of the relevant commodities by rather small percentages, which are unlikely to have much influence on world prices, perhaps with the exception of chilled beef. In summary, the assumption that Argentina has become a price taker in the world economy for most of her exportable goods, although not strictly true for all commodities, seems to be a useful and reasonable simplification which allows us to suppose that world prices are exogenously given and to concentrate on the analysis of the domestic supply and demand for

---

of the agricultural policy of the European Common Market and the position of the United Kingdom toward that institution.

[3] In practice, these considerations probably apply with greater force to price increases rather than to price decreases due to the asymmetry introduced by the protectionist agricultural policies followed by most potential customers of Argentina.

exportables, which are thus considered to be the only endogenous factors explaining the changes in the value of exports.

The Domestic Supply of Exportables

It was pointed out in Chapter 3 that for all practical purposes during the period under discussion the whole of the agricultural and livestock sector may be considered to make up almost all of the

TABLE 4.3
STRUCTURE OF THE TOTAL VALUE OF GROSS OUTPUT OF THE ARGENTINE AGRICULTURAL AND LIVESTOCK SECTOR
(*In percentages*)

	1950– 1952	1953– 1955	1956– 1958	1959– 1961
Total Agricultural Sector	47.5	52.8	56.2	49.9
Cereals and linseed	15.7	22.1	20.3	22.2
(wheat)	(7.6)	(11.4)	(8.6)	(8.1)
(maize)	(4.1)	(5.0)	(6.0)	(7.7)
(linseed)	(1.4)	(1.1)	(1.8)	(2.3)
(other cereals)	(2.7)	(4.6)	(3.9)	(4.1)
Industrial crops	18.0	16.1	22.7	18.1
Fruits	4.4	4.5	4.5	2.7
Flowers, garden vegetables, and other	9.4	10.1	8.7	6.9
Total Livestock Sector	52.4	47.3	43.8	50.2
Beef cattle	25.2	27.0	21.4	30.9
Other cattle	6.2	5.4	5.4	4.5
Wool	8.2	4.1	6.0	5.2
Milk, poultry, eggs, and other	12.8	10.7	11.0	9.5

Source: Statistical appendix of Aldo Ferrer and Alberto Fracchia, *La Producción, Ingresos y Capitalización del Sector Agropecuario en el Período 1950–1960*. (Research prepared for CAFADE, Buenos Aires, April 1961). This source has been supplemented by unpublished data on the national accounts of the Consejo Nacional de Desarrollo. Original figures were in current prices; percentages were computed for each year, and averages were then taken for the years indicated in the table.

exportable goods category. Table 4.3 presents the structure of the value of gross output of this sector for 1950–1961. A closer look at some of these categories, especially industrial crops, would reveal that several commodities in them have characteristics of what have been called home goods in earlier chapters. Such commodities are produced primarily for the domestic market and are sheltered from foreign competition in ways similar to those used to protect manufactured goods, although their occasional surpluses are disposed of in world markets. Yet such commodities represent a relatively small part of rural production and often remain closely linked to the prices of exportable commodities through the prices of the inputs which both categories of commodities use (for instance, land). The three groups of commodities which have the highest degree of "exportableness" — beef cattle, wool, and cereals and linseed — have accounted on the average for slightly more than half of the gross value of total rural production during the period under study.

Most of the agricultural commodities are obtained from crops with a production process that lasts about a year. Although some flexibility regarding changes in plans is allowed by the existence of inventories and more energetic harvesting of already planted crops, it seems that substantial short-run changes in production plans for most agricultural crops are unfeasible. For example, a devaluation that raises the domestic prices of exportables in January will have little effect on the maize crop harvested between March and June, as it was planted in September and October of the previous year. Similar examples could be given for wheat, oats, barley, sugar cane, sunflower, and so forth.

The short-run response of production for livestock products with respect to changes in relative prices is also likely to be rather small, if not apparently perverse. Some commodities, such as wool, resemble agricultural goods in that they also have once-a-year "crops." In the case of beef, it will be shown that the short-run response to an increase in its price will be a *decrease* in current slaughtering, resulting in a short-run drop in marketable supplies that may last more than one year.

In summary, the structure of the exportable sector of Argentina suggests that in the short run the domestic supply of exportables is likely to be quite inelastic with respect to changes in relative prices, if not apparently backward bending. At least until 1961 it seemed that changes in relative prices were not enough to induce new branches of production, especially those in manufacturing, to enter into the category of exportables. A substantial presence of manufactured goods in that category would have reduced significantly its short-run price inelasticity.

The study of the short-run responses of the domestic supply of exportables should be placed in the context of the long-run evolution of this sector in Argentina during the last forty years. Table 4.4 shows indices for total agricultural and livestock output and for some of the most important branches. The picture that emerges from this table is one of very low growth (lower than the growth of population) and even decline, especially for those branches of production that have the greatest degree of "exportableness." Although it is beyond the scope of this book to analyze in detail the factors which have accounted for this long-run behavior of the rural sector, perhaps the most important single factor hampering Argentine growth during the last thirty years, a few comments on this

TABLE 4.4
OUTPUT INDICES FOR AGRICULTURE AND LIVESTOCK IN ARGENTINA
($1960 = 100$)

	1925–1929	1935–1939	1945–1949	1950–1952	1953–1955	1956–1958	1959–1961
Total Agriculture and Livestock	78	86	92	83	100	98	100
Total Agriculture	86	96	86	72	95	94	98
Cereals and linseed	149	152	98	60	99	92	96
Industrial crops	35	46	74	85	87	97	99
Total Livestock	71	79	100	93	105	102	101
Cattle	71	79	98	92	105	103	103
Wool	79	83	107	95	98	91	99

Sources: *Cuentas Nacionales de la República Argentina*, Consejo Nacional de Desarrollo, Presidencia de la Nación, República Argentina, Buenos Aires, April 1964, p. 196; *Producto e Ingreso de la República Argentina en el Período 1935–1954*, Secretaría de Asuntos Económicos, Poder Ejectivo Nacional, pp. 144, 145; *Análisis y Proyecciones del Desarrollo Económico*, V, *op. cit.*, Statistical Appendix, pp. 7, 9. Indices with different base years were linked without adjusting for weights. For agriculture, output figures refer to the year when crops are harvested; for instance, the crop year 1960/1961 is allocated fully to 1961.

topic seem to be required to place recent developments in historical perspective. The great depression of the nineteen-thirties and the discriminatory and protectionist policies adopted at that time by the United Kingdom and other industrialized countries were the first major blows received by the Argentine rural sector, which were, however, offset to some extent by the effects of droughts in North America during the years 1935 to 1940. Shipping difficulties during the Second World War caused further damage, especially to agricultural crops. From 1946 until around 1953, government policies discouraged rural production by lowering the domestic relative prices of those products, even in years when their world prices reached very high levels. At the same time, it became extremely costly and difficult for rural producers to obtain modern inputs, the use of which could have enabled them to offset the low output prices via cost-reducing technological change. During these years, resources continued to be shifted into crops directed mainly to home consumption, as prices and other facilities, such as credit, tended to be relatively more advantageous in this sector.

The serious drought of 1951/1952 dramatized the deterioration that had taken place in the rural sector producing exportables. After 1952 some attempts were made to change the official policies toward exportables, although it was not until late in 1955 when such new attitudes began to be implemented with vigor, using devaluations of

TABLE 4.5
INDICES OF WHOLESALE PRICES OF RURAL PRODUCTS RELATIVE TO WHOLESALE PRICES OF MANUFACTURED GOODS
($1939 = 100$)

	All Agricultural and Livestock Products	Agricultural Products	Livestock Products
1947–1949	89	89	97
1950–1952	75	67	88
1953–1955	75	70	82
1956–1958	86	90	80
1959–1961	94	87	102

Sources: Obtained from wholesale price indices found in the *Boletín Estadístico*, Banco Central de la República Argentina, September 1962, and the *Boletín Mensual de Estadística*, of the Dirección Nacional de Estadística y Censos, several issues.

the exchange rate and other means to stimulate their production. Table 4.5 shows indices of wholesale prices for agricultural and livestock products relative to wholesale prices of other goods. Comparing such price indices with the output indices presented in Table 4.4, it may be noted that the aggregate supply of exportables has not expanded since 1953–1955 in proportion to the increase in aggregate rural prices; and indeed it does not appear to have expanded very much beyond the recovery from the drought, which explains the unusually low levels of production reached during 1950–1952. On the other hand, it may be noted in Table 4.5 that the relative prices of agricultural and livestock products moved rather independently and in different directions from one period to the next since 1950–1952. Yearly figures of relative prices would show not only this difference in behavior but also a good deal of erratic year-to-year fluctuations that no doubt have decreased the incentive value of the higher average levels of real prices.[4]

There are a great number of difficulties in trying to estimate or judge the nature of the aggregate supply of exportables. The aggregate level of rural output was influenced during the period under study not only by the level of relative prices but also by technological change, soil erosion, weather, availability of inputs, social overhead facilities, and credit, and by the expectations of rural producers regarding the length of time favorable prices would be maintained — a factor of great importance in a country where since the Second World War devaluations have occurred on the average once every three or four years, but where the domestic price level has been increasing more or less continuously at an unpredictable rate. Rather than estimating the aggregate supply of exportables, an attempt will be made to estimate supply responses for three groups of commodities: cereals and linseed, wool, and beef. Such estimations should cast further light on the possible short-run reaction of the total supply of exportables to a devaluation.

Supply Responses for Cereals and Linseed and Wool

These commodities may be said to face a total demand (domestic plus foreign) that is perfectly elastic,[5] thus implying that the single equation least-squares estimating technique should yield a true measurement of the elasticity of supply, assuming there are no other sources of bias present. Supply schedules have been estimated for the years 1935–1962, with a total of 28 observations. The following variables, all of which are expressed as natural logarithms with the exception of time, were used:[6]

[4] During 1962–1964 there has been a substantial increase in agricultural output, but it remains to be seen whether such an increase represents a delayed payoff to the policies followed since 1955 or just the result of unusually favorable weather conditions.

[5] Transport costs and other frictions are likely to destroy perfect elasticity of demand even when there is free trade in these commodities and the Argentine share in world trade of these goods is small. This is because the transport costs allow the domestic price of these commodities to fluctuate within some range independently of world prices. Within such a range, observed prices will be the result of the interplay of the domestic supply schedule and the imperfectly elastic demand schedule. For cereals and wool it is assumed that such range is small and can be neglected. The years for which the government arbitrarily set the level of prices paid to farmers present no special difficulty, for the government then in effect created a perfectly elastic demand at the official prices.

[6] For a description of the sources and methods used to obtain these variables,

Q_c = index of output of cereals and linseed
Q_w = index of output of wool
P_c = index of wholesale prices of cereals and linseed relative to wholesale prices of industrial goods
P_w = index of wholesale prices of wool relative to wholesale prices of industrial goods
P_y = index of wholesale prices of cattle relative to wholesale prices of industrial goods
Z = index of rainfall in selected regions of the Pampean zone
TM = time trend

A superscript t or $t-1$ will be used to indicate the year to which the variables refer. The estimated supply schedule for cereals and linseed is as follows:

$$Q_c^t = -4.86 - 0.27 P_c^t + 0.26 P_c^{t-1} + 0.17 P_w^t - 0.45 P_w^{t-1}$$
$$ (0.29) \quad (0.33) \quad\quad (0.17) \quad\quad (0.20)$$
$$+ 0.89 P_g^t + 0.48 P_g^{t-1} - 0.20 Z^t + 0.90 Z^{t-1}$$
$$ (0.50) \quad\quad (0.48) \quad\quad (0.28) \quad\quad (0.30)$$
$$- 0.022\, TM \quad\quad R = 0.84 \quad\quad (4.1)$$
$$(0.006) \quad\quad\quad d = 2.32$$

As all variables except time have been transformed into natural logarithms, the supply elasticities may be read directly from the coefficients of the price variables. At the 5 per cent level, only the coefficients for P_w^{t-1}, Z^{t-1}, and TM are significantly different from zero, with the coefficients for P_c^t and P_c^{t-1} failing to reveal any significant elasticity of output to its own price. The significant negative coefficient for P_w^{t-1} implies that some rural producers shift between crops and wool depending on relative prices, the decision being taken at the time of planting the crops (t refers to the year when the crops are harvested while $t-1$ refers to the year of planting). If only the variables at the time of planting are taken to explain the output results we obtain

$$Q_c^t = -4.70 + 0.25 P_c^{t-1} - 0.26 P_w^{t-1} + 0.87 P_g^{t-1}$$
$$ (0.21) \quad\quad (0.16) \quad\quad (0.42)$$
$$+ 0.90 Z^{t-1} - 0.022\, TM \quad R = 0.80 \quad (4.2)$$
$$(0.28) \quad\quad (0.006) \quad\quad d = 2.38$$

see the statistical appendix to this chapter, which also presents the time series employed in the regressions.

In Equation 4.2, the coefficient for $P_w{}^{t-1}$ loses its significance, while the coefficient for $P_g{}^{t-1}$ becomes barely significant at the 5 per cent level. This positive coefficient for $P_g{}^{t-1}$ is puzzling, as it implies that crops and cattle raising are on the whole complementary occupations. While it is true that the quantity index for cereals and linseed includes some crops which are complementary to cattle raising (oats, barley, rye, and to a lesser extent maize), such items have been in most years small relative to wheat and linseed, which appear to be lines of production that are competitive with cattle raising. Greater disaggregation and more refined data would be needed to clarify the precise interrelationships among different rural lines of production, but such a detailed study is not necessary for our purposes.[7] As they stand, Equations 4.1 and 4.2 imply that even allowing for the lag between the time of planting and the time of harvesting, changes in relative prices during the period under study do not appear to have resulted in significant and substantial changes in output. If all the price coefficients in Equation 4.2 are taken at face value, it can be said that a 1 per cent increase in *all* of the relative prices of the exportables considered at the time of the planting of cereals and linseed will yield a less than 1 per cent increase in the output of cereals and linseed at the time of harvesting, other things being equal. For example, a devaluation that raises the relative prices of both wool and cereals and linseed would, according to Equation 4.2, leave the output of the latter roughly unchanged.

The significant coefficient for *TM* implies that the result of conflicting forces on the supply schedule through time has been a secular shift to the left. Thus, any technological change that may have occurred during 1935–1962 appears to have been more than offset by forces such as erosion, unfavorable long-run expectations, shortages of critical inputs not reflected in the prices paid by farmers, and so on. The coefficient implies that these factors brought a yearly decrease of the aggregate output of cereals and linseed of 2.2 per

---

[7] When the output index for cattle is correlated with the relative prices of cereals and linseed we obtain the following *negative* simple correlation coefficients: —0.42 for $P_c{}^t$ and —0.50 for $P_c{}^{t-1}$. The simple correlation coefficient between $Q_c{}^t$ and $P_c{}^{t-1}$ is 0.39, while that between $Q_c{}^t$ and $P_g{}^{t-1}$ is 0.37. It may be noted that $P_g{}^{t-1}$ and $P_c{}^{t-1}$ show a simple correlation coefficient of 0.53. A possible extension of the analysis of rural-supply responses would involve different assumptions regarding the basis for farmers' expectations about future prices. For such an extension, government support prices announced at planting time could turn out to be the key variables.

cent.[8] Within the cereals and linseed category, however, some crops such as wheat have shown a secular increase in yields.

The results obtained in the estimation of the supply schedule for wool are very poor, and not a single coefficient is significant at the 5 per cent level. The independent variables used were the same employed in Equation 4.1. Thus, once again it appears that the short-run supply response to changes in relative prices is very weak. The simple correlation coefficients between Q_w and P_c^t and P_c^{t-1} tend to support the results obtained previously regarding the compettiveness at the margin between grain and wool production; they are −0.57 and −0.58, respectively.

The Special Short-Run Supply Response of Beef

While it was reasonable to assume that wool and cereals and linseed faced a perfectly elastic total demand during most of the period under discussion, such a simplifying assumption seems harder to justify in the case of beef (which accounts for about 86 per cent of the total output of meat in Argentina). Not only does Argentina have a high share in the total world exports of beef but also the domestic market for beef shows a great deal of independence from the world market because of the high transport costs involved in beef and the many frictions and imperfections that exist in the marketing of this commodity in world trade. Thus, while the domestic market for wool and grains could be treated on the whole as a relatively unimportant appendage to the world markets of those goods, the domestic market for beef in Argentina should be given greater attention, as it has a good deal of autonomy in setting domestic prices. These considerations imply that if in the period under study the Argentine beef market had operated freely, the relevant supply and demand schedules should have been estimated simultaneously to obtain unbiased estimates of the elasticity of the supply schedule for beef. However, during most of the postwar period (until 1959) the government set maximum prices, which in effect substituted the market demand for beef for an artificial schedule

[8] The significance of the index of rainfall is mildly surprising, as it is well known that the relationship between weather and crop yields is very complex and different for each crop. For a description of the crude rainfall index used, see the appendix to this chapter. For a description of the complicated links between weather and wheat yields in Argentina see *Agroclimatología del cultivo de trigo en la República Argentina*, by A. J. Pascale and E. A. Damario (Buenos Aires: Imprenta de la Universidad de Buenos Aires, 1961).

that was perfectly elastic in the relevant range. Thus, for those years an estimate can be made on the basis of observed prices and quantities of the supply schedule for beef without taking the true market-demand schedule into account.

At any rate, for the purposes of this study it will not be necessary to estimate the long-run supply schedule for beef. Rather, it will be shown that regardless of the size of the true long-run supply elasticity, an increase in the relative price of beef will result in the short run in a *decrease* in the slaughtering of animals and thus in a reduction of available beef supplies. No elasticity pessimist in his moments of deepest gloom ever dreamed of a backward-bending schedule for total supply availability of exportables. Yet, for the short run this is a distinct possibility for a country whose predominant exportable is beef, or an agricultural or livestock commodity having a similar type of production function.[9]

The production of beef in Argentina, as well as in other countries, follows a cycle of its own because of the special nature of the beef production function, which is examined later. The result is a "super-cobweb" effect in the beef market. Such an effect has some of the long-run properties of the well-known cobweb effect found in agricultural commodities such as coffee, whose grain-producing trees have long gestation periods. But the "super-cobweb" effect also has another aspect that gives the beef market added instability (and that yields a perverse short-run supply response): besides regular inputs, the beef industry requires large amounts of its own output as an input in the production process. In other words, a Leontief input-output table would show a high value for the diagonal element of the beef industry, while such coefficient would be small for the coffee industry.[10]

---

[9] By "available supply of beef" we mean a measure of the slaughtering for both export and domestic consumption. From a long-run or a national accounts point of view, total production of beef should include not only slaughtering but also the increments to the stock of livestock. It may be noted that the existence of a backward-bending supply curve for exportables in the short run would raise interesting possibilities. For example, if the domestic demand for exportables has a smaller absolute price elasticity than the "perverse" supply curve in the relevant price range, the beef-exporting country would hope that the foreign demand for its beef is inelastic for the short run. Devaluation would result in an almost certain improvement in the terms of trade. And so on. But it will be remembered that beef exports are only one of the several leading exports of Argentina.

[10] Professor C. P. Kindleberger has pointed out another example of cobweb-like effects in agricultural production, which centers around the choice between production for current use and investment for future output expansion. When

The theoretical underpinnings of a short-run, negatively sloped supply schedule and of a long-run cycle in the production of beef can be sketched as follows. Let us assume that we have a cattle industry with given stocks of cattle at a given point in time of S_t. The cattlemen, depending on cost conditions and the rate of profits that could be earned in alternative occupations, have a schedule linking the desired meat output for the current period with the ruling price of meat. It could be expected that such a schedule would have the normal positive slope of most supply schedules, so that

$$q_t^\circ = f(P_t) \qquad (A)$$

where

$$\frac{\partial q_t^\circ}{\partial P_t} > 0$$

The symbol q_t° represents the output, or current slaughtering, which cattlemen *desire* in a given year, given cost conditions, while P_t represents the actual ruling price. It must be emphasized that the supply schedule takes into account the possibility of alternative investment opportunities, or normal rates of return in other parts of the economy. The higher the price of cattle, the more the cattlemen would desire to produce, other things being equal.

The technical or physiological relation between the stock of cattle and the current production which would allow the stock of cattle to remain unchanged can be denoted thus:

$$q_t = v \cdot S_t \qquad (B)$$

If both S_t and q_t are measured in terms of homogeneous animals, v denotes the percentage of the herd which may be slaughtered in any given year to maintain the herd constant.[11]

---

cotton prices rose in the United States during the eighteen-thirties, labor was reallocated from cotton production to the clearing of land, which would allow for more cotton cultivation and thus future increases in cotton output. But as long as it takes only small amounts of present cotton (say in the form of seeds) to produce cotton in the future, it is possible to increase *both* present cotton output and investments to bring about future increases in cotton output by withdrawing labor from other sectors of the economy, whose prices have dropped relative to that of cotton. For most agricultural commodities such as coffee, wheat, or corn, the short-run response of output to price increases will be small, but never perverse.

[11] For Argentina, the value of v has been estimated at about 0.233, or 23.3 per cent of the herd. See *The Review of the River Plate*, October 9, 1956. A more thorough analysis would take into account the structure of the herds by ages and by different types of cattle. It should also be noticed that there are other inputs besides today's cattle that go into the production of tomorrow's cattle.

Equations A and B imply that for any given ruling price of beef there is a desired or optimum size for the cattle stocks:

$$S_t^\circ = \frac{f(P_t)}{v} \qquad (C)$$

It is possible, and quite likely, that S_t° and q_t° may, in the short run, be incompatible, that is, the realization of an actual slaughtering of $q_t = q_t^\circ$ may lead to a depletion of herds so that $S_t < S_t^\circ$. On the other hand, the realization of $S_t = S_t^\circ$ may imply $q_t < q_t^\circ$. Only after a period of time has elapsed with no disturbances emerging from price changes, cost changes, and so on, will S_t° and q_t° be compatible goals ("a steady state"). If the need for choice between q_t° and S_t° arises, which goal will a rational, profit-maximizing cattleman aim for? A little reflection will show that S_t° will always be chosen. Beginning with a position of equilibrium, we know that (given the size of v per year) cattlemen as a group cannot at the same time increase both slaughterings and herds. Now consider an increase in the price of beef. It will be assumed that cattlemen expect the new higher price to remain at the same level for all future periods. Increasing the slaughtering would imply disinvestment in cattle. If the funds thus obtained were reinvested in some other sector of the economy, it would be at lower rates of profits than those existing in the cattle industry because the only change in the equilibrium situation has been an increase in the price of beef, raising the profits in cattle. A similar argument would apply for a drop in the price of beef starting from an equilibrium situation and assuming the price change is expected to be permanent.

Thus, the actual production of beef (slaughtering) at any given period can be written:

$$\begin{matrix} q_t = (S_t - S_t^\circ) + v \cdot S_t & \text{, if } (1+v)S_t > S_t^\circ \\ q_t = 0 & \text{, if } (1+v)S_t < S_t^\circ \end{matrix} \qquad (D)$$

For the sake of simplicity, Equation D assumes that the adjustment to the optimum cattle stock takes place within a year. In the "steady state," $S_t = S_t^\circ$ and current production will be such as to keep the herds at the same level. What will the impact of a change in price of beef be on the current production of beef? Differentiating D with respect to P_t and remembering that for a given time the existing stock is a given constant we obtain (when $q_t \neq 0$)

and from C

$$\frac{\partial q_t}{\partial P_t} = -\frac{\partial S_t^{\,\circ}}{\partial P_t} \qquad (E)$$

$$\frac{\partial q_t}{\partial P_t} = -\frac{f'(P_t)}{v} \qquad (F)$$

We know that $f'(P_t)$, the slope of the schedule relating actual prices and *desired* output, is positive. Therefore $\partial q_t/\partial P_t$ is negative in sign, that is, an increase in the price of beef will lead to a decrease in the short-run production or slaughtering of cattle. The smaller v is, the sharper the drop in slaughtering.

The difference between this problem and the classical problem in capital theory as to "when to cut down the tree" should be noticed. The problem under consideration is more akin to the choice of investing in different projects promising different income streams. The problem is not so much whether to kill the cow today or tomorrow but rather whether to invest in cattle instead of in something else.[12]

For simplicity, the model just sketched assumes that the price of beef is independent of the level of output. To construct a long-run model for free markets with a classical cobweb effect we would of course have to take into account a demand schedule that is less than perfectly elastic. It has also been assumed that following a price change the expectations of cattlemen are that the new price will be a permanent one (or that at least it will remain above the old price); other assumptions regarding expectations would naturally yield different results.

Empirical evidence tends to support the theoretical conclusions advanced in Equations A through F rather well for the years 1944–1959. Comparing changes in available beef supplies (ΔQ_b) and changes in the relative wholesale beef prices received by producers (ΔP_b) for those sixteen years we obtain

$$\Delta Q_b = 50.9 - 0.97\,\Delta P_b \qquad R = 0.57 \qquad (4.3)$$
$$(0.38) \qquad\quad d = 2.10$$

When changes in the price of beef during the previous year and

---

[12] However, the change in the price of cattle will also change the slope of the curve showing the total value of a single animal through time at any given point in time. With a constant interest rate given, the decision regarding when to kill the animal will thus also be affected by the change in the price of beef, with any single animal being allowed to live longer than before the increase in price.

the relative prices of dairy products[13] (ΔP_d) are taken into account, the following result is obtained:

$$(\Delta Q_b)_t = 35.4 - \underset{(0.33)}{0.75} (\Delta P_b)_t - \underset{(0.56)}{1.07} (\Delta P_b)_{t-1} + \underset{(0.48)}{1.25} (\Delta P_d)_t$$

$$R = 0.80$$
$$d = 1.23$$

(4.4)

Equation 4.4 suggests that the adjustment period of changes in cattle stocks in response to changes in prices takes more than one year, although the coefficient for $(\Delta P_b)_{t-1}$ is not significant at the 5 per cent level. The significant coefficient for $(\Delta P_d)_t$ implies that an increase in the relative prices of dairy products induces a greater amount of slaughtering, presumably as producers shift from raising beef cattle to keeping cows suited for milking, the latter requiring a smaller, longer-lived stock of animals. A more thorough discussion of the significance of this coefficient would require an analysis of the many interrelationships existing among the production functions of livestock and agricultural products; such an analysis is beyond the scope of this study.

It may be concluded that a devaluation can expect little help in the short run from the response of beef production; not only will available supplies fail to expand in the short run but they are actually likely to decrease. This tendency toward a decrease in the short-run availability of beef would probably be checked to the extent that the relative prices of other exportables also increase, thus reducing the incentives to expand the beef sector (by cutting down present slaughtering) at the expense of other exportables. If following a devaluation, direct government controls and discriminatory taxes on beef prices and exports bring larger increases in domestic prices for noncattle exports than for those of beef, the result may well be (as it was after the 1955 devaluation) a perverse increase in

[13] Other regressions were estimated, taking into account the changes in the relative prices of wool, mutton, and cereals and linseed. Their coefficients, however, were found to be insignificant. It may be noted that the correlation coefficients obtained in regressions which related the changes in output to the changes in beef prices were higher than those obtained in regressions which took the level of beef output and prices as their variables. It should also be noted that the methodology used may not have avoided completely the "identification problem," as in some years random events, such as drought, could have increased slaughtering sharply, driving the price of beef below the maximum prices set by the government.

the current availabilities of beef at the expense of disinvestment in cattle herds and the long-run productive potential of this industry.

Supply Response of Exportables: Summary

The assumption made in Chapter 2 regarding the inelasticity of the short-run domestic supply response of F goods to an increase in its relative prices seems justified by the analysis of the likely supply response of rural exportable goods. The positive short-run supply response of noncattle commodities is likely to be rather small, and could very well be offset by the negative response of beef. It has been shown that even in periods of more than one year the over-all supply of rural exportables appears to be rather price inelastic. However, the historical record on this issue is far from clear, as it could be argued that during the postwar years relative prices of rural products have shown such erratic year-to-year fluctuations that the incentive arising from higher prices in one year was to a large extent offset by the fear of lower relative prices for the next year, as well as by the deterioration of social overhead facilities serving the rural sector and by the lack of critical inputs. Furthermore, it does appear that at least part of the higher profits received by the rural sector as a result of more favorable relative prices since 1953–1955 have been invested in new rural machinery, equipment, and other capital goods.[14] But such increases in the capital stock of the rural sector seem to have been offset from the point of view of total production by lower inputs of other types, especially labor.

Some observers have blamed chiefly the land tenure system for the failure of rural output to increase significantly, at least until very recent years. It is pointed out that because the total area which can be devoted to rural production is already being fully used, future expansions of output must come from more intensive production

[14] Since the beginning of 1956 until the beginning of 1960, the fixed reproducible capital stock in the agriculture and livestock sectors (measured in constant prices) increased by a total of 20 per cent, with the stock of machinery growing by 79 per cent and that of vehicles by 33 per cent. Data obtained from A. Ferrer and A. Fracchia, *La Producción, Ingresos y Capitalización del Sector Agropecuario en el Período 1950–1960, op. cit.*, Statistical Appendix. The equivalent figures for 1950 until the beginning of 1956 were +13 per cent for all reproducible fixed capital; +70 per cent for machinery and a *decrease* of 20 per cent in the stock of vehicles. Unpublished figures of the Consejo Nacional de Desarrollo show a decline in the total number of persons employed in agriculture and livestock of 14 per cent between 1950 and 1961. These trends in the capital and labor employed in the rural sector appear to have continued during the period 1961–1964. As mentioned before, agricultural output showed significant increases during 1963/1964.

techniques, and the existing pattern of land tenure is not conducive to such technological innovation. Without attempting to evaluate the importance of this argument as an explanation of long-run rural output trends, it may be said that while it appears that the land tenure system in Argentina is not optimum from the point of view of maximizing technological change, it does not seem to be so harmful as to prevent innovations, so that additional reasons must be sought to explain the observed historical output trends shown in Table 4.4.[15]

While the historical record shows that resources have not moved readily between rural and nonrural activities in response to relative prices, there is scattered evidence of much greater flexibility and fluidity of resources within the rural economy, where crops such as corn and sunflower, wheat and linseed keenly compete for existing land, and where livestock producers choose among alternative production possibilities depending on the relative output prices. Shifts between agriculture and livestock also seem to take place, although such shifts are probably smaller than those within each of these two major rural sectors.[16]

[15] In recent years, the expansion of production of exportable commodities into new areas of the country previously considered unfit for such activities suggests that the "end-of-the-frontier" thesis explaining rural stagnation in Argentina seriously underestimated potential output growth by the incorporation of new areas to production. For a very interesting summary and discussion of the principal factors which account for the stagnation of the rural sector see Walter F. Kugler, *Ideas que Animarán la Acción de la Secretaría de Agricultura y Ganadería en el Período 1963-1969*, Buenos Aires, October 1963. Arthur L. Domike, an expert of the Food and Agriculture Organization of the United Nations, has estimated on the basis of his unpublished research, that as much as half of Argentina's farmland is poorly or inadequately exploited for reasons related to inadequacies in the tenure structure. Even if one accepted land tenure as the key explanation for the stagnation of rural output in 50 per cent of the farmlands, the very low output growth rate in the rest would remain to be explained by other reasons.

[16] This periodic reallocation of resources is desirable to the extent that, when a fixed total amount of resources devoted to rural production is given, relative rural prices reflect true competitive market conditions (national and international). Under such circumstances these shifts among rural lines of production maximize rural output and also potential foreign exchange earnings. Unfortunately, relative rural prices have often been set rather arbitrarily by the government, and the shifting back and forth among different commodities may have slowed down technological change in some cases. The marginal investment and the change in production methods involved in switching from one activity to another within the rural sector are likely to be much less than in the case of switching from urban to rural activities; the same reasoning applies mutatis mutandis to production decisions involving agriculture versus livestock. These considerations help to explain the different supply responses to different relative prices, especially in a highly uncertain environment.

Nonrural exportables formed a very small fraction of total exports, and at least until 1961 the observed changes in relative prices failed to expand this category. In particular, Argentine industry, which has developed during the last thirty years primarily on the basis of import substitution, has not been able to contribute significantly to the exportable category, thus perpetuating its dependence on the rural sector for the foreign exchange it needs to purchase from abroad critical industrial inputs.

The Domestic Demand for Exportables

While the domestic production of exportables has grown very slowly during the last thirty-five years in Argentina, the rising population and per capita incomes have caused domestic demand for these commodities to expand at a higher rate. The result has been a steadily decreasing availability of exportable surpluses, not only relative to total exportable production but also in absolute amounts. Such is the background to the balance-of-payments difficulties of Argentina during the last fifteen years from the point of view of exports, which also accounts for the rather surprising fact that the level of the export quantum reached during 1955–1959 was only 75 per cent of that reached in 1935–1939.

Even if a devaluation does not induce any increase in the short-run availability of exportable commodities, it may still result in an increase of total exports if it reduces the domestic demand for exportables, either by inducing people to substitute home goods for previously consumed exportables or by reducing the real income of the population, especially of those with a high propensity to spend on exportables. Thus, it would be desirable to obtain some idea regarding the price and income elasticities of the domestic demand for exportables in Argentina, with separate estimates for wage earners and non-wage earners. Unfortunately, the same factors that made it difficult to obtain statistical results of a high degree of reliability for the import function appear again with special strength. The key difficulty arises from the reliance of the government during most of the period under study on ad hoc rationing mechanisms to allocate between exports and domestic consumption. Such systems usually imply that people are not "on their curves," thus complicating the analysis and casting doubts on the statistical results. Because of these complications, no thorough statistical analysis of the demand for exportables will be attempted.[17] Rather, this section will rely on the study of the structure of such demand and on a few isolated statistical estimations to obtain some information regarding the likely reaction of the domestic demand for exportables to a change in income distribution.

During 1950–1959, 78 per cent of the total output of the agricultural and livestock sector of Argentina went into domestic absorption compared with 50 per cent in 1920–1929.[18] Table 4.6 shows the share of the output used domestically for some of the most important exportables. In contrast with most Latin American countries, Argen-

TABLE 4.6
SHARE OF OUTPUT OF SELECTED EXPORTABLE COMMODITIES
ABSORBED DOMESTICALLY, 1950–1961
(*In percentages*)

Wool	37*
Wheat	60
Maize	62
Linseed	7†
Beef	80
All Meat	80

* For 1949–1958.
† For 1957–1962.
Sources: Percentages obtained from data on output and exports, both in physical magnitudes, found in *Estadísticas Básicas,* Junta Nacional de Carnes, Buenos Aires, 1963; *Revista de la Bolsa de Cereales,* several issues; *Boletín Mensual de Estadística,* several issues; and *The Review of the River Plate,* several issues. The percentages given refer to apparent domestic absorption, as they have been obtained by taking the difference between output and exports.

tina absorbs significant shares of most of the commodities which it exports, thus providing a powerful link by which devaluation can affect the whole economy, in spite of the relatively small ratio of actual exports to gross domestic product.

[17] While the existence of government-imposed maximum prices received by producers allowed us to use the single-equation, least-squares technique to estimate supply responses, especially in the case of beef, the maximum official prices applied to the sale of exportables to the domestic market destroy the possibility of estimating the true price elasticity of demand. If black-market prices had been recorded, and if such markets were representative of the total domestic market, it would have been possible to estimate the true price elasticity of demand by making the black-market prices the dependent variable of the estimated regression equation, assuming a perfectly inelastic supply schedule for the commodities flowing into the black market.
[18] See *Economía Agropecuaria Argentina, Problemas y Soluciones,* Oficina de Estudios para la Colaboración Económica Internacional, Buenos Aires, 1964, Tomo I, p. 106.

According to the Argentine national accounts, consumption of agricultural and livestock products amounted to 23 per cent of the gross national product during 1950–1961.[19] This percentage includes value added by the manufacturing and service sectors, and it may be compared with the 15 per cent of the gross domestic product[20] accounted for by value added in the agricultural and livestock sectors. As practically all of the rural commodities flow into consumption, the relative weight of such goods in total consumption is higher than in total national product. It is of greater interest from

TABLE 4.7
STRUCTURE OF THE BASIC BUDGET OF A TYPICAL WORKING-CLASS FAMILY IN BUENOS AIRES IN 1960
(*In percentages of total expenditure*)

Foodstuffs and Drink	59.2
Bread and cereals	7.2
Beef	15.0
Other meat	4.1
Oils and lard	1.9
Milk and dairy products	8.7
Fruits, garden vegetables, and potatoes	9.8
Nonalcoholic beverages, sugar, sweets, and spices	5.9
Alcoholic beverages (mainly wine)	4.3
Other	2.3
Clothing, Housing, Services, and Other	40.8

Source: *Costo del Nivel de Vida en la Capital Federal, Nueva Encuesta sobre Condiciones de Vida de Familias Obreras, Año 1960*, Dirección Nacional de Estadística y Censos, Buenos Aires, February 1963, pp. 23–32.

the point of view of this study to consider the weight of these exportables in the consumption of wage earners and other groups in the society.

Engel's Law and a priori considerations suggest that exportable commodities have a greater weight in the expenditures of wage earners than in those of non-wage earners. Table 4.7 lends support to such considerations, showing the results of a study made by the

[19] See *Cuentas Nacionales de la República Argentina, op. cit.*, pp. 182–183. This percentage includes a small component of imported products, and it may be broken down in the following way: meat consumption 6 per cent of GNP; manufactured food, drink, and tobacco 13 per cent; and other agricultural and livestock products 4 per cent.

[20] During the period under discussion the differences between gross national and gross domestic product in Argentina were very small and do not affect the comparability of the percentages here discussed.

National Statistical Office of Argentina regarding the budget of typical working class families in the city of Buenos Aires. Just beef and bread, two commodities which fall unambiguously in the exportable category, account for about 20 per cent of the expenditures (and probably of the total income) of working-class families. Practically all of the commodities in the food and drink category are either unambiguously exportable or very closely related to this category of goods, so that a devaluation is likely to have a very quick and significant impact on the average price of the consumption basket of working-class families, even after allowing for the fact that a substantial part of the price paid for the exportable commodities shown in Table 4.7 embodies value added by manufacturing and services, which are of the home-good type. Under the clothing category, the influence of exportables is also likely to be felt, via the price of wool, hides, and to a lesser extent cotton. Although published budget studies for non-wage earners are lacking, it does not seem unrealistic to suppose that the expenditures of these groups on exportables, especially foodstuffs, represent a much lower percentage of their income than in the case of wage earners.[21] Thus, it may be stated that in Argentina exportables are primarily wage goods, thus setting the stage for a quasi-Ricardian conflict between the industrial sector, especially wage earners, and the rural sector, which is often at the root of balance-of-payments difficulties in Argentina.

The fact that Argentine exportables can on the whole be considered wage goods also has some implications for the elasticity of their domestic demand with respect to changes in their relative prices. If the price elasticity takes only into account pure substitution effects,[22] such elasticity is likely to be rather low for exportables taken as a whole, as the possibilities of substituting exportable foodstuffs for other nonexportable commodities is likely to be limited, given the wide range of foodstuffs included under exportables.[23]

[21] A recent survey of urban expenditure carried out under the joint sponsorship of the Organization of American States, the Interamerican Development Bank and the Consejo Nacional de Desarrollo of Argentina supports this conclusion.

[22] It is important here to break down price effects into income and substitution effects, as was done in Chapter 2, even if it is difficult to estimate empirically those two effects. If wage earners spend all of their income on exportables, for example, before and after a change in their relative prices, a Marshallian demand curve of wage earners for these products would show a price elasticity of demand of -1, which however could arise with a substitution effect of zero. A further empirical limitation on the estimation of the pure substitution relative price elasticity arises from the necessity of estimating such variables for wage earners and non-wage earners lumped together.

[23] Some possibilities do, however, exist, as between beef and fish and in

A rough attempt has been made to estimate an equation expressing the nature of the total domestic demand for exportables. As shown in the appendix to this chapter, for 1950–1961 there are data on the value of total final domestic consumption of foodstuffs, drink and tobacco, and other rural products. Such data embody not only the value added by the sector producing exportables but also processing and merchandising costs, which reflect value added by sectors in the home-good category. In spite of this limitation, a comparison among the per capita consumption of these commodities (C_e) and wage (W) and nonwage income (T) per wage earner and non-wage earner, respectively, as well as the implicit relative prices of the commodities under discussion (P_e) can serve as a check on the presumption that wage earners have a higher propensity to spend on exportables than non-wage earners, and that the price elasticity of the domestic demand for exportables is rather low. Taking the twelve years for which data are available (1950–1961), we obtain

$$C_e = 7{,}736 - 5.19\, P_e + 0.25\, W + 0.05\, T \quad R = 0.90$$
$$\phantom{C_e = 7{,}736 -\ } (1.73) \quad\ (0.08) \quad\ (0.02) \quad d = 1.63$$

(4.5)

The fit is remarkably good: the coefficients for P and W are significant even at the 2 per cent level, while the coefficient for T is significant at the 5 per cent level. As variables C_e, W, and T have been expressed in 1960 pesos, the coefficients for W and T show approximately the marginal propensities to spend on the exportable-type commodities of wage earners and non-wage earners once they are weighted by the ratio of total population to the population of wage earners and non-wage earners, which is 1.43 and 3.32, respectively. Such an adjustment yields marginal propensities of approximately 0.36 for wage earners and 0.16 for non-wage earners. Thus, Equation 4.5 not only supports the presumption that the average propensity of wage earners to spend on exportable-type goods is higher than that of non-wage earners but also shows that such difference is maintained at the margin.

Comparing the results implied by the coefficient for W in Equation 4.5 with the average propensity implied in Table 4.7, one emerges with the not unreasonable result that the income elasticity of the

---

general between goods with a high degree of "exportableness" and those with a lower degree of "exportableness." Unfortunately, in many cases traditional Argentine tastes conspire against easy substitutability among exportable and nonexportable foodstuffs.

demand of wage earners for exportables is less than one. It may also be noted that the simple correlation coefficient between C_e and W is $+0.74$, while it is only $+0.10$ for C_e and T.[24]

Based on the average values of P_e and C_e for the years covered by Equation 4.5, the price elasticity implied by the significant P_e coefficient is considerably less than one: -0.35. However, for the reasons discussed previously, such an estimate cannot be taken as conclusive proof of low substitution effects in the consumption of exportables arising from changes in relative prices.[25]

Another effort has been made to gain information regarding the domestic demand for exportables by estimating the domestic-demand schedule for beef for the period 1935–1962, at least with regard to the income variables. Taking wages and nonwages per wage earner and non-wage earner, respectively, and the per capita domestic consumption of beef (C_b), all expressed in 1960 prices, we obtain

$$C_b = 2{,}138 + \underset{(0.012)}{0.073\,W} - \underset{(0.006)}{0.012\,T} \qquad \begin{array}{l} R = 0.78 \\ d = 0.90 \end{array} \qquad (4.6)$$

While both coefficients for W and T are significant at the 5 per cent level and the regression fit is reasonably good, the Durbin-Watson statistic indicates that there exists positive serial correlation of the error terms in the regression (taking into account that there are 28 observations and two independent variables). The estimated coefficients, however, confirm the conclusions reached on the basis of Equation 4.5, that wage earners have a higher marginal propensity to spend on exportables than non-wage earners (once the coefficients are weighted by population). Indeed, the coefficient for T in Equation 4.6 indicates that beef is an inferior good for the high-income classes.[26]

---

[24] The simple correlations between P_e and W, and P_e and T are also of some interest. While the former is -0.40, the latter is positive and equal to 0.64. These results indicate that periods of high relative prices for exportables, which could be due to a devaluation of the exchange rate, are associated with a redistribution of income toward nonwage income. It should be observed that both W and T were deflated by the same price index. The simple correlation between W and T is -0.13 for 1950–1961.

[25] On the other hand, the fact that the implicit prices for these commodities were obtained by dividing indices of total value by the quantum index used as dependent variable tends to bias the estimated price coefficient toward -1, and tends to improve the fit of the regression.

[26] Using the retail price of beef (P_{br}) deflated by the cost-of-living index as an additional independent variable, we obtain

The Domestic Demand for Exportables: Summary

The domestic demand for exportables presents an interesting contrast to that for importables: while it was demonstrated in Chapter 3 that in the latter case, non-wage earners appear to have a greater weight than wage earners, the opposite is true for the demand for exportables. But the statistical results obtained are too rough to allow us to reach a firm conclusion regarding the relative weights of wage income and nonwage income in the total domestic demand for F goods (importables plus exportables). Although in Chapter 3 we were able to obtain an estimate for the *marginal* propensities to import of wage earners and non-wage earners, little could be said about the average import propensities of each social group; however, it appears that wage earners have both a higher average and marginal propensity to spend on exportables than do non-wage earners. Perhaps it can be presumed that wage earners have on balance a higher *average* propensity to spend on F goods than non-wage earners, but even discounting part of the rather high marginal propensity to import of non-wage earners estimated in Chapter 3, such a revised figure certainly would match the high marginal propensity of wage earners to spend on exportables.[27] The

$$C_b = 2{,}753 - 0.89 P_{br} + 0.049 W - 0.002 T \quad R = 0.92$$
$$\phantom{C_b = 2{,}753 -\ } (0.15) \phantom{P_{br} +\ } (0.009) (0.004) \quad d = 0.60 \quad (4.7)$$

The price elasticity implied by the significant coefficient for P_{br} is -0.31 (taking the average values for P_{br} and C_b for the period 1935–1962), a value remarkably close to the price elasticity estimated in Equation 4.5 for the demand of all exportables. However, the Durbin-Watson statistic again implies that the strong serial correlation of the error terms casts serious doubts on the validity of the results, which at any rate could have been challenged with regard to the price coefficient for reasons discussed previously.

[27] Using the same source of data employed in the estimation of Equation 4.5, an attempt was made to explain the per capita consumption of durable goods (C_d), which as seen in Chapter 3 generates a substantial part of the demand for imports of raw materials and intermediate products, as a function of W and T, for 1950–1961. The following was the result, with all variables expressed in 1960 pesos:

$$C_d = -6{,}225 + 0.09W + 0.10T \quad R = 0.91$$
$$\phantom{C_d = -6{,}225 +\ } (0.08) (0.01) \quad d = 1.80 \quad (4.8)$$

While the coefficient for W is not significantly different from zero, that for T is significant even at the 1 per cent level. The simple correlation between C_d and T is 0.90; that between C_d and W is 0.03. These results serve to stress the contrast between the nature of the demand for exportables and that for importables; together with the information provided in Chapter 3 on the import requirements of industries producing durable consumer goods, it supports the presumption that a good share of the imports of intermediate products and raw materials represents disguised luxury imports.

size of the standard errors of the coefficients and the data and conceptual difficulties encountered in estimating the regressions do not permit us, however, to say any more regarding the relative sizes of what in Chapter 2 were called $\partial f_1/\partial W$ and $\partial f_2/\partial T$.

The scanty evidence on price elasticity of demand for exportables, for both wage earners and non-wage earners lumped together, indicates a price elasticity of less than one, although perhaps higher than the price elasticity of the total domestic demand for importables. Thus, some improvement in the trade balance may occur after devaluation even in a short run characterized by a perfectly inelastic supply for F goods and even if there is no redistributive effect. Such an improvement based on the price elasticity of demand for exportables is, however, likely to be very small. A drop in domestic output arising from the redistributive effect will have a more powerful effect in reducing the domestic demand for both importables and exportables, working through the leverage provided by the high marginal propensities to spend on F goods.[28] As shown in Chapter 2, the existence and importance of the redistributive effect and its impact on the trade balance depends essentially on the gap between the marginal propensities to save of wage earners and non-wage earners. The next chapter turns to this critical issue, as well as to other related features of the Argentine economy.

Statistical Appendix to Chapter 4

The tables in this appendix present the data utilized in the regressions discussed in Chapter 4.

Table S.1: Basic Data Used to Estimate the Supply Response of Cereals and Linseed

The variables, which were transformed into natural logarithms to obtain regressions 4.1 and 4.2, and their sources are

[28] If it is assumed that the marginal propensities to spend on F goods are the same for wage earners and non-wage earners, Equation 2.13 of Chapter 2, showing the impact of devaluation in a short run characterized by a zero supply elasticity for the F good and zero substitution effects becomes

$$\frac{dB}{dk} = \frac{a}{D}\left\{\frac{\partial F}{\partial Y} \cdot F_d\right\} \qquad (2.13b)$$

The expression $\partial F/\partial Y$ represents the common marginal propensity to spend on F goods, and F_d the total domestic demand for F goods; a is the marginal propensity to save (hoard) and D is an income multiplier, which now becomes equal to $a(1-s) + \partial F/\partial Y$.

1. Index of rainfall in selected locations of the Pampean zone (Z'). The figures for annual rainfall for the following communities were the basic raw materials: Rufino (Santa Fe); La Carlota (Córdoba); Victoria F.C.E.R. (Entre Ríos); Pergamino (Buenos

TABLE S.1
BASIC DATA USED TO ESTIMATE THE SUPPLY RESPONSE OF CEREALS AND LINSEED

	Z'	P'_c	P'_w	P'_g	Q'_c	Q'_w
1935	763	959	795	998	1935	845
1936	1092	1191	1160	1081	1503	775
1937	690	1309	1387	993	1627	815
1938	865	1226	934	1052	1072	862
1939	1202	1000	1000	1000	1450	867
1940	1339	817	1080	936	1527	990
1941	1011	629	1009	899	1861	1064
1942	926	486	756	877	1594	1104
1943	1089	525	583	784	846	1136
1944	1030	480	521	763	1650	1129
1945	969	601	530	718	781	1129
1946	1376	1176	664	802	857	1129
1947	982	963	683	929	1228	1122
1948	1095	891	937	836	1203	1021
1949	855	781	839	749	890	966
1950	897	679	1420	768	594	962
1951	896	651	1874	853	801	1001
1952	989	613	602	899	399	899
1953	1180	725	679	892	1087	978
1954	1012	699	666	871	940	1009
1955	1140	657	727	793	936	958
1956	1401	753	1188	775	804	873
1957	1244	752	1522	703	978	966
1958	1090	768	967	814	985	943
1959	1180	744	1175	1169	1054	954
1960	913	854	1106	1092	1000	1000
1961	869	924	961	948	819	1002
1962	679	1020	647	919	952	941

Aires); Saladillo (Buenos Aires); Villa María (Córdoba); General Saavedra (Buenos Aires); Trenque Lauquén (Buenos Aires); Tandil (Buenos Aires); Santa Rosa (La Pampa); Quemú-Quemú (La Pampa); and Río Colorado (Río Negro). The figures on rainfall were obtained from the files of the Servicio Meteorológico Nacional for 1935–1959; for more recent years they were obtained from several issues of *The Review of the River Plate*. For each locality an index was constructed with its average rainfall during 1920–1950 set equal to 1000. The figures shown in Table S.1 represent the simple averages of those twelve indices for each year.

2. Relative prices for cereals and linseed (P'_t). This index (1939 = 1000) was obtained by dividing the index for wholesale prices for cereals and linseed by the index for wholesale nonrural prices (both national and imported). For 1939 to 1962 the source of these indices is the same as shown for Item 6 in the statistical appendix to Chapter 3. For earlier years, indices were obtained from the *Revista Económica* of the Banco Central de la República Argentina, several issues during 1937–1940. Indices with different bases were linked on the earliest year for which the old series overlap the new ones. The same sources and methods were used in obtaining the relative wholesale prices of wool (P'_w) and cattle (P'_g). These wholesale prices reflect the quotations (either free or government controlled) ruling in the major organized markets where rural producers sell their products. During periods of government control of prices the indices only reflect the official prices.

3. Indices of output of cereals and linseed (Q'_c) and wool (Q'_w). The output index for cereals and linseed refers to the year when crops were harvested. The sources for these indices are the same ones indicated in Table 4.4. Worksheets of the Consejo Nacional de Desarrollo were also used as sources for these series. It may be noted that the index for cereals and linseed may underestimate slightly the growth of output in recent years, as it does not take into account crops such as sorghum which have expanded very rapidly during the last decade (in the case of sorghum, it replaced maize domestically as animal feed, freeing maize for export). The aggregate index for agriculture shown in Table 4.4 would also underestimate production, but not by significant amounts.

Table S.2: Data Used to Estimate the Short-Run Supply Response of Beef

The variables, whose year-to-year differences were taken to obtain regressions 4.3 and 4.4, and their sources are

1. Relative prices for beef (P_b). This index (1939 = 1000) was obtained by dividing the index for wholesale prices for bovine cattle in the Liniers market by the index for wholesale nonrural prices (both national and imported). The index for wholesale prices for bovine cattle at Liniers was obtained from *Estadísticas Básicas*,

op. cit., p. 13. Source for wholesale nonrural prices same as for Item 6 in the statistical appendix to Chapter 3.

2. Relative prices for dairy products (P_d). This index (1939 = 1000) was obtained by dividing the wholesale-price index for dairy products (Productos de granja) by the index for wholesale nonrural prices. Sources as for Item 6 in the statistical appendix to Chapter 3.

TABLE S.2
DATA USED TO ESTIMATE THE SHORT-RUN SUPPLY RESPONSE OF BEEF

	P_b	P_d	Q_b
1943	821	615	1602
1944	812	635	1619
1945	761	642	1456
1946	750	765	1682
1947	898	984	2024
1948	845	1047	1958
1949	777	1046	2003
1950	742	978	2044
1951	801	831	1879
1952	827	792	1788
1953	914	833	1765
1954	909	807	1815
1955	826	752	2147
1956	775	724	2475
1957	693	704	2459
1958	854	733	2541
1959	1308	682	1944

3. Quantity of beef produced (Q_b). This variable presents the weight of slaughtered bovine cattle in thousands of tons. Data obtained from *Estadísticas Básicas, op. cit.*, p. 6.

Table S.3: Data Used to Estimate the Domestic Demand Schedule for Exportable-Type and Importable-Type Commodities

These variables, used to estimate the results shown in regressions 4.5 and 4.8, and their sources are

1. Relative prices to consumers of exportable-type commodities (P_e). This index (1960 = 1000) was obtained by dividing the implicit prices of exportable-type commodities by the implicit price deflator for the gross national product. Both were obtained from *Cuentas Nacionales de la República Argentina, op. cit.* Implicit prices were obtained by dividing current value figures by the corresponding figures measured at 1960 prices.

2. Per capita (per wage earner and non-wage earner) wage income (W) and nonwage income (T) in 1960 prices. As in Items 4 and 5 in the statistical appendix to Chapter 3.

3. Per capita consumption of exportable-type commodities, measured in 1960 pesos (C_e). This group includes consumption by families of meat, other nonprocessed rural products and manufactured foodstuffs, drink, and tobacco. Data obtained from *Cuentas Nacionales de la República Argentina, op. cit.*, pp. 182–183. These figures were divided by population data obtained as in Item 1 in the statistical appendix to Chapter 3.

TABLE S.3
DATA USED TO ESTIMATE THE DOMESTIC DEMAND SCHEDULE FOR EXPORTABLE-TYPE AND IMPORTABLE-TYPE COMMODITIES

	P_e	W	T	C_e	C_d
1950	784	25,196	65,655	13,111	2,116
1951	733	23,457	69,331	12,733	2,453
1952	821	23,734	59,220	11,994	1,848
1953	880	23,659	64,538	12,409	1,826
1954	853	24,767	65,523	12,382	2,203
1955	838	24,868	73,336	13,254	2,557
1956	783	23,759	71,104	13,450	2,622
1957	887	23,558	74,649	12,925	3,458
1958	850	26,934	78,851	13,695	3,621
1959	950	21,996	80,493	11,887	3,008
1960	1,000	22,500	81,149	12,063	3,552
1961	935	24,314	80,099	12,621	4,144

4. Per capita consumption of importable-type commodities, mainly durable consumer goods, measured in 1960 pesos (C_d). This variable includes purchases by families of vehicles and appliances, both electrical and nonelectrical, and other goods made out of wood and metal. Sources and methods as in the previous item.

Table S.4: Data Used to Estimate the Domestic Demand Schedule for Beef

The variables, used to estimate regressions 4.6 and 4.7, are

1. Index (1936–1939 = 1000) of relative retail prices to consumers of beef (P_{br}). The index of retail prices for beef was deflated by the cost-of-living index to obtain P_{br}. Retail prices for beef and cost-of-living index obtained from *Estadísticas Básicas, op. cit.*, p. 13.

2. Per capita (per wage earner and non-wage earner) wage income (W) and nonwage income (T) in 1960 prices. As in Items 4 and 5 in the statistical appendix to Chapter 3.

TABLE S.4
Data Used to Estimate the Domestic Demand Schedule for Beef

	P_{br}	W	T	C_b
1935	1,009	15,873	59,352	2,658
1936	1,060	16,530	61,256	2,582
1937	985	17,309	69,988	2,716
1938	976	17,032	63,751	2,709
1939	976	16,931	64,538	2,726
1940	1,001	16,604	64,473	2,654
1941	1,006	17,032	67,822	2,630
1942	1,037	16,655	71,958	2,355
1943	1,068	16,806	70,120	2,245
1944	1,141	18,847	76,357	2,321
1945	1,000	17,738	70,645	2,417
1946	900	19,779	77,932	2,723
1947	837	22,374	84,629	2,977
1948	740	25,221	83,513	3,132
1949	683	26,027	68,937	3,153
1950	662	25,196	65,655	3,228
1951	744	23,457	69,331	3,163
1952	888	23,734	59,220	2,881
1953	960	23,659	64,538	2,867
1954	925	24,767	65,523	2,902
1955	824	24,868	73,336	3,115
1956	726	23,759	71,104	3,304
1957	873	23,558	74,649	3,239
1958	940	26,934	78,851	3,215
1959	1,543	21,996	80,493	2,379
1960	1,398	22,500	81,149	2,458
1961	1,194	24,314	80,099	2,823
1962	1,127	23,029	76,028	2,719

3. Per capita domestic consumption of beef in 1960 prices (C_b). Data on per capita consumption of beef expressed in kilos were multiplied by the retail price of beef per kilo in 1960. Physical per capita consumption of beef and retail price for 1960 obtained from *Estadísticas Básicas, op. cit.*, pp. 11, 13.

5

Savings, Investment, and the Inflationary Process in Argentina

The previous two chapters have examined the key relationships of the external sector of Argentina, primarily the domestic demand and supply of importables and exportables. It was seen in Chapter 2, however, that while such relationships are naturally very important in determining the impact of devaluation on the balance of trade, the short-run redistributive effect is based essentially on the saving propensities of the different social classes. It was then shown that so long as non-wage earners have a larger marginal propensity to save than wage earners, the balance of trade will improve in the short run dominated by the redistributive effect, regardless of the propensities of the different social groups to spend on importables and exportables, although the degree of improvement will of course be influenced by the latter. This chapter will examine the validity of the assumption that in Argentina non-wage earners have a higher marginal propensity to save than wage earners. Even if this is the case, however, it could be argued that the increased savings may induce non-wage earners to augment their investment expenditures, so that the redistributive effect may or may not increase hoarding. Thus, the structure and nature of gross capital formation in Argentina will also be examined to try to ascertain the net impact on hoarding of the redistributive effect. Finally, since the Argentine devaluations have taken place in the context of severe inflationary conditions, some of the basic characteristics of the inflationary process will be sketched at the end of this chapter.

The Structure and Nature of Domestic Savings

The observed *ex post* domestic savings of Argentina during 1950–1961 are shown in Table 5.1 expressed as percentages of the gross national product. The amount of total domestic savings is influenced by a large number of variables in any given year: level and distribution of income, the rate of inflation and expectations regarding its future course, real interest rates, and so on. For any year, or even for several years, *ex post* savings may embody a

TABLE 5.1
STRUCTURE OF GROSS DOMESTIC SAVING IN ARGENTINA, 1950–1961
(*In percentages of gross national product at market prices*)

	1950–1952	1953–1955	1956–1958	1959–1961
Total Gross Domestic Saving	18.5	19.1	18.0	20.5
Gross Public Saving	5.0	2.8	3.2	3.5
Gross Private Saving	13.6	16.3	14.8	17.1
Families	8.9	11.3	9.6	11.7
Depreciation allowances	4.0	4.4	4.5	3.8
Net savings of incorporated enterprises	0.7	0.6	0.7	1.5

Sources and methods: Cuentas Nacionales de la República Argentina, Consejo Nacional de Desarrollo, Presidencia de la Nación, República Argentina, Buenos Aires, April 1964, and other data, unpublished, of the Consejo Nacional de Desarrollo. Gross public savings include net savings of government enterprises; all depreciation allowances have been allocated to the private sector. Net foreign saving is excluded from total gross domestic savings. Percentages were taken for each year on the basis of current prices; the percentages shown represent the averages of such yearly percentages.

significant amount of forced savings, thus making difficult the estimation of *ex ante* schedules on the basis of observed data. The relatively high rates of domestic savings observed in Argentina during 1950–1961 coupled with the inflation which existed in those years suggest that part of those observed savings was "forced" or unintended. The fact that during 1950–1958 the public and the private rates of savings moved in different directions from period to period could be interpreted to lend support to such a presumption. However, bearing this limitation in mind, an attempt will be made to isolate the marginal propensities to save of wage earners and non-wage earners, on the assumption that unintended savings were not sufficiently large during 1950–1961 to bias the estimated difference in *ex ante* propensities of these two social groups in any systematic way.

Table 5.1 shows that during 1950–1961 gross public savings accounted for 3.6 per cent of the gross national product, or roughly 20 per cent of all gross domestic savings. Although devaluation and income redistribution will induce some changes in the level of public savings, other things being equal, mainly via changes in tax revenues, such changes are likely to be swamped in practice by government fiscal measures taken at the time of devaluation.[1] Thus, public savings will be considered to be exogenously determined.

In previous chapters, it has been estimated that per capita non-wage income was about three times per capita wage income. It does not seem unreasonable to assume that given such differences in real income, the average and marginal propensities to save of non-wage earners will be higher than that of wage earners. Taking for 1950–1961 per capita gross private savings (A) and comparing it with wages per wage earner (W) and nonwages per non-wage earner (T), all variables expressed in 1960 pesos, the following regression equation is obtained:

$$A = -9{,}171 + 0.30\,W + 0.12\,T \quad R = 0.74$$
$$\phantom{A = -9{,}171 + {}} (0.22) \phantom{W +{}} (0.04) \quad d = 1.58 \qquad (5.1)$$

While the coefficient for W is not significantly different from zero, that for T is; adjusting it for the ratio of total population to the population of non-wage earners, it yields a marginal propensity of non-wage earners to save of 0.41. While this latter value should be taken as a very rough approximation, Equation 5.1 does seem to confirm the presumption on which the redistributive effect rests. While the simple correlation coefficient between A and W is only $+0.21$, that for A and T is $+0.68$. If instead of using per capita variables total values are used (denoted by A', W', and T'), the following obtains:

$$A' = -8{,}078 + 0.30\,W' + 0.28\,T' \quad R = 0.83$$
$$\phantom{A' = -8{,}078 + {}} (0.31) \phantom{W' +{}} (0.12) \quad d = 1.64 \qquad (5.2)$$

---

[1] Considering the present Argentine tax structure, we would expect that the endogenous forces arising from a devaluation would tend on balance to decrease real tax revenues. As most taxes are collected with a lag of about one year, the increase in the price level would decrease the real value of tax revenues, while the devaluation induced drop in domestic output would tend to reduce the revenues of taxes collected currently.

Equation 5.2 tells roughly the same story as 5.1: the significant coefficient for T' now implies a marginal propensity to save for non-wage earners of 0.28, but the coefficient for W' is still not significantly different from zero.

The roughness of the data and the difficulties arising from changes in the legal and institutional framework of the private sector do not permit a more disaggregated study of gross private savings. The breakdown shown in Table 5.1 for gross private savings reflects changes in laws regarding corporations, depreciation allowances, and so on, more than any economic factor. An interesting breakdown would have been between rural and nonrural private savings; data for such classification are not available. However, it may be noted that the simple correlation between A' and total rural nonwage income is only slightly higher than that between A' and other nonwage income: $+0.77$ compared with $+0.73$, all variables being expressed in 1960 pesos.[2]

The Structure and Nature of Domestic Gross Capital Formation

A devaluation is expected in the long run to induce greater investment in industries producing importables and exportables either at the expense of investments in home-good industries or in a context of a greater over-all rate of capital accumulation. A redistribution of income toward nonwages arising from a devaluation will tend not only to induce greater capital formation in F industries but will also tend to change the consumption-and-investment mix of national income in favor of the latter. In semi-industrialized economies, where capital markets are weak, a devaluation will not only result in price incentives for the expansion of the output of exportables and importables; it will also give rise to a strong financial stimulus by providing entrepreneurs in those sectors with liquid funds with which to finance the expansion.

These long-run considerations raise the question of whether the investment incentives generated by a devaluation are so strong as

---

[2] The simple correlation coefficient between rural nonwage income and other nonwage income is $+0.68$, which drops to $+0.42$ when both variables are expressed in per capita terms. Such relatively low correlation coefficients are due among other things to the fact that following a devaluation the profits of home-good industries (included in other nonwage income) fall or stagnate while rural profits increase.

to induce, even in the short run, an upsurge of capital formation that will more than offset the marginal propensity to save of non-wage earners and yield a negative net propensity to hoard. In other words, the possibility exists that the new incentives will stimulate non-wage earners even in the short run to dip into accumulated cash balances, to borrow from banks, and so on, in spite of their higher level of income. If this is the case, the redistributive effect will not result in an improvement in the balance of trade in the short run, although it may still yield a drop in domestic output if the additional expenditures of non-wage earners have a very low home-good component (for instance, because of a high-import component, which would also aggravate the short-run deterioration of the balance of trade).[3]

For such a situation to develop in the short run it will be necessary for gross investment expenditures on F-good industries to expand more rapidly than the rate at which gross investment expenditures on H-good industries contract as a result of the drop in their relative profitability. In spite of the higher relative share of nonwage income in total national product which results from the devaluation, such a result is unlikely. As a matter of fact, observers of several stabilization programs characterized by such income redistribution have pointed out that gross investment in H-good industries will diminish rapidly following a devaluation while those investments that become more profitable after devaluation and stabilization increase only after an unavoidable time lag,[4] thus yielding an increase in hoarding in the short run. It may be noted that there is a conflict between the short- and the long-run improvement in the balance of trade following a devaluation; for any given rate of decrease in investment in H-good industries, the faster the increase of investment in F-good industries the smaller the short-run improvement but the greater the long-run improvement in the balance of trade. The precise nature of such a trade-off will depend on several variables, including the gestation periods of different projects, their import requirements,

---

[3] The possibility of a "foreign trade accelerator" which causes a negative marginal propensity to hoard has been emphasized by C. P. Kindleberger and S. S. Alexander. See Charles P. Kindleberger, *International Economics* (Homewood, Ill.: Richard D. Irwin, Inc., 1958), pp. 186–187; Sidney S. Alexander, "Effects of a Devaluation on a Trade Balance," International Monetary Fund *Staff Papers*, Vol. II, No. 2 (April 1952), pp. 263–278.

[4] See Graeme S. Dorrance, "The Effect of Inflation on Economic Development," International Monetary Fund *Staff Papers*, Vol. X, No. 1 (March 1963), pp. 1–47. It is conceivable that in some countries entrepreneurs could be so alert that the opposite result could be obtained, however.

and so on. Similar factors will also determine how in the long run the declining rate of investment in H-good industries and the growing rate of investment in F-good industries will affect the balance of trade and the growth rate of the economy.

Some further light can be cast on the probable investment behavior following a devaluation by examining the actual investment structure in Argentina during 1950–1961. Table 5.2 shows gross capital formation and its main components as percentages of gross

TABLE 5.2
STRUCTURE OF GROSS DOMESTIC INVESTMENT IN ARGENTINA, 1950–1961
(*In percentages of gross national product at market prices*)

	1950–1952	1953–1955	1956–1958	1959–1961
Total Gross Domestic Investment	20.0	18.9	20.1	22.4
Gross Public Investment	6.0	5.0	4.3	4.8
Gross Private Investment	14.1	13.9	15.8	17.6
Changes in selected inventories	— 0.2	0.8	— 0.4	0.4
Residential housing	6.1	5.2	5.2	3.4
Other fixed investment	8.1	8.0	11.0	13.8

Sources and methods: Same as in Table 5.1. Investment in residential housing obtained from very rough estimates made in some worksheets of the Consejo Nacional de Desarrollo. The difference between gross domestic saving and gross domestic investment represents net foreign investment. Percentages were taken for each year on the basis of current prices; the percentages shown are the averages of such yearly percentages. It should be noted that because of the high level of and changes in the relative prices of capital goods in Argentina the figures of Table 5.2 have to be adjusted before using them for analyzing international comparisons of investment rates and year-to-year changes in real capital formation in Argentina.

national product; the high level of relative prices of capital goods in Argentina accounts for the relatively large percentages shown. Public capital formation, which includes investment of public enterprises, accounted for about 25 per cent of total gross domestic investment; another 25 per cent of all capital formation went into residential housing, leaving 50 per cent for other private capital formation.[5]

Public investment may be considered to be exogenously deter-

---

[5] Comparing Tables 5.1 and 5.2 it may be seen that for the whole period 1950–1961 public investment exceeded public saving in an amount roughly equal to net foreign investment, as private saving was about equal to private investment. Net foreign investment includes net decreases of foreign-exchange reserves.

mined, as public savings were assumed to be. To measure the short-run impact of changes in nonwage income on gross private investment, the year to year changes in nonwage income per non-wage earner (ΔT) and the changes in the income velocity of circulation (ΔV) were compared with the changes in gross private fixed investment per capita (ΔPI). The income velocity of circulation, defined as the ratio of the gross national product to the average holdings during the year of currency and demand deposits by the public, has been used as a proxy variable to reflect the availability of credit, for during most of the period under study interest rates were subject to government controls and failed to reflect the degree of liquidity existing in the money market at any given time. The following result was obtained using these variables, where both ΔPI and ΔT are expressed in 1960 pesos:

$$\Delta PI = 409 - \underset{(0.69)}{0.73\,\Delta V} + \underset{(0.06)}{0.06\,\Delta T} \quad \begin{array}{l} R = 0.43 \\ d = 1.55 \end{array} \quad (5.3)$$

The fit is rather poor; neither of the coefficients is significantly different from zero, implying that there is no stable short-run link between nonwage income and private investment. Such a link, however, is likely to exist in the long run. To test such a presumption, the following two regressions were estimated using levels instead of changes and subdividing the per capita level of gross private investment into housing (PIH) and nonhousing (PIO):

$$PIH = 2{,}164 - \underset{(0.09)}{0.21\,V} + \underset{(0.013)}{0.009\,T} \quad \begin{array}{l} R = 0.72 \\ d = 1.03 \end{array} \quad (5.4)$$

$$PIO = -2{,}369 + \underset{(0.42)}{0.70\,V} + \underset{(0.06)}{0.06\,T} \quad \begin{array}{l} R = 0.83 \\ d = 1.53 \end{array} \quad (5.5)$$

In both 5.4 and 5.5, the coefficients for T are insignificant, implying no stable link between nonwage income and private investment even in the long run. However, the estimating technique is too rough to reach any firm conclusion regarding this link; thus, if only the simple correlation between PIO and T is examined, we emerge with a correlation coefficient of $+0.77$, which by itself suggests the existence of some such link.[6] Furthermore, the equations estimated in

---

[6] For the years 1950–1961, the estimation of the private investment function is hindered by a high correlation coefficient between the two independent variables, V and T, which equals $+0.81$.

Chapter 3 showed a significant marginal propensity to import capital goods out of nonwage income, which supports the hypothesis that nonwage income will influence private investment in the long run, even though such influence is likely to be small in the short run. It is also possible that greater disaggregation by sectors of production (for example, agriculture, manufacturing, and so on) would reveal stable long-run links between investment and nonwage income.

The significant coefficient for V in Equation 5.4 suggests that monetary policy has substantial influence on investment in housing, a result which is in line with some of the known characteristics of mortgage credit in Argentina. Until 1959, it may be estimated that new gross credits of the government-owned National Mortgage Bank and related institutions accounted for between 40 and 60 per cent of the total value of investment in housing. These credits were given at rates of interest of about 6 per cent and maturities often extending for thirty years, while the price level increased at an average annual rate of more than 20 per cent. Under these circumstances, the government decisions to expand or contract available official mortgage credit would have a sharp and direct impact on housing investment, perhaps the most important single H- good type of capital formation.

In summary, the presumption that the redistributive effect will result in a net increase of hoarding in the short run appears justified from available evidence on investment behavior. Such hoarding may be reinforced by tighter monetary policies that keep down the level of investment, especially in construction. In any one year the forces that significantly influence the level of private investment expenditure, in addition to domestic credit availability and the level of nonwage income, are many: direct and indirect foreign investment (as during 1960–1961), the value of investment projects under way from the previous year, special government policies on tax concessions to stimulate investment (also important during 1960–1963), changes in the level of protection and in regulation controlling imports of capital goods, political uncertainties, excess capacity, the relative prices of capital goods, and so on. It is then not very surprising that in the short-run changes in nonwage income have not been found to have by themselves a significant impact on the level of private investment.[7]

---

[7] The presumption in favor of a net increase in hoarding in the short run is strengthened by the fact that a large part of the increase in nonwage income goes into the hands of rural entrepreneurs, who are likely to be more conservative in their real investment behavior than their industrial colleagues.

A Digression: A Rough Calculation of the Impact of Devaluation on Domestic Output in the Short Run

The marginal propensities estimated in this and the last two chapters are of course too rough to allow any precise quantification of the pure redistributive effect on the level of domestic output, other things being equal. However, it may be useful to obtain from them an indication of the magnitude of the short-run drop in domestic output. Taking as a starting point Equation 2.15, we can write the percentage change in domestic output arising from a given percentage change in the exchange rate k, (E_{yk}) as follows:

$$E_{yk} = \frac{1}{D} \left[\frac{F_d^w}{Y} \left(\frac{\partial f_1}{\partial W} - \frac{\partial f_2}{\partial T} \right) - \frac{F_u}{Y} \cdot a \right] \quad (2.15a)$$

On the basis of the estimated regressions the following alternative values may be assumed for the key short-run parameters:[8]

	Assumption A	Assumption B
$\partial f_1/\partial W$	0.20	0.25
$\partial f_2/\partial T$	0.30	0.45
a	0.25	0.40
F_d^w/Y	0.15	0.20
F_u/Y	0.25	0.30
s	0.40	0.50

When these values are given, E_{yk} will equal -0.19 under assumption A and -0.29 under assumption B, implying that a devaluation of 10 per cent will tend to reduce domestic output by about 2 per cent, other things being equal. It should be remembered that this percentage is high because of the simplified assumptions: no changes

---

[8] The expression D, representing the income multiplier, was shown in Chapter 2 to be equal to:

$$(1-s)\left(a + \frac{\partial f_2}{\partial T}\right) + s \cdot \frac{\partial f_1}{\partial W}$$

Variable s can be interpreted to be the share of money wages in total money income at predevaluation prices; it is assumed to have a value between 0.4 and 0.5. We assume here as in Chapter 2 that by an appropriate choice of physical units all prices were originally set equal to one; thus dk can be taken to represent the percentage change in the exchange rate, defined as units of domestic currency per unit of foreign currency. Even as a rough approximation, the estimated value of E_{yk} will only be valid for relatively small values of dk.

in money-wage rates, no increase in the output of F goods, neglect of the government sector, marginal propensities for each group adding up to one, and so on. The introduction of the government sector, accounting for about one fourth to one fifth of total income and assumed to have a level of real expenditures exogenously determined, would naturally reduce considerably the value of E_{yk}. Yet the tentative values shown for the relevant parameters indicate that the redistributive effect is likely to be a powerful force in the short run in depressing the level of domestic output, *ceteris paribus*, and not just a second-order effect.

The Inflationary Process, Devaluation and Income Distribution

During 1945–1962, the wholesale-price index and the cost-of-living index for Buenos Aires workers rose yearly by an average of about 26 per cent. Such a rise was highly irregular: for those years the standard deviation of the yearly rates of inflation was roughly equal to the mean rate of inflation. Exchange rate devaluations are important in this irregular inflationary spiral, at times appearing to passively follow previous price increases and at other times appearing to stimulate the upward movement of the price level. The Argentine inflation is worthy of detailed consideration, but we will analyze here only those features relevant to this study.[9]

The Argentine inflation since 1945 is often divided into two major periods: from 1945 (or 1943) to 1949 and from 1949 to the present.[10] The first stage was characterized by rapid increases in over-all real per capita income and available supplies (national product plus imports), made possible by very favorable terms of trade and large foreign-exchange reserves accumulated during the war, which help to explain why the price level did not rise even faster following massive increases in wages, government expenditures and private investment, in a context of easy money policies and world-wide price inflation. During the three boom years 1946–1948, the money supply held by the public rose by an annual rate of 27 per cent and hourly

[9] For more extensive studies, see Javier Villanueva, *El Proceso Inflacionario Argentino (1943–1962)*, mimeographed, Buenos Aires, 1963, and Julio H. G. Olivera, "El caso de la Argentina," in *Inflation and Growth*, Vol. IV, mimeographed, Santiago, Chile: Economic Commission for Latin America, 1962.

[10] See, for example, the 1957 *Annual Survey* of the United Nations Economic Commission for Latin America.

money-wage rates in industry rose at a rate of 35 per cent per year, while the wholesale-price index rose by "only" 12 per cent a year and the cost of living by 15 per cent.[11] Real supplies of goods and services, on the other hand, rose at an annual rate of more than 11 per cent during those boom years.

The industrial sector as a whole was the main beneficiary during the first stage of the inflationary process.[12] Its gains in real income went beyond the increments in real output and the improvement in the terms of trade achieved by the Argentine economy during 1943–1949, thus cutting into the *absolute* level of real income of the rural sector that was producing exportables and of government employees, rentiers, and other groups of the economy. These years also witnessed a fast increase in industrial employment and a decline in rural employment; after taking into account the expansion of industrial employment it appears that real wages per industrial worker rose by between 50 per cent and 60 per cent between 1943 and 1949. The improvement in the domestic terms of trade of the industrial sector was so strong that it seems that it allowed real profits in industry to expand in the face of massive wage increases. Other non-rural entrepreneurs, especially in commerce, probably benefitted also from the inflationary conditions.

The improvement of the domestic terms of trade for industry during 1943–1949 in the face of an opposite trend in world prices was achieved primarily by the use of official price ceilings for many nonindustrial goods and services established by decree and enforced by government agencies, including a centralized marketing board for most exportable rural produce. In the rural sector producing exportables, nonwage income bore the brunt of these policies, as rural real wages also rose during this period although by less than industrial real wages. Among rentiers, those receiving income from the renting of dwellings were the hardest hit by inflation as a result of rent-control laws. Although data on these matters are scarce, it appears that nonunionized white-collar workers in general, and government employees in particular, also suffered losses in real income during this first stage of the inflationary process.

From 1946–1949 to 1950–1952, the external terms of trade of

[11] These percentages are simple averages for the yearly increases for 1946–1948. The sources of the data are presented in the Statistical Appendix to this chapter.

[12] It appears that during this early stage of the inflationary process rural entrepreneurs producing industrial crops for the domestic market also achieved substantial improvements in their real income.

Argentina deteriorated by about 25 per cent; by 1956–1958, the terms of trade index was 37 per cent below the level of 1946–1949. Such external conditions plus the inability of the domestic economy to cope successfully with the resulting foreign exchange shortages resulted in a very low rate of growth of domestic output during 1949–1962. The drop in the capacity to import and in foreign-exchange reserves plus the low growth rate of domestic output yielded an annual rate of growth of total available real supplies (national product plus imports) of about 2 per cent for this period, a figure only slightly above the rate of growth of population. This second stage is characterized by a counteroffensive of the sectors which suffered a cut in their real incomes during the first stage of the inflation, especially the rural sector, whose ultimate weapon in this struggle is its ability to wreck the balance-of-payments position of Argentina. Argentine industrialization policies failed to encourage substantial manufactured exports, thus leaving the industrial sector to depend on the foreign exchange earned by rural exports to finance its imports of raw materials and capital goods. Since 1951/1952 and under the pressure of declining exports, the need to increase the real income of producers of exportables from the 1947-1952 levels was officially recognized. The social conflict then centered on who in the industrial sector (and to a lesser extent the commerce sector) should give up part of their real income, at least in the short run, as other weaker social groups had already been squeezed before 1950, and little more real income could be obtained from them unless they were to be completely wiped out. The low rate of growth during 1949–1962 of available supplies, especially of foodstuffs that can be either exported or consumed domestically, accounts for the bitterness of the social conflict during the nineteen-fifties, with urban workers, especially those in industry, fighting to maintain and expand the real income gains obtained during 1946–1949 against both the rural and industrial entrepreneurs. Although some minor skirmishes involving other social groups, such as transport workers and civil servants, have taken place in the fight for larger shares, the fundamental issue in the inflation since 1949 has been the struggle among the three powerful groups of rural producers and industrial wage earners and non-wage earners. The inflationary impact of the struggle among these three groups may be temporarily slowed down by a further decrease in the real income of other less powerful groups, but once the real income of such smaller groups has been cut to the bone, as it seems to have been the case in the early stages of the inflation, further struggles among the heavyweights will result in a faster inflationary pace, especially under conditions of a stagnant national output.

During 1949–1962, the wholesale-price index rose by an average annual rate of about 30 per cent, while the cost-of-living index rose at an average annual rate of 29 per cent. In contrast to the earlier period, hourly money-wage rates in industry rose by less than the

TABLE 5.3
INCOME DISTRIBUTION ACCORDING TO FACTOR
SHARES IN ARGENTINA, 1950–1961
(*In percentages of gross national product*)

	1950–1952	1953–1955	1956–1958	1959–1961
Wage Income	41.9	41.7	39.6	35.8
Agriculture and livestock	4.1	4.6	3.5	3.2
Mining and manufacturing	13.1	12.7	13.2	12.2
Government	7.4	8.0	7.1	6.3
Other sectors	17.2	16.3	15.7	14.0
Nonwage Income	45.5	46.4	48.3	51.3
Agriculture and livestock	9.2	11.5	11.0	11.9
Mining and manufacturing	12.3	12.6	14.8	17.4
Other sectors	24.0	22.3	22.5	22.0
Payments by producers to government, plus net profits of government enterprises less subsidies and interest on the public debt	12.6	11.8	12.0	12.9

Sources: Basic data obtained from *Cuentas Nacionales de la República Argentina, op. cit.* Wage income includes employees' social security contributions. Other payments by families to government are also included under either wage or nonwage income. Nonwage income includes income of the self-employed.

price indices, at an annual rate of 27 per cent, while the rate of growth of the money supply also lagged behind, growing at an average annual rate of 23 per cent. Exchange-rate devaluations, however, became more frequent and severe during these years, especially since 1955, and once again the domestic terms of trade moved counter to the external terms of trade, as domestic prices of rural exportable products rose at a faster rate than domestic prices of industrial products.

The recovery of rural real income from the rock-bottom levels of

1950–1952 (which were adversely influenced by severe droughts) has not proceeded in a smooth way, but rather it has witnessed sizable erratic year-to-year fluctuations. Table 5.3 presents the main features of income distribution according to factor shares in Argentina for 1950–1961, taking three-year averages that help to reduce some of the erratic gyrations of the income shares. Table 5.3, however, tends to hide the improvement that has occurred since 1950–1952 in the real income of the rural sector, as it is influenced by the faster output growth of nonrural sectors of the economy. A clearer

TABLE 5.4

IMPLICIT PRICES OF VALUE ADDED BY SECTORS OF THE ARGENTINE ECONOMY RELATIVE TO IMPLICIT PRICES OF GROSS DOMESTIC PRODUCT

$(1960 = 100)$

	1950–1952	1953–1955	1956–1958	1959–1961
Agriculture and Livestock	79.3	85.5	90.9	98.1
Fishing	152.7	96.7	123.2	87.9
Mining	111.3	99.0	110.1	103.1
Manufacturing	94.3	91.2	93.4	97.9
Construction	129.6	125.0	121.5	106.0
Commerce	100.4	91.7	97.3	99.8
Transport	100.5	97.7	104.3	101.0
Communications	85.5	95.8	96.6	104.1
Electricity and Gas	99.2	97.6	84.3	95.9
Banking and Insurance Services	131.3	130.5	128.5	105.0
Housing Services	147.4	154.9	147.0	94.2
Government Services	110.6	124.2	113.2	105.7
Other Services	114.8	116.4	106.9	103.2

Sources: *Cuentas Nacionales de la República Argentina, op. cit.*, pp. 212–213.

picture emerges from Table 5.4, which shows the implicit prices per unit of net output produced by the various sectors of the economy during 1950–1961. These tables underline the broad trends present in the second stage of the inflationary process: a recovery of the position of the rural sector primarily at the expense of real-wage income, especially since 1955. It seems that during 1950–1955, real wages managed to keep such an adverse trend to a minimum, with the burden of economic decline and the modest gains of the rural sector falling primarily on the shoulders of urban entrepreneurs. Since 1955, however, real wages appear to have borne most of the burden of transferring real income to rural producers, while urban nonwage income recovered a substantial part of its 1950–1955 losses. Table 5.4 shows that real rents from housing continued to decline during the second stage of the inflation, while real wages in the government sector moved erratically, but with a tendency to continue to decline since 1953–1955.

In the seesaw battle for income shares which has taken place since the Second World War in Argentina, devaluation of the exchange rate has been a key instrument in changing relative prices in favor of the rural sector producing exportables. Such policy has been used more frequently since 1955, but as a rule it was only undertaken as a measure of last resort, with foreign-exchange reserves nearly depleted and in an atmosphere of almost financial panic. The sharp improvements brought about by these devaluations for the relative prices of rural exportable goods began to be offset after a few quarters, at least partially, by increases in industrial prices. Under pressure from trade unions which complain of devaluation-induced increases in the prices of foodstuffs hourly money-wage rates in industry tend to increase after a time lag, although as a rule by less than the increase in prices brought about by devaluation, and such increases in costs are swiftly reflected in higher industrial prices. The precise increase in industrial prices will depend on the bargaining power at that point in time of trade unions and the market position of industrial firms. The latter, it may be noticed, as a rule have a very substantial degree of market power buttressed by prohibitive tariffs. This sequence of events will produce rather unstable relative prices; indeed, because of this and other reasons the Argentine inflation has been characterized by substantial changes in relative prices from year to year.

The proposition that high rates of inflation will be associated with sharp changes in relative prices is supported by the Argentine experience. To test this hypothesis, the weighted sum of the *absolute* values of year-to-year percentage changes in the relatives prices of the fourteen sectors of production making up the gross domestic product was regressed against the rate of change of the price level.[13]

[13] The relative prices refer to the implicit price deflator for each of the fourteen sectors of production divided by the implicit price deflator for the gross domestic product. The weights used in the summation of the year-to-year percentage changes of these relative prices (treating all changes as positive) are the following: 0.089 for agriculture; 0.087 for livestock; 0.002 for fishing; 0.010 for mining; 0.236 for manufacturing; 0.064 for construction; 0.175 for commerce; 0.084 for transport; 0.010 for communications; 0.010 for other public services; 0.046 for housing; 0.024 for finance; 0.079 for personal services and 0.085 for government services. These weights represent the relative importance

For the period from 1935 to 1961, the correlation coefficient between these two variables equaled +0.84, the F-ratio amounting to 55.5. Thus, it may be stated that in the Argentine inflation, the higher the pace of inflation, the greater were the changes in relative prices. The economic interpretation of this statistical result is not unambiguous; it can be argued that due to downward rigidity of prices and the resistance of sectors whose interests were being hurt, any change in relative prices desired and sought by the economic authorities (for instance, by devaluation of the exchange rate) provoked stronger inflationary pressures; but it can also be pointed out that given the rigidity of money prices in many sectors of the economy (for instance, rents, public services), the greater the autonomous inflation the larger will be the induced change in relative prices for those sectors. It seems clear that both of these types of considerations contribute to the statistical result shown above. However, more recently when years of rapid price increases have been closely associated with devaluations, the first explanation of the close link between inflation and changes in relative prices, which makes the changes in relative prices the independent variable, appears to be more appropriate. At any rate, the fact that high rates of inflation have been associated with unstable relative prices indicates a strong presumption that the high rates of inflation have induced a considerable degree of economic inefficiency.

The Dynamics of the Argentine Inflation

The inflationary pressures in Argentina have arisen from three principal immediate sources: excessive credit expansion by the banking sector, including the Central Bank, to finance either public or private financial deficits but especially the former; massive wage increases and devaluation of the exchange rate. At different stages of the inflationary spiral, one of these sources appears to be the autonomous force behind the inflationary pressure, while the others seem to follow passively, but taking the period 1943–1961 as a whole no such generalization is possible. Furthermore, these immediate

of the different sectors in the gross domestic product around 1946–1950. The rate of growth of the implicit deflator of the gross domestic product was taken as the measure of inflation. Basic data were obtained for 1950–1961 from *Cuentas Nacionales de la República Argentina, op. cit.*; and for 1935–1950, from *Producto e Ingreso de la República Argentina en el Período 1935–1954*, Secretaría de Asuntos Económicos, Poder Ejecutivo Nacional, Buenos Aires, 1955. For the years 1950–1961, the wholesale-price indices for agriculture and livestock were used instead of the implicit prices, as the latter were not available.

sources of inflationary pressure are in turn influenced by real economic and social causes, some of which have been mentioned previously.[14] Finally, in some years droughts, foreign prices, and so on have acted as additional sources of inflation.

While it does not appear feasible, nor indeed desirable, to break into the inflationary spiral and isolate a single monetary or real variable as the fundamental cause of the whole problem, it may be useful to obtain a quantitative idea of how the different sources of inflationary pressure interacted through time and to what extent they can "explain," in a statistical sense, the observed increases in the price level. Such analysis may also shed some light on the issue of whether autonomous increases in money wage rates or autonomous expansion in bank credit and the money supply bore greater responsibility for the accelerating pace of inflation. This issue is of special interest in the light of the practice of several Argentine governments to increase the money wages of very large numbers of workers in the private sector by decree.[15]

The analysis of the dynamics of inflation aims to explain statistically the rate of growth of the level of prices. In this section, several price indices have been considered, the two principal ones being the wholesale-price index and the cost-of-living index. Yearly rates of change have been used for the period 1945–1962. The independent variables included in the multiple regression analysis are

1. Annual rate of change of the money supply in the hands of the public (m'). For any one year, an average of the money supply held by the public at the end of each month was taken; comparing year-to-year percentage changes in those average figures the variable m was obtained.[16] This variable should be interpreted primarily as a proxy for the rate of increase of bank credit, which gives an indication of injections into the stream of purchasing power beyond the "normal" flow that arises from current factor payments available for

---

[14] For example, the stagnation in the output of exportable rural goods while the rest of the economy continued to expand was a key factor in forcing periodic exchange-rate devaluations. The failure of the industrial sector to generate substantial manufactured exports can also be blamed for the foreign-exchange shortage.

[15] For a study of the dynamics of the Chilean inflation, many of whose techniques and ideas are followed in this section see Arnold C. Harberger, "The Dynamics of Inflation in Chile," in *Measurement in Economics: Studies in Mathematical Economics and Econometrics in Memory of Yehuda Grunfeld*, Carl Christ et al., eds. (Stanford: Stanford University Press, 1963).

[16] For the sources of the basic data see the statistical appendix to this chapter.

expenditure. A key element in credit expansion during the period under discussion was borrowing by the public sector from the banking system (primarily the Central Bank) to cover budget deficits. An idea of the importance of such borrowing relative to the rest of the economy may be obtained from Table 5.5, which expresses net public sector borrowing from the banking system as a percentage of gross national product in current prices; as a rule, public-sector liabilities accounted for between 35 and 40 per cent of the con-

TABLE 5.5

Net Borrowing of the Public Sector from the Banking System as a Percentage of Gross National Product
(*Average of percentages for three years*)

1944–1946	1.3
1947–1949	4.4
1950–1952	0.6
1953–1955	2.2
1956–1958	2.3
1959–1961	1.6

Sources and methods: Net public borrowing is defined as the increase in public sector liabilities in the hands of the banking sector minus the increase in public-sector deposits with the banking sector. Monetary data obtained from Banco Central de la República Argentina, *Estadísticas Monetarias y Bancarias, Años 1940–1960*, Suplemento del *Boletín Estadístico* No. 6, Buenos Aires, June 1962, and from later issues of the *Boletín Estadístico*. Gross national product figures obtained as in previous tables; the pre-1950 percentages shown represent slight overestimations in comparison with post-1950 percentages, as the pre-1950 figures for gross national product are underestimated in comparison with the new series for 1950–1961. A considerable part of the net government borrowing during 1946–1949 was not reflected in increases in the money supply, as it was used directly to obtain foreign exchange from the Central Bank to pay for nationalized foreign real assets; such transactions simply led to a change in the asset structure of the banking system.

solidated assets of the banking sector during 1950–1961. It should be clear, however, that no simple link can be established between inflation and public-sector borrowing from the banking system; indeed, in some years, such as 1951 and 1956, negative public sector borrowing was accompanied by substantial increases in the price level, while in other years, such as 1947, large public-sector borrowing took place while the price level increased only moderately. A more complete picture of the factors that account for the expansion of the money supply is given by Table 5.6; although this table presents only an *ex post* picture of the process of credit and monetary expansion, it highlights some important monetary trends and can serve as a point of reference for further discussion of monetary policy in recent years.[17]

2. Annual rate of change of hourly money-wage rates in industry (w'). In their struggle to first expand and then maintain their level of real wages, industrial workers in Argentina relied during the

TABLE 5.6
CHANGES IN THE CONSOLIDATED BALANCE SHEET OF THE BANKING SYSTEM IN ARGENTINA
(*In billion pesos*)

	1943–1949	1949–1952	1952–1955	1955–1958	1958–1961
Changes in Assets	21.39	18.65	32.82	75.54	185.70
Net credit to the public sector	10.47	1.68	9.42	26.77	40.75
Credit to the private sector	12.03	18.40	21.99	51.74	125.91
Net gold and foreign exchange	— 1.11	— 1.42	1.41	— 2.96	19.03
Changes in Liabilities	21.39	18.65	32.82	75.54	185.70
Money supply	13.23	12.84	21.20	47.21	106.62
Quasi money and others	8.16	5.81	11.62	28.33	79.08
Addendum					
A. Changes in gross national product	37.63	47.67	57.90	222.96	780.06
B. Credit to the private sector as a percentage of A	32.0	38.6	38.0	23.2	16.1

Sources and method: As in Table 5.5. Changes in monetary data are taken from December to December, for instance, December 1943 until December 1949, and so on. Changes in the gross national product at current prices are taken using the figures for the whole corresponding year, for instance, 1943 to 1949, and so on. The changes for 1943–1949 and 1949–1952 are taken from the data found in *Producto e Ingreso de la República Argentina en el Período 1935–1954, op. cit.*

period under study primarily on periodic massive money-wage increases decreed by the federal government and covering very large fractions of the industrial labor force. It is conceivable that such

---

[17] For a detailed and interesting analysis of monetary developments since 1935 in Argentina see José María Dagnino Pastore, *Ingreso y Dinero; Argentina, 1935–1960*, mimeographed, Buenos Aires, 1964. See also Adolfo César Diz, *La Oferta de Dinero en la República Argentina (1935–1962)*, mimeographed, Tucumán, 1963.

wage policy could be blamed for generating cost-push inflation at least for some of the years under study.

3. Annual rate of change of the exchange rate, expressed as the price of one United States dollar in terms of Argentine pesos (k'). No further justification seems necessary of the potentially autonomous role that this variable can have in the inflationary spiral.

4. Annual rate of change of real available supplies, defined as the gross domestic product plus merchandise imports (s'). Other things being equal, the greater the rate of increase of available supplies, either from domestic production or imports, the lower will be the rate of inflation.

These four independent variables, both lagged and unlagged, were used to explain the following measures of inflation for the period 1945–1962:

$p'_1 =$ annual rate of change of the over-all wholesale-price index

$p'_2 =$ annual rate of change of the wholesale-price index for rural products

$p'_3 =$ annual rate of change of the wholesale-price index for non-rural domestically produced products

$p'_4 =$ annual rate of change of the wholesale-price index for imported products

$p'_5 =$ annual rate of change of the cost-of-living index for the city of Buenos Aires

The first result to note is that when both the lagged and unlagged independent variables were included in the regressions, the coefficients for the lagged variables (the lag being of one year) were always insignificant, and often of the wrong sign. When the only lagged variable included in the regressions was the rate of increase of the money supply in year $t-1$, in addition to the change in that variable during period t, the coefficient for m'_{t-1} was insignificant and had the wrong sign in all regressions. These results suggest that on the average the price level adjusted within a year to changes in the sources of inflationary pressures.[18]

[18] This result may be contrasted with that of A. C. Harberger for Chile, where it was found that m'_{t-1} had a significant coefficient in the regression explaining the annual rate of change of the consumer-price index. See A. C. Harberger, "The Dynamics of Inflation in Chile," *op. cit.* It should be noted, however, that Harberger used a slightly different definition for m'.

Besides the four basic independent variables listed, other variables were employed without success in trying to explain the pace of inflation. Such variables include the income distribution in any one year between wages and nonwages, the changes in such income distribution, and the index of quantitative restrictions on imports developed in Chapter 3.

First, with the wholesale-price indices, the following results are obtained, where all variables refer to the same time period:

$$p'_1 = -14.3 + 1.13\,m' + 0.31\,w' + 0.30\,k' - 1.05\,s'$$
$$ (0.41) \quad\ (0.24) \quad\ (0.08) \quad\ (0.51)$$
$$R = 0.93$$
$$d = 1.98$$
$$(5.6)$$

$$p'_2 = -15.9 + 1.43\,m' + 0.07\,w' + 0.42\,k' - 0.53\,s'$$
$$ (0.63) \quad\ (0.36) \quad\ (0.12) \quad\ (0.77)$$
$$R = 0.88$$
$$d = 1.91$$
$$(5.7)$$

$$p'_3 = -14.1 + 0.99\,m' + 0.49\,w' + 0.22\,k' - 1.07\,s'$$
$$ (0.38) \quad\ (0.22) \quad\ (0.08) \quad\ (0.47)$$
$$R = 0.93$$
$$d = 1.90$$
$$(5.8)$$

$$p'_4 = -20.2 + 1.40\,m' + 0.09\,w' + 0.60\,k' - 1.75\,s'$$
$$ (0.46) \quad\ (0.26) \quad\ (0.09) \quad\ (0.56)$$
$$R = 0.96$$
$$d = 2.11$$
$$(5.9)$$

The general fit in these four equations is rather good, in all cases explaining at least 77 per cent of the observed changes in the price level. The significant coefficients for variable m' imply that a 1 per cent increase in the money supply in the hands of the public will result, other things being equal, in an increase in the level of prices of slightly more than 1 per cent for rural (p'_2) and imported (p'_4) products, and of roughly 1 per cent for the over-all wholesale-price index (p'_1) and for the index of nonrural domestically produced goods (p'_3). The values of the standard errors are such, however, that none of these coefficients can be said to be significantly different from one. In the case of the index of imported prices, the fact that changes in the money supply have a coefficient significantly different from zero imply that during at least part of the period under study domestic demand conditions, as well as foreign prices and the exchange rate, influenced these prices, a situation that resulted primarily from quantitative restrictions on imports. Similarly, the significant coefficient for m' in Equation 5.7 implies that besides foreign prices and the exchange rate, domestic demand conditions also influenced the level of prices for rural products, which were largely exportables.

The coefficients for the wage variable are insignificant except for Equation 5.8. It is in this equation, which tries to explain the rate of change of domestically produced nonrural goods, that one would have expected the variable w' to have its greatest impact via the cost-push mechanism. According to Equation 5.8, a 1 per cent increase in hourly industrial money-wage rates will, *ceteris paribus*, result in an increase of one half of 1 per cent in the prices of domestically manufactured goods. The insignificant coefficients for w' in Equations 5.7 and 5.9 were to be expected on a priori grounds, on the assumption that while m' reflects primarily the pull of aggregate demand, w' reflects one of the cost-push pressures that originates in the industrial sector.

The coefficients for k', the rate of change of the exchange rate, are significant in all equations. As one would expect, the absolute size of the coefficients for rural and imported goods are highest, although far from the value of 1.00, which should have resulted if these categories had represented pure exportable and importable elements and frictions (whether government inspired or not) had not existed to hamper the free flow of goods entering and leaving Argentina during this period. It may be noticed that the coefficient for k' in Equation 5.6 tends to support the rough estimate made in Chapter 3 for the relative importance of importable and exportable goods in the Argentine economy and the probable impact of a devaluation of the exchange rate on the price level; this equation implies that a devaluation of 10 per cent will increase the level of wholesale prices by roughly 3 per cent, *ceteris paribus*.

Except for Equation 5.7, the coefficients for s', the rate of growth of the total real supply of goods and services, are significant. In Equations 5.6 and 5.8, the size of the coefficients imply that a 1 per cent increase in aggregate real supply will lead to a 1 per cent drop in the price level, other things being equal: a not unreasonable result. The fact that s' has a significant coefficient in the equation explaining the domestic price of imports has an explanation similar to that given to the significance of the m' coefficient in the same equation. Indeed, for the basic explanation to appear reasonable both coefficients must be significant.

A disturbing aspect of Equations 5.6 through 5.9 is the relatively large size of the constant term. Taken at face value, it implies that if m', w', k', and s' were in any one year equal to zero, the price level could be expected to drop by around 14 per cent. The most plausible explanation for the large size of the constant term is that there is a considerable amount of overlapping and double-counting of inflationary pressure in variables m', w', and k'. In other words, the average size of the constant term, regardless of its statistical significance, casts some doubt on the procedure of interpreting the coefficients of each of the independent variables as its true contribution to the inflationary process independently of the behavior of the other independent variables. However, it does not seem to limit the usefulness of these equations in isolating the *relative* importance of each of the sources of inflationary pressure.

The following result is obtained when the cost-of-living index is used as the dependent variable:

$$p'_5 = -10.5 + \underset{(0.35)}{0.93\,m'} + \underset{(0.20)}{0.50\,w'} + \underset{(0.07)}{0.15\,k'} - \underset{(0.43)}{1.05\,s'}$$

$$R = 0.93$$
$$d = 1.84$$

(5.10)

All coefficients are significant and the fit is as good as the one for the over-all wholesale-price index shown in Equation 5.6. The coefficient for s' is identical for both equations, while the coefficient for m' is not significantly different from 1.00 in both regressions. In contrast to the results obtained by Harberger for the Chilean case, the coefficient for w' is significant in explaining changes in the cost-of-living index, while insignificant in explaining changes in the over-all wholesale index. The coefficient for k' in Equation 5.10 seems rather low, and it is surprising that it is lower than the corresponding coefficient in Equation 5.6. Considering the size of the standard errors, however, we cannot attach much importance to the difference between 0.30 and 0.15.

It may be of interest to examine the simple correlation coefficients between independent variables. The following array shows these coefficients for the independent variables taken at the same time periods:

	w'	k'	s'
m'	+0.58	+0.52	−0.07
w'	—	+0.36	−0.23
k'	—	—	−0.33

As one could expect from a situation characterized by an inflationary spiral, there is a substantial degree of correlation between m' and w', as well as between m' and k'. However, the lack of homogeneity in the Argentine inflation keeps these values way below what one is likely to observe in inflations where all monetary variables grow in a "balanced" fashion, a fortunate fact from the point of view of isolating the short-run impact of each of the major immediate sources of inflationary pressure.

The relationship between k' and s' is also worth exploring. Although the correlation coefficient is small, it indicates that devaluations are associated with a drop in the sum of national production plus imports, a result consistent with the model developed in Chapter 2. Also consistent with that model is the simple correlation coefficient obtained between k' and *changes* in the wage share of gross national income; such correlation coefficient was found to equal −0.55.

The correlation coefficients between lagged and unlagged independent variables may yield some clues as to the mechanics of the inflationary process. While the simple correlation coefficient between m'_t and w'_{t-1} is +0.53, that between w'_t and m'_{t-1} is only +0.15. The practice of Argentine governments during most of the period under study to make available to the private sector plentiful bank credit after each government-decreed massive wage increase seems to account for the observed tendency of the money supply to follow wage increases rather than vice versa.[19] The apparent futility of the

---

[19] With quarterly data for the period 1950–1960, better fits were also obtained when changes in the money supply were used as the dependent variable and wage changes as the independent variable (using the lagged rates of change for four quarters) rather than the other way around. The same type of result was obtained in the quarterly data when comparing rates of change in prices and the money supply, that is, better explanations were obtained for the behavior of the data if it is assumed that the expansion of the money supply followed price increases in a permissive manner rather than vice versa.

policy of granting these massive wage increases, especially after 1949, is indicated by the lack of correlation between increases in money-wage rates and the wage share in the national income, as well as between increases in money-wage rates and changes in such share; the correlation coefficient for the former pair of variables is −0.16 while it is +0.16 for the latter.[20]

The results obtained in Equations 5.6 through 5.10 imply that during the Argentine inflation of 1945–1962 both demand-pull elements (reflected primarily by variable m') and cost-push elements (reflected by w' and k') have been at work. This conclusion seems warranted by the fact that the coefficients for m', w', and k' are all significant in the key regressions 5.8 and 5.10. However, it appears that since 1955 devaluations of the exchange rate have gained in relative importance as a source of upward pressure on the price level; more generally, since 1949 the cost-push features appear to have become dominant in the Argentine inflation, and the highest rates of inflation have been observed in years when the exchange rate was devalued and relative prices turned in favor of the rural sector. During this second stage of the inflationary process, monetary expansion has played a more or less permissive role; when price increases originating in increases in industrial wage rates or exchange-rate devaluations were not followed by sufficiently ample expansions of the money supply, the result was primarily a tendency for real output to shrink, rather than the price level to drop. The increasingly cost-push nature of the Argentine inflation is best illustrated by the not uncommon experience in recent years of high rates of inflation existing while the real national product was falling (the years 1949, 1952, 1959, and 1962 are examples of this disquieting experience).

From the point of view of income distribution and the balance of payments, it of course makes a great deal of difference whether the cost push on the level of prices arises from a change in industrial wage rates or a devaluation. Generally speaking, the first round of inflation generated by a devaluation will be accompanied by an improvement in the relative prices of exportable and importable

---

[20] The existence of some wage lag after devaluation appears justified by the low correlation coefficient obtained between w'_t and k'_{t-1}: +0.19. The irregular nature of the Argentine inflation is revealed by the low correlation between the key independent variables with their corresponding lagged values. Thus, the correlation coefficient between m'_t and m'_{t-1} is +0.20; between w'_t and w'_{t-1} is +0.26 and between k'_t and k'_{t-1} is +0.04.

goods, and thus, *ceteris paribus,* will tend to improve the balance-of-payments position of the country. The inflation generated by increases in money-wage rates in industry, if a level for the exchange rate is given, will naturally have the opposite effect. The increase in money wages in industry leads to an increase in industrial prices and, reversing the mechanism presented in Chapter 2, to a decrease in the aggregate hoarding of the economy, thus increasing the domestic absorption of importables and exportables. The interplay of these two sources of inflationary pressure in the context of a low rate of growth of real output is at the heart of the problem of a rapidly rising price level in Argentina since 1949.[21]

Statistical Appendix to Chapter 5

The tables in this appendix present the data utilized in the regressions discussed in Chapter 5.

Table S.1: Data Used to Estimate Private Saving Responses

The variables used to estimate regressions 5.1 and 5.2 and their sources are

1. Gross private savings per capita, in pesos at 1960 prices (A). Total gross private savings at current prices were obtained by subtracting from total gross domestic savings the following items: gross savings of the general government, net savings of public enterprises, and net foreign savings. The basic source of data is *Cuentas Nacionales de la República Argentina, op. cit.;* and worksheets of the Consejo Nacional de Desarrollo were used to obtain net savings

---

[21] It may be objected that it is not appropriate to consider a devaluation of the exchange rate as a cost-push element in the Argentine inflation, as it comes about as a result of general excess demand which spills over into excess demand for exportables and importables; and thus the price increases it generates may be considered to be a delayed response to demand-pull forces. Yet such response may be delayed for such a long period that it seems better to consider the devaluation as the *immediate* cause of the observed price rises. Thus, the fact that Argentina absorbs domestically a sizable share of its output of exportables tends to weaken the link between excess demand and price increases, as the link usually goes through balance-of-trade deficits and the devaluations they provoke. It should be noted that the concept of aggregate demand pressing on existing capacity loses a great deal of its operational validity in an economy such as the Argentine, which is characterized by bottlenecks and a low capacity to transform. Under those circumstances, "full capacity" for the economy as a whole becomes a rather ambiguous concept. This problem acquires special importance when a sector as critical as agriculture and livestock, or electricity and railroads, is the one with low-output ceilings and price-inelastic supply schedules.

of public enterprises. Figures at current prices were divided by the deflator of the gross national product (1960 = 100) and by total population.

2. Per capita (per wage earners and non-wage earners) wage income (W) and nonwage income (T) in 1960 prices. As in Items 4 and 5 in the statistical appendix to Chapter 3.

TABLE S.1
DATA USED TO ESTIMATE PRIVATE SAVING RESPONSES

	A	W	T	A'	W'	T'
1950	7,209	25,196	65,655	123.23	300.75	338.28
1951	5,442	23,457	69,331	95.31	286.48	365.63
1952	4,833	23,734	59,220	86.48	296.42	319.12
1953	6,867	23,659	64,538	125.18	300.83	354.23
1954	7,215	24,767	65,523	133.91	321.01	366.37
1955	7,336	24,868	73,336	139.60	312.91	417.49
1956	6,084	23,759	71,104	117.11	319.24	412.45
1957	5,754	23,558	74,649	112.82	322.69	441.10
1958	8,986	26,934	78,851	179.39	375.28	474.26
1959	8,448	21,996	80,493	171.63	311.80	492.40
1960	8,399	22,500	81,149	173.57	324.83	505.48
1961	7,299	24,314	80,099	153.42	356.71	506.92

3. Total gross private savings (A'), wage income (W'), and nonwage income (T') in billion pesos at 1960 prices. As in Items 1 and 2 of this appendix.

Table S.2: Basic Data Used to Estimate Private Investment Responses

The basic variables used to estimate regressions 5.3, 5.4, and 5.5 and their sources are

1. Fixed gross private investment per capita, in pesos at 1960 prices (PI). Total fixed gross private investment at 1960 prices obtained from *Cuentas Nacionales de la República Argentina, op. cit.* Total figures were divided by total population.

2. Gross private investment per capita in housing in pesos at 1960 prices (PIH). These figures were arrived at on the basis of rough current prices estimates for private gross investment in housing found in worksheets of the Consejo Nacional de Desarrollo. It was assumed that the same price deflator could be applied to both housing and nonhousing construction. Total figures were divided by total population.

3. Nonhousing fixed gross private investment per capita, in pesos at 1960 prices (*PIO*). Obtained as a residual from Items 1 and 2 in this appendix.

4. Income velocity of circulation (*V*). Obtained by dividing the gross national product at current prices by the average money supply held by the public. The average money supply was obtained by

TABLE S.2
Basic Data Used to Estimate Private Investment Responses

	PI	PIH	PIO	V
1950	6,713	2,103	4,611	3.653
1951	7,050	2,067	4,983	4.126
1952	6,217	1,962	4,255	4.224
1953	6,216	1,721	4,495	3.839
1954	5,964	1,734	4,230	3.648
1955	6,806	1,906	4,901	3.747
1956	7,266	1,983	5,283	3.992
1957	7,973	2,176	5,797	4.412
1958	7,673	1,922	5,751	5.123
1959	6,927	1,668	5,259	6.240
1960	9,377	1,423	7,954	6.220
1961	10,067	1,452	8,615	6.303

taking an average of the money supply at the end of each of the twelve months of the year. In the regressions this variable entered multiplied by 1,000; for instance, for 1950, V was equal to 3,653, and so on. Sources for the monetary data are the same as in Table 5.6 of this chapter.

5. Nonwage income per non-wage earner in 1960 prices (*T*). Sources are the same as in Table S. 1.

Table S.3: Data Used to Analyze the Dynamics of Inflation: Independent Variables

The independent variables used to estimate regressions 5.6 through 5.10 and their sources are

1. Annual percentage rate of growth of the money supply (m'). The money-supply figures on which this variable is based represent the average for the money supply held by the public at the end of each of the twelve months of the year. Sources are the same as in Table 5.6 of this chapter.

2. Annual percentage rate of growth of industrial money hourly wage rates (W'). The index of money-wage rates on which this

variable is based refers to yearly averages. The index of hourly money-wage rates has been obtained by dividing total industrial money wages paid by the index of hours worked. The source of these indices is the Dirección Nacional de Estadística y Censos, *Boletín Mensual de Estadística*, several issues. It is well known that the industrial sample on which these indices are based has become

TABLE S.3
DATA USED TO ANALYZE THE DYNAMICS OF INFLATION:
INDEPENDENT VARIABLES

	m'	w'	k'	s'
1945	19.1	14.6	— 2.7	— 3.0
1946	25.7	24.3	0.8	12.1
1947	25.4	42.2	1.9	17.2
1948	28.6	39.7	0.0	5.0
1949	30.0	37.5	2.2	— 4.5
1950	25.0	20.0	27.1	— 0.1
1951	26.8	7.7	35.8	5.4
1952	12.5	45.2	5.2	— 7.7
1953	24.7	8.6	— 1.9	3.6
1954	17.0	14.5	3.3	5.6
1955	16.3	11.1	11.4	8.0
1956	18.1	14.0	127.6	1.7
1957	17.1	33.7	31.3	6.2
1958	21.2	37.8	23.9	4.7
1959	55.8	69.9	164.0	— 5.2
1960	31.1	31.4	9.7	7.6
1961	18.3	24.7	0.1	6.2
1962	12.1	25.7	36.6	— 4.3
Mean	23.6	27.9	26.5	3.3
Standard Deviation	9.6	15.5	44.6	6.3

obsolete; thus, the hourly money-wage rates obtained from this source should be considered as an indication only of wage rates in so-called vegetative industries (the older industries which compose the sample). Changes in hourly money-wage rates in these industries, however, may be assumed to reflect with a fair degree of accuracy similar changes in other industrial sectors.

3. Annual percentage rate of growth of the average exchange rate applied to merchandise trade (k'). The exchange rate is defined as the price of one United States dollar in Argentine pesos. During most of the period under study multiple exchange rates were in effect; k' is based on the exchange rate obtained by dividing the

SAVINGS, INVESTMENT, AND INFLATION 129

value of imports plus exports in pesos by the value of imports plus exports in United States dollars. Basic data obtained from Dirección Nacional de Estadística y Censos, *Comercio Exterior,* several issues.

4. Annual percentage rate of growth of total real supplies (s'). This variable is based on annual figures for the sum of the gross domestic product plus merchandise imports, both expressed at constant prices. Basic data obtained as in Items 1 and 9 in the statistical appendix to Chapter 3.

Table S.4: Data Used to Analyze the Dynamics of Inflation: Dependent Variables

The dependent variables used to estimate regressions 5.6 through 5.10 and their sources are

1. Annual percentage growth of the over-all wholesale-price index (p'_1), the wholesale-price index for rural products (p'_2), the wholesale-price index for nonrural domestically produced goods (p'_3), and the wholesale-price index for imported goods (p'_4).

TABLE S.4
DATA USED TO ANALYZE THE DYNAMICS OF INFLATION: DEPENDENT VARIABLES

	p'_1	p'_2	p'_3	p'_4	p'_5
1945	9.0	16.8	6.5	7.1	19.7
1946	15.8	59.0	6.8	— 9.4	17.7
1947	3.5	— 0.3	12.6	— 11.9	13.5
1948	15.5	11.7	18.0	15.2	13.1
1949	23.0	14.1	29.3	20.7	31.1
1950	20.2	16.6	23.5	15.4	25.5
1951	49.1	52.4	44.2	61.2	36.7
1952	31.2	18.4	38.4	30.3	38.7
1953	11.6	20.7	9.5	4.1	4.0
1954	3.2	1.0	4.2	— 1.4	3.8
1955	8.9	5.3	10.0	11.7	12.3
1956	26.0	42.1	17.5	62.9	13.4
1957	24.1	25.5	24.5	10.6	24.7
1958	31.0	33.2	30.7	22.6	31.6
1959	133.5	150.8	124.0	179.9	113.7
1960	15.7	13.1	17.2	11.7	27.3
1961	8.3	5.8	10.1	— 3.2	13.5
1962	30.4	37.0	27.5	32.9	28.1
Mean	25.6	29.1	25.3	25.6	26.0
Standard Deviation	28.5	33.8	26.4	42.4	23.5

Source of the basic indices used to obtain these variables is the same as in Item 6 in the statistical appendix to Chapter 3.

2. Annual percentage growth of the cost-of-living index for the city of Buenos Aires (p'_5). Source of the basic index used to obtain this variable is the same as in Table 4.7.

6

The Impact of Devaluation, 1955-1961

From an average of around 7.5 pesos per United States dollar in 1955, the Argentine exchange rate moved to a level of above 82 pesos per dollar at the end of 1961. This chapter will analyze the impact of such a devaluation on the Argentine economy in the light of the theoretical and empirical results of earlier chapters. Special attention will be devoted to examining the devaluation announced in December 1958 and the stabilization program adopted simultaneously with that measure.

Before embarking on the discussion of the impact of devaluation during 1955–1961 and of earlier stabilization efforts, it may be useful to review briefly some key empirical results and observations made in earlier chapters. It has been found that the Argentine economy has a very high short-run marginal propensity to import, which is closely linked to the relatively high import content of domestic investment and a high marginal propensity to import of non-wage earners. The nature of most imports and the lack of resource mobility led to the conclusion that the short-run price elasticity of the demand for imports is likely to be very low. The aggregate supply of exportables is also suspected of having a low price elasticity, especially in a short run of less than a year. In spite of this fact, the supply of exports may be increased even in the short run via the income mechanism (that is, real domestic deflation), but with doubtful results if only the relative prices of exportables are increased with respect to home goods. It has been found that the private saving and investment responses are such in the Argentine economy that a devaluation–cum–wage lag is likely to lead to a result predicted by the model developed in Chapter 2: real income deflation, via price inflation and the redistributive effect. The real deflation will tend to reduce the domestic demand for importables and exportables, although the drop will not be so large as it would have been if the demand of non-wage earners for imports had not been greater than that of wage earners. The existence and duration of the wage lag is of course of critical importance; if the strongly unionized industrial workers succeed in obtaining wage increases shortly after devaluation by the full extent of the increase in the price level, neither income distribution nor domestic relative prices is likely to remain changed for a period sufficiently long to have a significant influence on the balance of payments. The stage would then be set for a new round of devaluation and inflation.

The price elasticities which are of importance in determining the outcome of a devaluation may be grouped into two broad categories: (a) those based on tastes and production capabilities beyond the influence of "our" country, and (b) those based on the tastes, and more important, the production capabilities of "our" country. Previous chapters have emphasized the elasticities of the second group. Thus, we are not primarily concerned with whether the sum of the elasticities of demand for exports and imports is more or less than one, but rather with the flexibility and fluidity of the domestic productive resources, which will be reflected *ceteris paribus* in high or low elasticities in the demand for imports and the supply of exportables. The key question is whether or not a devaluation will succeed in triggering off such reallocation of domestic resources that will make feasible (given an appropriate level of absorption) equilibrium in the balance of trade plus full employment of resources for the whole economy. A policy of straightforward income deflation is a sure way to achieve equilibrium in foreign accounts. High price elasticities of type (a), especially a high elasticity in the foreign demand for our exportables, will help to make the necessary adjustments smoother. But it is only when price elasticities of type (b) are high that the twin goals of full employment and balance-of-trade equilibrium can be obtained in the long run, even for a very small country with no influence on its terms of trade. If the structure of production of a country is frozen the choice is very likely to be either deflation and unemployment or balance-of-payments disequilibrium, even for a country blessed with an infinitely price-elastic foreign demand for its exports.

Pre-1955 Stabilization Efforts

The post-1955 policies aimed at achieving balance-of-payments equilibrium and price stability were foreshadowed by similar policies undertaken since around 1950 by the government headed by General Juan D. Perón. A major difference between these two periods was the lesser emphasis given to exchange-rate devaluation in the pre-1955 stabilization efforts.[1]

Under pressure from falling net foreign-exchange reserves, a condition partly arising from the disastrous weather conditions during 1950 and 1951 which caused severe crop failures, the Argentine government turned to deflationary policies early in 1952 to halt the drain of reserves and to check price inflation. However, higher domestic prices for the production of exportables, to be financed by subsidies from the government, were also decreed. Increases in money-wage rates were slowed down considerably, especially during 1953, and industrial real-wage rates fell from the levels reached in 1951 (which were already below the level of 1950). The tightly controlled banking system reduced credit expansion to the private sector in 1952 and the early part of 1953; credit expansion to the public sector was also reduced during 1952. Real consumption and construction expenditures of the general government were curtailed, and import restrictions were tightened, especially on goods other than raw materials and intermediate products.

As a result of these policies, manufacturing production fell, although not as sharply as construction activity. Imports followed suit during 1952 and 1953, reaching in the latter year their lowest level for the 1947–1962 period. Net official foreign-exchange reserves, which amounted to $184 million at the end of 1952, increased to $377 million at the end of 1953. The exercise in deflation showed clearly that quick results in cutting down imports, and to a lesser extent, expanding available exportable surpluses, could be obtained by deflating domestic real income, and especially by curtailing investment. Handsome foreign-exchange reserve increments plus

[1] Following the devaluation of the pound sterling in 1949, the peso was devalued vis-à-vis the United States dollar during 1950 and 1951. Until October 1955, the multiple exchange rates were then held steady with only minor modifications; but by allowing exporters to negotiate an increasing share of their exchange receipts at the more favorable rates, *de facto* minor devaluations were carried out during 1951–1955. During these years exchange control, used in Argentina since 1931, was the favored policy to achieve balance-of-payments equilibrium.

relative price stability could be achieved, the first at the expense of future increases in the productivity of the economy and the second by a policy of wage and credit restraint.

The deflationary policies were coupled with only very mild efforts to alter the structure of production and reallocate resources. The higher prices offered to farmers for the 1952/1953 crops plus unusually good weather brought satisfactory crops during 1953. But pressures from the industrial sector resulted in a renewal of expansionary policies late in 1953; another massive wage increase decreed in May 1954 upset the price stability achieved during 1953 and eroded the improvement obtained by the relative prices of the rural sector during 1952/1953. By 1955, the relative implicit prices of the value added by the rural sector were even below the 1951 and 1952 levels. The upswing in production that started in 1953 soon began to hit against the old bottlenecks in transportation, energy, and so on; while after a brief period of hope the rural output continued to stagnate and its level of technology showed little improvement. However, a more favorable attitude toward foreign capital coupled with a greater emphasis on the more complex branches of manufacturing resulted in further advances in the field of import substitution. When the stop-go cycle of 1952–1955 came to its end in late 1955 under pressure of falling net reserves, the real gross domestic product was about 12 per cent above the level of 1951.

The Prebisch Plan and the Cycle 1955–1958

The military junta which came to power in September 1955 asked Dr. Raúl Prebisch, of the United Nations Economic Commission for Latin America, to prepare a series of recommendations regarding the economic policies the provisional government should follow. An immediate result of the Prebisch proposals was the exchange reform involving the devaluation of the peso undertaken in late October 1955. These reforms replaced the old official exchange rates for a single official rate and created a free market for exchange where most transactions not covered by the official rate could be carried out. The official rate was set at 18 pesos per dollar, while the free rate stood at around 37 pesos during 1956. The degree of effective devaluation which these exchange reforms implied may best be judged by examining the average rate of exchange applied to total exports and imports during 1955 and 1956. The average rate of exchange for merchandise exports was 7.9 pesos in 1955 and 19.2

pesos per dollar in 1956; those for merchandise imports were 7.6 pesos in 1955 and 16.2 pesos in 1956.²

The new exchange rates were accompanied by a variety of new nonuniform surcharges and taxes on imports and exports. Furthermore, the proportion of exchange which could be negotiated in the free market for different types of transactions was subject to change by the exchange authorities. Thus, in effect many of the features of a multiple-exchange system were maintained, including the possibility of devaluing the average exchange rate applied to merchandise imports and exports without having to change the basic official rate. This characteristic of the exchange system was used during 1956–1958 to further devalue the peso.

The exchange reform freed about one third of all imports from quantitative restrictions, by introducing automatic granting of licenses for some imports of raw materials and intermediate products, together with the creation of the legitimately free market rate where exchange could be purchased to pay for many imports. Most invisible and capital transactions were permitted through the free exchange market. However, quantitative restrictions were maintained on most imports and flat prohibitions on some, mainly consumer and capital goods. Thus, the exchange reform of October 1955 represented only a partial step toward the goal of a unitary free rate and the removal of all quantitative restrictions over trade and capital flows.

The Prebisch plan³ explicitly stated the need for a transfer of real income from the industrial and urban sectors to the rural sector, both to stimulate production and to finance investment in the latter sector. The plan foresaw that devaluation would lead to higher prices, and estimated an increase of about 10 to 15 per cent.⁴ Prebisch faced

---

² Because of outstanding import and exchange permits of the old system, the effect of the devaluation on the effective average exchange rate for merchandise imports was felt gradually. Thus, the average rate for merchandise imports was 11.8 pesos during the first quarter of 1956, 15.4 pesos in the second quarter, 17.6 pesos in the third quarter and 20.0 pesos in the last quarter. Data obtained from several issues of *Comercio Exterior,* of the Dirección Nacional de Estadística y Censos.

³ As presented in three documents submitted to the Argentine government: *Provisional Report* of October 24, 1955; *Final Report and Economic Recovery Programme,* and *Sound Money or Uncontrolled Inflation* of January 20, 1956. These reports show an aspect of Dr. Prebisch's economic thinking not widely known among Anglo-Saxon economists, who often have a rather distorted idea of his points of view. For English translation of these reports see *The Review of the River Plate,* October 31 and November 11, 1955, and January 20, 1956.

⁴ It is interesting to note, however, that Prebisch explicitly recognized the

squarely the issue of who in the industrial sector should suffer the short-run drop in income necessary to increment rural real income, suggesting that money wages of industrial workers should be increased by roughly the same percentage as the rise in the cost of living, while the government made sure that such wage increases would not be passed on to consumers in the form of even higher industrial prices. In other words, additional real income for rural producers was to be obtained by a cut in industrial profits and from an expected increase in industrial average labor productivity of 10 per cent during 1956.[5] Further wage increases were to be strictly limited to those made feasible by further increments in labor productivity.

Although in general favoring the elimination of price controls, Prebisch advised a cautious and gradual movement toward free prices. Many of the old price-control measures were maintained, as for example, in the case of beef and housing rents, dampening the impact of devaluation on the cost-of-living index, especially in 1956.[6]

Prebisch also stressed the desirability of avoiding deflationary policies and unemployment. For 1956, he foresaw that available foreign exchange would be used up by imports of raw materials, intermediate products, and replacements of capital goods required by a relatively high level of industrial production. Thus, he explicitly linked any potential acquisition of machinery and equipment for expanding existing industrial capacity to the outcome of efforts to attract foreign capital into Argentina. Spare parts and some equipment were to be admitted through the free-exchange market, while the importation of other capital goods was prohibited unless financed by foreign capital. This reluctance to sacrifice the level of industrial production, and thus imports of raw materials and intermediate products, for the sake of obtaining capital equipment to expand the potential output of the import-competing and the export sectors reflects an awareness of the structural relationships discussed

---

existence of a "Sohmen-effect" following the removal of some of the more cumbersome import restrictions, which would tend to exert a downward pressure on domestic prices, primarily by eliminating the excess per unit profits of lucky holders of scarce import licenses.

[5] "There is no sound alternative to the stipulation that [the increase in wages and salaries] must be borne by the profits of management and by a higher rate of productivity." *Sound Money or Uncontrolled Inflation, op. cit.*

[6] While in December 1955, it had been decided to free most prices from controls, this policy was reversed in February 1956, when a new extensive price control system was established.

in Chapter 3. It was seen there that a cut in total real consumption, especially of wage earners' consumption, of a given amount will tend to reduce imports by much less than a similar cut in domestic investment. Thus, given a certain availability of foreign exchange, Argentina would find the substitution in the import bill of investment goods for noncapital goods an especially burdensome process in terms of living standards and employment. Yet the expansion of investment in key sectors of the economy was a long-run necessity to expand output simultaneously with balance-of-payments equilibrium. This dilemma led Prebisch to recommend some form of state cooperation with foreign capital in the development of oil resources, as well as in other industrial sectors. The plan also recommended a consolidation of external short-term debts, which had been growing steadily during earlier years.

In summary, the Prebisch plan hoped to escape the sequence predicted for after devaluation by the model of Chapter 2 by substituting the wage lag with a cut in the industrial rate of profits, and by an increase in total available supplies forthcoming from a greater inflow of foreign capital and a sharp increase in industrial productivity during 1956. The latter was to be obtained by a rationalization of the working rules and habits which had arisen during earlier years, but without an expansion of the capital stock. It was not expected that the balance of payments could be brought completely into equilibrium in 1956, but it was hoped this could be achieved during 1957, at which time further steps could be taken toward liberalizing foreign trade and the domestic economy, perhaps including new peso devaluations. It may also be noted that the expansion in the money supply during 1956 was to be limited, according to the plan, to about 15 per cent. The following pages will discuss briefly the fate of the Prebisch plan and of the high and difficult goals at which it aimed.[7]

Table 6.1 indicates the degree of devaluation undergone by the Argentine peso, not only immediately after October 1955 but also during 1957 and 1958. Tables 6.1 and 6.2 indicate that, as expected,

---

[7] Dr. Prebisch never had more than an advisory role in the provisional government which claimed to be implementing his plan. A year after the October 1955 devaluation Dr. Prebisch, back in the headquarters of the Economic Commission for Latin America in Santiago de Chile, expressed serious doubts about how his plan was being implemented. In particular, he considered the wage increases granted to industrial and other workers during 1956 (which were reflected mainly in money-wage statistics for 1957) to be excessive. See *The Review of the River Plate*, October 30, 1956.

the devaluations raised the relative prices of the rural sector and of imported goods in 1956. The picture for 1957 is more ambiguous; but with the implicit prices of the value added in the rural sector as the most reliable guide, it appears that a further small improvement took place. By 1958, in spite of the additional small doses of devaluation, domestic industrial prices caught up and increased

TABLE 6.1
PERCENTAGE CHANGES OF KEY EXCHANGE RATE, PRICE AND WAGE VARIABLES IN ARGENTINA, 1955–1958

	Third Quarter 1955 to Third Quarter 1956	Third Quarter 1956 to Third Quarter 1957	Third Quarter 1957 to Third Quarter 1958
Average Merchandise-Import Exchange Rate	129.5	42.0	11.1
Average Merchandise-Export Exchange Rate	168.1	20.7	21.2
Over-all Wholesale-Price Index	30.5	26.2	29.6
Wholesale Prices of Rural Products	50.4	24.8	29.5
Wholesale Prices of Nonrural Domestic Products	27.7	26.6	30.3
Wholesale Prices of Imported Products	71.8	8.5	17.4
Over-all Cost-of-Living Index	15.3	28.3	31.7
Foodstuffs Prices: Retail	14.4	42.4	35.1
Hourly Money-Wage Rates in Industry	12.2	32.7	57.4
Money Wages per Worker in Industry	14.4	28.6	62.2

Sources and method: Basic indices obtained from *Comercio Exterior, Boletín Mensual de Estadística,* and other publications of the Dirección Nacional de Estadística y Censos; also from International Monetary Fund, *International Financial Statistics,* several issues.

at a faster rate than rural and imported prices, under pressure from the large increases in money wages decreed by the new constitutional government which came to power in May 1958.

The increases in the prices of imported and rural goods during 1956 were less than the increase in the price of the dollar; besides changes in international prices and differences arising from coverage, such divergence is explained for rural goods by the taxes, retentions, and price controls adopted or maintained after October 1955. Furthermore, the government deposed in September 1955 had set up domestic prices for many rural products that were above those corresponding to the old exchange rate multiplied by world prices, covering the difference by subsidies from the Treasury. A devaluation accompanied by a removal of such a system will naturally result in a less than proportional increase in the domestic prices of these products. In the case of imported goods, the removal of the harsher features of import control seems to have exerted a downward influence on these prices.[8]

TABLE 6.2

Percentage Changes of Implicit Prices in the National Accounts, 1955–1958

	1955 to 1956	1956 to 1957	1957 to 1958
Gross Domestic Product	20.9	22.1	38.2
Value added by rural sector	32.3	28.1	35.0
Value added by manufacturing	12.4	25.7	41.9
Value added by commerce	27.7	28.3	28.6
Value added by government services	9.2	10.5	61.9
Private Consumption Expenditure	21.2	27.5	30.4
Meat	4.6	40.9	39.4
Other nonmanufactured rural products	23.8	30.4	25.7
Manufactured goods	26.1	30.4	27.8
Services	15.8	15.6	36.2
Gross Fixed Investment	38.7	21.2	32.1
Construction	25.6	9.7	36.0
Domestic machinery and equipment	15.1	20.2	31.5
Imported machinery and equipment	105.6	76.0	25.2

Sources and methods: Basic data obtained from *Cuentas Nacionales de la República Argentina*, Consejo Nacional de Dessarrollo, Presidencia de la Nación, Buenos Aires, April 1964. The implicit prices are obtained by dividing figures expressed in current prices by the corresponding items expressed at 1960 prices.

It was clearly understood by most informed observers that the success or failure of the Prebisch stabilization plan would depend to a very large extent on the wage and price policy the provisional government followed. A renewal of massive wage increases, which

---

[8] These considerations illustrate the simple point that while in the model developed in Chapter 2 the domestic prices of importables and exportables moved by the same percentages as the devaluation of the exchange rate, the many frictions present in reality destroy such precise correspondence. In general, two types of slippage may be isolated for prices of importables and exportables: that between world prices multiplied by the exchange rate and the corresponding domestic wholesale prices, and that between domestic wholesale and retail prices. Transport costs, commercialization margins, taxes, and government controls over foreign trade create slippages of both types.

could lead as in the past not to lower profit margins in industry and commerce but to higher industrial prices, would erode the real-income improvement obtained by the rural sector after the devaluation. The resistance of the provisional government to trade union pressure weakened steadily throughout 1956, so that late in the year large wage increases, beyond the limits set by Prebisch, were granted. But on balance it appears that real industrial wages fell slightly in 1956, recovering in 1957 and rising strongly during 1958. A similar evolution seems to have taken place by nonwage income in industry; in spite of the price-control measures adopted early in 1956 to enforce the recommendation that wage increases should not be reflected in higher industrial prices, it appears that no significant drop in profit margins occurred during these years. According to national income statistics the share of wage income in total value added by manufacturing, excluding employers' social security contributions, was only fractionally higher in 1956 than in 1955. Thus, while the improvement in real income obtained by the rural sector in 1956 was achieved in part at the expense of both real industrial wages and nonwages, that burden was completely shouldered in 1957 by wage earners in the noncommerce service sectors in general (including government employees, whose real wages fell drastically) and also by the construction sector. The shaky nature of available data does not warrant a more careful quantification of these trends; but it appears that during 1957 both the industrial and the rural sectors managed to improve their relative position at the expense of the groups in the service sectors with the weakest bargaining position.[9]

The improvement of real income of the rural sector was concentrated in agriculture rather than livestock, a sector which in earlier years had benefitted relative to other rural sectors. Relative prices for livestock products hardly increased at all after the 1955 devaluation because export taxes were especially severe on its products, foreign prices fell, and price controls were maintained on the domestic marketing of beef. The contrast between grain and livestock prices sparked a massive slaughter of cattle by rural producers wishing to switch into agriculture.

The extent of the redistribution of income set off by the devaluation of October 1955 and the *de facto* devaluations following in

---

[9] Most of the government employees at work during 1956–1957 had been appointed by the government overthrown in September 1955.

1956–1958 appears to have been relatively small. The fact that beef was kept under price control played no small part in softening the impact of devaluation on real wages, industrial and nonindustrial. According to the national income statistics, the share of all gross-wage income (including employers' social security contributions) dropped only slightly between 1955 and 1956: from 47.0 per cent of gross domestic income at factor cost to 46.4 per cent. This share fell further in 1957 to 44.8 per cent, but rose to 46.3 in 1958.

The fiscal and monetary policies of the government during these years lacked consistency. While during 1956 net borrowing from the banking system by the public sector was actually negative, amounting to an impressive −1.1 per cent of the gross national product for that year, in 1957 such net borrowing expanded substantially toward the end of the year, becoming +2.2 per cent of the gross national product, and in 1958 under a new administration reached +5.8 per cent of gross national product. Banking credit to the private sector expanded by 25 per cent from September 1955 to September 1956, and by 24 per cent from September 1956 to September 1957, figures which indicate that monetary policy followed on the whole a largely permissive role during these years. The hesitations in the economic policy of the provisional government are also noticeable here, however; at several points the authorities threatened to curtail credit to finance wage increases (especially late in 1957) only to give in when the pressure from the industrial community became too strong. The tight credit policies of late 1957 seem to have led to some decrease in the share of nonwage income in the manufacturing sector, as they forced entrepreneurs to finance out of profits some of the wage concessions made in late 1956 and early 1957. This display of firmness, however, came too late and was too weak to make much difference in the fate of the stabilization program. In defense of the economic authorities, it should be pointed out that during 1955–1957 the monetary instruments at their disposal were very weak and in a confused state because of the reorganization of the Central Bank and the banking system during those years.[10]

The increase by 10 per cent in industrial productivity that Prebisch had hoped would take place in 1956 did not occur. For the

[10] In August 1956, the charter of the Central Bank was revised to return to this institution some degree of independence from the authorities of the federal government. On December 1957, further banking reforms in turn increased the independence of commercial banks from the Central Bank.

economy as a whole employment increased slightly above the level of 1955, while real gross domestic product rose by only 2 per cent between 1955 and 1956, and by about 5 per cent in each of the following two years. Agricultural output actually fell in 1956 because of bad weather; and its recovery in 1957 was far from spectacular. The slaughtering of cattle resulted in sharp decreases in the output of the livestock sector during 1956 and 1957, the only consolation being that such activity raised the output of meat packing plants and the level of meat exports. In brief, during 1956–1958 little reallocation of resources seems to have taken place. Some further gains were achieved in the field of import substitution, but these reflect more the result of long-standing policies than of the devaluations.

The redistribution of income caused by the devaluations of 1955–1957 was not sufficiently important to have much influence on the level and composition of absorption, which remained in 1956 (in constant prices) at about the same level reached in 1955. The improvement in the balance of trade in 1956 relative to 1955 was much smaller than what the stationary absorption and the 2 per cent increase in gross domestic product would suggest, due to a deterioration in terms of trade between these two years. In United States dollars, the deficit in current account which reached $240 million in 1955 was reduced to $130 million in 1956. This deficit was mostly financed by an inflow of foreign capital, although a further drop in net gold and foreign-exchange reserves took place during 1956. However, in 1957 and 1958 the current-account deficits again grew far beyond the foreign capital inflow, further reducing exchange reserves and increasing the official external debt.

The quantum of merchandise imports remained during 1956 at the same level as the average for the previous two years, a slight decrease of capital goods imports being compensated by an increase of other imports. Imports for the last quarter of 1955 plus the first three quarters of 1956 showed a decrease of about 1 per cent relative to the previous four quarters. The quantum of imports soared in 1957, increasing by at least 12 per cent over the levels of 1956, under the influence of a sharp increase in capital formation and a more liberal granting of licenses for capital goods.[11] Thus, at best

[11] The over-all import quantum used in Chapter 2, based on data of the Economic Commission for Latin America, shows an increase of 20 per cent from 1956 to 1957, while the corresponding index of the Dirección Nacional de Estadística y Censos shows an increase of 12 per cent.

only a pause in the increase of imports was achieved by the measures of October 1955.

The quantum of merchandise exports increased by about 2 per cent in 1956 over the average for 1954/1955, and by a larger percentage over the depressed level of 1955. Further increases in the export quantum were registered in 1957 and 1958. Thus, at first sight it appears that the policy of devaluation had some success along this line. A closer look at the quantum indices of the major export items, however, shows that the increase registered in the over-all index for 1956/1957 compared to 1954/1955 arose from rather perverse reasons. Thus, exports of maize, wheat, and wool, commodities whose relative prices were among the most favored by the stabilization plan, showed substantial *decreases* between 1954/1955 and 1956/1957: 21 per cent for wheat, 27 per cent for corn, and 5 per cent for wool.[12] On the other hand, the export quantum for meat increased by 64 per cent between these two periods, while that for hides rose by 30 per cent; it will be remembered that relative prices for livestock products hardly rose at all during 1956 and 1957, which led to a substantial slaughter of cattle herds. Thus, the export picture improved during this phase of the swing from cattle into grains, even when grain exports did not expand for meteorological or other reasons; but increases in exports that deplete capital stock can hardly form the base for a sustained improvement in the balance of trade. The basic discouraging fact is that as shown in Table 4.4 neither agricultural nor livestock output rose during 1956–1958 relative to 1953–1955, in spite of the expansion of acreage devoted to exportable grains. Furthermore, there was little change in the over-all per capita domestic consumption of exportables, in spite of the removal in late 1956 and 1957 of some of the government subsidies to the domestic consumption of these items. And in some key commodities, especially meat, further increases took place in their domestic per capita consumption, which contributed to the raid on cattle herds.[13]

[12] The basic data for indices of export quantum have been obtained from International Monetary Fund, *International Financial Statistics*, several issues.

[13] Per capita consumption of beef rose by almost 10 per cent from 1953–1955 to 1956–1958. Stocks of bovine cattle, estimated at 46.9 million heads in 1956 dropped to 41.3 million heads in 1958. See *Estadísticas Básicas*, Junta Nacional de Carnes, Buenos Aires, 1963, pp. 1, 11. The case of meat suggests a possible elaboration of the model of Chapter 2. While exports were there simply set equal to the difference between the domestic production and consumption of exportables, a more realistic model would also include in this equation changes in the domestic stock of exportables, of which cattle herds are a special case.

While the stabilization program of October 1955 benefitted (in the short run) by the implications of the shift from cattle into grains, it faced a major primarily exogenous difficulty. As shown in Table 3.2, the terms of trade deteriorated by about 14 per cent between 1953–1955 and 1956–1958. However, even if foreign prices had remained at the levels of 1955, the balance-of-payments disequilibrium would have persisted for 1956–1958, although in a substantially reduced form.

By early 1958, it was clear that the stabilization program had failed to achieve its objectives of balance-of-payments equilibrium and price stability. The ambitious aim of achieving a redistribution of income in favor of the rural sector at the expense of industrial profits had met at best only with some very partial short-run success; 1957 and especially 1958 witnessed an increase in inflationary pressures as the rural sector tried to maintain its 1956 gains by seeking further devaluations, while organized urban workers sought successfully to obtain large money-wage increases, which were quickly passed on in higher prices by entrepreneurs unable or unwilling to allow a drop in their profit margins. In this inflationary free-for-all, many weaker groups suffered further cuts in their real income; but some of them (such as the civil servants), taking advantage of a Presidential campaign in early 1958, were able to obtain government-inspired increases in their money incomes. By the second semester of 1958, these inflationary pressures reached full force and net official gold and foreign-exchange reserves dropped into negative magnitudes.

The problem of increasing the output of exportables remained; many observers attributed the lack of response in aggregate rural output to the partial and fitful way in which rural relative prices had improved in 1956 and 1957. Considerable progress was achieved during 1956–1958 in the field of import substitution, but the politically sensitive oil problem had not been tackled in full force and during 1956–1958 nearly 23 per cent of the import bill was accounted for by fuels, mainly petroleum. Many blamed the policy of maintaining full employment at all costs for the inability of the economy to change its structure of production more readily in response to price incentives.

During the second half of 1958, it appeared that even the modest gains achieved in earlier years in liberalizing foreign trade were being undone; granting of new import licenses and authorizations for custom clearance were temporarily banned from May 2 to

August 1. The cycle 1955–1958 was coming to an end in the familiar pattern: mounting inflationary pressures, vanishing exchange reserves, and an atmosphere of financial and social chaos, as rumors of radical changes in government economic policy swept the land. Few remembered the closing warning by Prebisch in his final report, regarding the economic outlook if his recommendations were not implemented:

> Later, the Government would be irresistibly compelled to take more drastic steps than those which today may suffice. And however strong might be the spirit of self-denial among its members, it would nevertheless have to cope with an opposition, which quick to seize the opportunity of making political capital out of the unpopularity of the measures to be applied, would render the application of a strong antiinflationary policy difficult in the extreme.[14]

The Frondizi-International Monetary Fund Stabilization Plan and the Cycle 1959–1961

In spite of the "emergency" massive wage increase decreed shortly after the government headed by Dr. Arturo Frondizi took power in May 1958, the new administration soon began to give signs of an attitude toward the economic problems of Argentina which differed sharply from that implied by the speeches made during the presidential campaign. Toward the end of July 1958, the government suddenly announced a new oil policy, which under the guise of "work and service" contracts allowed the participation of private foreign capital in the exploration and production of Argentine oil.[15]

During the last week of December 1958, after several months of rumors which became particularly intense after each of the several visits made to Buenos Aires by officers of the International Monetary Fund, President Frondizi announced a new stabilization plan.[16]

---

[14] *Sound Money or Uncontrolled Inflation, op. cit.*

[15] The federal government awarded these contracts with a torrential speed, and without the benefit of comparing terms through a call for tenders. The government argued that it was imperative to increase oil production as soon as possible, and that a call for tenders, as well as Congressional approval of the new policy, would have been excessively time consuming. These oil contracts became a major source of political debate in Argentina and drew criticism even from sources favorable to the participation of foreign capital in oil production. The contracts were annulled by the administration of President Arturo Illia shortly after it came to power in October 1963.

[16] It is said that of several alternative stabilization plans suggested by staff economists of the International Monetary Fund, President Frondizi personally chose the harshest and most austere one. The interest of the new administration

In a radio broadcast on December 29, the President asked his countrymen for two years of austerity and sacrifices, and appealing to the example of Western Germany stated

> We must achieve an Argentine miracle; we must show that we too are capable of transforming despair into hope and the ruins of defeat into great victories . . . .[17]

All official quantitative controls were to be removed from foreign trade and the peso, whose value would be set by a single free foreign-exchange market and which would be allowed to fluctuate freely, with no government pledge of any pegged value. The government, it was announced, would limit its role in the exchange market to smoothing out "excessive" fluctuations but allowing the market to set the basic trend. Although all requirements for import licenses were abolished, new ad valorem import surcharges were decreed, thus providing a link with the old *de facto* and *de jure* multiple exchange rates for imports. Three basic lists of imports were originally drawn up which reflected the pressures of on the one hand the agricultural sector's demands for low rates on agricultural equipment and inputs, and on the other hand the industrial sector's demands for further protection, including low rates for its raw materials. Surcharges ranged from zero for some raw materials to 300 per cent for some items produced locally and nonessential goods.[18] Furthermore, advanced deposits on imports, which had

in attracting a large amount of foreign capital may have been the basic cause for such an attitude.

[17] *The Review of the River Plate*, December 30, 1958. The example of Western Germany appeared repeatedly in official statements and speeches, especially those of Ingeniero Carlos Alsogaray, a self-proclaimed disciple of Ludwig Erhard, who was to play a key role in the implementation of the stabilization plan when he became Minister of both Labor and Economy in June 1959.

[18] List No. 1 was composed of products previously imported at the official rate of exchange, such as petroleum, lubricants, newsprint, rubber, iron ore, coal and coke. These goods were exempted of any import surcharges. List No. 2 was composed of semi-finished products and some raw materials essential to agriculture, livestock and industry, previously imported under mixed official and free-peso rates. Items in list 2 were subject to a 20 per cent surcharge. Capital goods, such as electric motors and machinery, and other manufactured goods made up list No. 3. These items which were previously imported at the free-peso rate faced a surcharge of 40 per cent. All other goods not appearing on these lists, including luxury goods and machinery produced locally, were taxed at 300 per cent of their c.i.f. value. In the months following December 1958, these lists were often modified. Furthermore, special laws aimed at stimulating foreign capital exempted imports of machinery and other products from the surcharges and other duties under easily met conditions. Finished automobiles

been in effect since January 1958, were drastically increased. These deposits were to be held for 180 days from the date of customs clearance. About 80 per cent of the items listed in the import surcharge classifications were affected by the deposit requirement.

Export retentions were also announced: 10 per cent on the f.o.b. value of the export of most livestock products and 20 per cent on the value of the exports of most cereals and oilseeds as well as on quebracho and raw hide exports. Exports of manufactured goods were exempted from any tax. To siphon off some of the windfall gains caused by the devaluation, the government levied a temporary 15 per cent tax on the export of cereals and oilseeds made from existing stocks of the 1958/1959 crop. While the increase in import surcharges tended to increase the effective devaluation of the peso, the export taxes had, of course, an offsetting influence on the devaluation. However, most of these export taxes were removed totally or partially during 1960 and 1961, thus helping to maintain rural incomes at a time when industrial prices were pressing their postdevaluation counteroffensive.

New moves were also announced to restrict the growth of banking credit and the money supply. Starting January 1, 1959, commercial banks were required to hold minimum reserves of 30 per cent of their demand deposits and other sight liabilities, instead of the 20 per cent previously in force. Furthermore, the 30 per cent additional reserve requirement for deposits in excess of the level of those items as of October 31, 1958, a measure in effect since November 1958, was retained. In other words, the total reserve requirements against new net demand deposits became 60 per cent. It was also announced that the Central Bank would stop providing the official Mortgage Bank with loanable funds, which this institution would now have to raise on its own in the capital market. Commercial banks were also warned against increasing their mortgage loans beyond the level of December 1958.

Further announcements regarding the stabilization plan emphasized the determination of the government to eliminate most internal price controls, a process which had already started in December 1958 with the freeing of all beef prices. The main exceptions to the removal of price controls were urban rents and the interest rates charged and offered by the banking system. The fares

---

continued to have their own prohibitive import surcharges. See Banco Central de la República Argentina, *Memoria Anual* for 1958 and 1959, where a detailed description of these measures is presented.

and fees for public services (urban transport, electricity, railroads, postal service, and so on) were to be substantially increased, in an effort to curtail the large deficits of state-owned enterprises, which were blamed for the over-all government deficit. The plan also called for a reduction in the size of the governmental bureaucracy.

A key preoccupation of the Frondizi administration was to attract foreign capital into Argentina. The receipt of a package of foreign loans amounting to $329 million dollars was announced simultaneously with the stabilization measures; these loans represented mainly short- and medium-term aid to bolster gross exchange reserves.[19] Other measures, besides the oil contracts, were taken during 1958 and 1959 to improve the investment climate for foreign private firms. The plan also expressed its commitment to multilateral trade and announced that bilateral payments would be terminated at the earliest possible date.

The stabilization plan of December 1958 presents an interesting contrast to that of October 1955; it appears that the failure of the earlier "softer" plan led key authorities to the conclusion that a quicker rush toward a free enterprise economy had to be made, and that it could not be expected that the transfer of real income to the rural sector could come out of any other group than the urban working class. A postdevaluation money-wage lag was to be sought and defended as part of the stabilization plan.

No significant effort was made by the Argentine government to prepare public opinion for the December 1958 announcement; as in the case of oil policy, the shock treatment was followed, perhaps under the fear that preparatory discussions would allow opponents of the stabilization plan to organize an invincible resistance. As could be expected, the stabilization plan opened up an era of severe social and political difficulties. Thus, while examining the economic impact of the devaluation, it should be remembered that such developments occurred in the context of social and political disturbances which were unusual even for postwar Argentina.[20]

---

[19] The International Monetary Fund, the leading external influence behind the stabilization plan, provided $75 million; the United States Treasury pledged to purchase pesos for dollars up to $50 million; the Export-Import Bank provided $125 million, and the United States Development Loan Fund lent $25 million. Ten private United States banks and one Canadian bank lent $54 million.

[20] The announcement and early implementation of the plan struck even conservative observers as ". . . ruthless and indeed almost politically provocative . . ." *The Review of the River Plate*, May 29, 1959. President Frondizi was not trusted by the powerful Armed Forces of Argentina because of his tacit

The Economic Impact of Devaluation

The clean-cut nature of the measures announced on December 1958 provides a good test of the usefulness of the model developed in Chapter 2 as a guide to the analysis of the short-run impact of devaluation in a semi-industrialized country. The following pages will examine the behavior during 1959 and later years of the key variables stressed by the model of Chapter 2, as well as of other variables which that simplified model did not take explicitly into account. It will be shown that generally the extensions to the theory of devaluation developed in Chapter 2 appear justified by the Argentine experience of 1959–1961.[21]

1. Exchange Rates, the Price Level and Relative Prices

As shown in Table 6.3, the price of one United States dollar in terms of Argentine pesos increased by roughly 190 per cent between the third quarter of 1958 and the third quarter of 1959.[22] The free rate oscillated around 66 pesos during January 1959, compared with an average exchange rate for merchandise imports and exports of about 28 pesos in the third quarter of 1958 and an average rate of

---

alliance with followers of General Perón during the 1958 elections, while on the other hand he alienated most of his earlier supporters by his sudden change of viewpoints on economic policy in general and on oil policy in particular. He also faced hostility from important provincial governors.

[21] For other interpretations of the experience of these years, which also stress the redistributive effect, see Aldo Ferrer, "Reflexiones acerca de la política de estabilización en la Argentina," *El Trimestre Económico*, Vol. XXX(4), No. 120 (October–December 1963), pp. 501–504 (México), and by the same author, "Devaluación, Redistribución de Ingresos y el Proceso de Desarticulación Industrial en le Argentina," *Desarrollo Económico*, Vol. 2, No. 4 (January–March 1963), pp. 5–18 (Buenos Aires). The Argentine experience of these years is also reflected in Raúl Prebisch, "Economic Development or Monetary Stability: The False Dilemma," *Economic Bulletin for Latin America*, United Nations, Vol. VI, No. 1 (March 1961), pp. 1–26. For the application of the redistributive model to an experience outside Latin America, see Andreas S. Gerakis, "Recession in the Initial Phase of a Stabilization Program. The Experience of Finland," International Monetary Fund *Staff Papers*, Vol. XI, No. 1 (November 1964), pp. 125–149. A recent survey of Argentine economic policies since the Second World War, covering much of the same ground as this monograph, is found in Eprime Eshag and Rosemary Thorp, "Economic and Social Consequences of Orthodox Economic Policies in Argentina in the Post-War Years," *Bulletin of the Oxford University Institute of Economics and Statistics*, Volume 27, No. 1 (February 1965), pp. 3–44.

[22] Because of the effective devaluation of the peso during the last quarter of 1958 and of other economic measures taken during that same quarter, it will be useful to consider the third quarter of 1958 as the base period for comparisons of price changes whenever quarterly data are available.

37 pesos in the last quarter of 1958. The free rate moved up rapidly during the early months of 1959, reaching quotations above 100 pesos during a few frantic days in early June, but settling down to a rate between 82 and 83 pesos after September 1959. With the support of the Central Bank, which entered the market as buyer and seller when the rate diverged from these limits, the exchange rate

TABLE 6.3
PERCENTAGE CHANGES OF EXCHANGE RATES AND
PRICES IN ARGENTINA, 1958–1961

	Third Quarter 1958 to Third Quarter 1959	Third Quarter 1959 to Third Quarter 1960	Third Quarter 1960 to Third Quarter 1961
Average Merchandise Import-Exchange Rate	181.2	6.1	0.2
Average Merchandise Export-Exchange Rate	199.1	— 1.3	0.1
Over-all Wholesale-Price Index	147.7	4.6	11.0
Wholesale Prices of Rural Products	177.3	0.4	9.7
Wholesale Prices of Nonrural Domestic Products	132.9	6.6	12.6
Wholesale Prices of Imported Products	207.7	3.5	— 3.8
Over-all Cost-of-Living Index	124.5	15.9	16.6
Foodstuffs Prices: Retail	143.4	11.2	13.0
Dollar Prices of Imports	— 5.9	2.1	1.0
Dollar Prices of Exports	6.9	2.8	— 2.7

Sources and Method: Same as in Table 6.1.

remained at that level until the second quarter of 1962.[28] It seems clear that the exchange authorities regarded the freely fluctuating rate of the early months of 1959 as nothing more than a temporary expedient to be used in avoiding a commitment to any single rate until domestic prices became stabilized and net foreign-exchange reserves were built up.

[28] As in 1955, the existence of outstanding import and exchange permits at the old exchange rate caused the average import rate for actual merchandise imports to lag behind the free rate. The implicit average rate for merchandise imports was 36 pesos in the last quarter of 1958, 49 pesos in the first quarter of 1959, 70 pesos in the second quarter, 78 pesos in the third quarter, 81 pesos in the last quarter of 1959 and 82 pesos in the first quarter of 1960. The implicit average rate for merchandise exports reached 83 pesos by the second quarter of 1959.

As could be expected from the discussion in Chapters 3 and 4, the drastic devaluation of early 1959 had a significant impact on the price level. Consider first the prices of importables and exportables, as approximated by the wholesale prices for rural and imported products shown in Table 6.3. On the basis of the change in the average exchange rate for imports and in foreign prices, one could have expected an increase in the prices of imported goods of about 165 per cent from the third quarter of 1958 to the third quarter of 1959. Two other major factors influenced the level of domestic prices for imports: the increase in import surcharges just described and, in an opposite direction, the complete removal of quantitative restrictions. The observed increase of 208 per cent in the level of import prices suggests that the first factor was more than enough to offset any downward pressure on prices which could have arisen from the removal of quantitative restrictions.[24] The domestic prices of exportables could have been expected to increase by 220 per cent on the basis of the movements of the exchange rate and foreign prices. Wholesale prices of rural products, only a crude approximation to the concept of the domestic price level of exportables, rose by a smaller amount: 177 per cent. At least part of this gap is explained by the special export taxes and retentions adopted simultaneously with the devaluation. These taxes appear to have more than offset an opposite influence on the domestic price of exportables which arose from the freeing of several commodities, especially beef, from price controls.

The increase during 1958/1959 in the wholesale prices of non-rural domestic products, primarily manufactured goods, was as expected smaller than the price increase for importables and exportables, but also rather substantial. Part of this increase arose from the dismantling of most official controls over domestic prices and the increase that took place in the prices charged by public utilities and transportation facilities. Furthermore, domestic industry during this period suffered sharp increases in other costs; money-wage rates had risen substantially during the second semester of 1958, and naturally the prices of inputs into domestic manufacturing originating in either the import or export sector increased with the devaluation.

---

[24] If it is assumed that the removal of quantitative restrictions had a zero effect, it would follow that the level of effective ex-post average import surcharges was raised by about 26 per cent during 1959, yielding the additional 43 per cent increase in import prices.

It may be seen in Table 6.3 that after the third quarter of 1959 the exchange rate was practically constant throughout 1960 and 1961. During these years, the tendency was for prices of domestic manufactured products to rise faster than the prices of either importables or exportables, thus whittling down the gains achieved by the relative prices of these goods in the short run following the devaluation. This tendency accelerated during the last quarter of 1961 and the first quarter of 1962, when the remarkable price

TABLE 6.4
Percentage Changes of Implicit Prices in
the National Accounts, 1958–1961

	1958 to 1959	1959 to 1960	1960 to 1961
Gross Domestic Product	97.9	20.3	12.3
Value added by rural sector	134.3	11.7	— 2.6
Value added by petroleum and mining	144.1	— 5.4	— 7.8
Value added by manufacturing	90.8	30.0	13.8
Value added by commerce	120.5	14.5	6.0
Value added by government service	56.9	25.0	35.8
Private Consumption Expenditures	99.7	25.5	11.4
Meat	236.1	10.6	— 4.6
Other nonmanufactured rural products	79.1	31.1	7.9
Manufactured goods	98.2	27.7	11.6
Services	70.0	24.1	19.6
Gross Fixed Investment	91.2	15.5	11.6
Construction	87.8	11.9	20.8
Domestic machinery and equipment	91.5	23.8	7.6
Imported machinery and equipment	130.0	7.9	4.6

Sources and methods: Same as in Table 6.2.

stability achieved during 1960 and early 1961 began to crumble under pressure from money-wage increases and an expanding level of real economic activity. It may also be noted from Table 6.3 that the cost-of-living index appears to have lagged behind the wholesale index in reflecting the price increases arising from the devaluation.

The implicit or net prices presented in Table 6.4 shows even more clearly the pattern of a short-run improvement in the relative position of the rural sector after devaluation, followed by an erosion of such position as prices in other sectors of the economy, especially manufacturing, construction and some services, started their counteroffensive. By 1961, the implicit price for the value added by the rural sector relative to the price deflator for the the gross domestic product was below the predevaluation 1958 level. However, taking three-year averages of the relative prices of the value added by the rural sector, it is seen that 1959–1961 showed an improvement over 1956–1958 (135 as compared with 125, with $1950 = 100$), while the latter period had shown an improvement over 1953–1955 (125 versus 117).[25]

The branches of production most closely identified with home goods naturally showed the smallest price increases between 1958 and 1959, tending to recover their relative position in later years. Most services, excluding commerce, plus construction and manufacturing showed that pattern. Within manufacturing, the more traditional branches which had long ago become home-good industries by virtue of prohibitive protection against foreign competition showed the smallest price increments immediately following devaluation, while those branches closest to the frontier of import substitution showed greater price rises.[26]

2. Income Redistribution; Wages and Wage Policy

Earlier discussion has put emphasis on the key role of money-wage behavior as a determinant of success or failure for stabilization policies. Following a devaluation, large increases in money wages would (a) wipe out any chances of cutting the absorption of wage recipients and (b) lead to further domestic price increases, unless entrepreneurs can be forced to finance such wage increases out of profits or, equally unlikely, a short-run increase in productivity is accomplished. Both of these results would reduce the effectiveness of

---

[25] The behavior of the implicit prices of the commerce sector, which rose more than the average immediately after devaluation, suggests that exporters may not pass on to rural producers all of the gains from the increase in the domestic price of exportables. Although available data are not sufficient to analyze this slippage in the redistribution of income, the fact that commercial activity in the import and manufacturing sector declined in 1959 while the implicit relative prices of the commercial sector rose in those years suggests that such an improvement probably arose in the commercialization of exportables. See Table 6.2 for a similar experience in 1956 and 1957. Total money gross nonwage income in the commerce sector rose by 37 per cent between 1955 and 1956, and by 111 per cent between 1958 and 1959. See *Cuentas Nacionales de la República Argentina, op. cit.*, pp. 126, 127. See also Table 6.7.

[26] The implicit prices for value added in "vegetative" branches of manufacturing (foodstuffs, tobacco, textiles, clothing, printing, leather and wood) rose by 86 per cent from 1958 to 1959, while those for "dynamic" branches, more closely identified with import substitution, rose by 101 per cent at that time. These figures were obtained from worksheets of the Consejo Nacional de Desarrollo.

devaluation in correcting the balance of trade (*a*) by failing to cut down on imports and domestic consumption of exportables and (*b*) mainly by increasing domestic costs and thus squeezing profit margins and decreasing the incentives of the export and import-competing production sectors. If a cut in absorption were all that was required for the long-run success of a devaluation, it would be possible, even in a democratic capitalistic economy, for all social classes to share equally in the burden of austerity. However, a reallocation of resources is also indispensable if the devaluation is to have a long-run success in making possible both full employment and balance-of-payments equilibrium. Therefore, even in the context of a general cut in absorption in a capitalist economy, better incentives, and higher real incomes must be offered to some sectors of production after a devaluation. The rural sector is one of the obvious condidates for such an increase in real income in Argentina. But reallocation is also needed within industry, and the likely outcome of such a situation is that while the working class is likely to face sharp drops in real income, many industrial entrepreneurs (although not necessarily all) are likely to receive increases in real income.

The economic authorities, no doubt influenced by the 1956 experience, decided early in the stabilization plan to make sure that the wage lag would be maintained at all costs. Cost-of-living clauses in wage contracts were suspended by decree, starting in January 1959. The Minister of Labor claimed to follow three rules regarding labor relations: (*a*) the government would no longer order payment of wages to striking workers; (*b*) the government would no longer undertake to promote negotiations while a strike was in progress; and (*c*) union delegates would not be allowed to disturb the order within factories. During the first half of 1959, the Army was often used to quell general and other strikes. State of siege powers were granted to the government to handle work stoppages and several union leaders were jailed. The government, of course, refrained from any new blanket wage increases. Relatively minor wage increases were granted by private employers strictly along collective bargaining lines, but with the public authorities loudly proclaiming that no bank credit would be allowed to finance excessive wage increases. The government even refused to allow banks to finance the traditional December wage bonus.

Table 6.5 shows the impact on real industrial wages of the devaluation plus the state-of-siege conditions. The 1959 drop in real wages fell on all urban workers with similar harshness; the recovery of real wages during 1960 and 1961 left real wages in many sectors below the levels reached during 1958. These trends are also reflected in the National Accounts data on wages, as shown in Table

TABLE 6.5
PERCENTAGE CHANGES OF MONEY AND REAL INDUSTRIAL WAGES IN ARGENTINA, 1958–1961

	Third Quarter 1958 to Third Quarter 1959	Third Quarter 1959 to Third Quarter 1960	Third Quarter 1960 to Third Quarter 1961
Hourly Money-Wage Rates in Industry	58.6	30.3	23.4
Money Wages per Worker in Industry	36.0	51.0	24.5
Real Hourly Money-Wage Rates in Industry	—29.4	12.5	5.9
Real Money Wages per Worker in Industry	—39.4	30.3	6.7

Sources and method: Real wages obtained by dividing money wages by the cost-of-living index. Sources are the same as in Table 6.1. It should be remembered that the index of wages shown above refers primarily to "vegetative" branches of the manufacturing sector. (See statistical appendix to Chapter 5.)

TABLE 6.6
PERCENTAGE CHANGES IN REAL WAGES PER EMPLOYED WAGE EARNER, 1958–1961

	1958 to 1959	1959 to 1960	1960 to 1961
All Sectors of the Economy	—17.7	8.3	12.3
Agriculture and livestock	— 6.6	3.7	0
Manufacturing	—20.4	19.3	12.2
Construction	—20.3	— 2.4	11.3
Commerce	—20.9	4.0	12.0
Transport	—13.9	4.7	11.4
General government	—21.5	3.3	35.0
Other sectors	—15.2	3.7	— 4.5

Sources and methods: Total and sectorial money wages were obtained from *Cuentas Nacionales de la República Argentina, op. cit.* Wages in this case include employers' social security contributions. All money wages were deflated by the implicit price deflator for the gross domestic product at factor cost, so as to not change the relative position of wages in that total when measured in constant prices. Thus, the deflated total wages only give a rough approximation to "true" real wages; especially for rural wages. Total real wages were divided by the number of wage earners in each sector to obtain real wages per employed wage earner. Data on employment are rough; they were obtained from worksheets of the Consejo Nacional de Desarrollo.

6.6, which suggest that rural wages fared better than urban wages during 1959. The urban working class was not only hit by lower real wages but also by dwindling employment opportunities during 1958–1961; as a result of these forces, the share of all gross wage income in the gross domestic income at factor cost fell from 46.3 per cent in 1958 to 40.4 per cent in 1959, rising slowly to 41.0 per cent in 1960 and 43.1 per cent during 1961.[27]

TABLE 6.7
PERCENTAGE CHANGES IN REAL TOTAL GROSS NONWAGE INCOME, 1958–1961

	1958 to 1959	1959 to 1960	1960 to 1961
All Sectors of the Economy	6.0	4.9	2.0
Agriculture and livestock	26.7	−9.3	−18.0
Manufacturing and construction	−2.3	12.3	9.6
Commerce and transport	6.6	10.1	4.9
Other	−3.9	4.7	8.4

Sources and methods: Same as in Table 6.6. Real nonwages are gross of both depreciation and taxes.

Tables 6.7 shows the changes in total and sectorial nonwage income, gross of taxes and depreciation allowances, and deflated by the implicit price deflator for the gross domestic product at factor cost. These changes in total real nonwage income reflect changes in the level of output of the various sectors as well as changes in profit or nonwage rates per unit of output. As expected, during 1959 the nonwage income of the rural sector rose dramatically, while that for the rest of the economy showed relatively minor change. In other words, it appears that practically the whole gain of real income of the rural sector was obtained at the expense of urban workers, and to a much smaller extent, from an improvement in the external terms of trade. The gain in the real-nonwage income of commerce and transport during 1959 may reflect a minor

[27] As the share of wage income in the rural sector is smaller than in the rest of the economy, a redistribution of income in favor of that sector will result in a decrease of the over-all wage share even if real-wage rates remain constant in all sectors of the economy. Table 6.6 clearly shows that the drop in the over-all wage share was due primarily to the decrease in real-wage rates throughout the economy, rather than just to the increase in the rural share. The latter factor, of course, also contributed to the drop in the over-all wage share. It may be noticed that the model of Chapter 2 assumed for simplicity the same wage share for all sectors of the economy; the redistributive effect is strengthened when the sector that gains from the devaluation also has a smaller than average wage share.

leak in this transfer of income, as pointed out in footnote 25. The rest of the economy, dominated by home goods, showed a drop in their real nonwages. However, real-nonwage income per unit of output appears to have increased in most key sectors of the economy during 1959, as may be gathered by comparing the figures of Table 6.7 with the decreases in real output which took place during 1959, shown in Table 6.11.[28]

In contrast with the experience of 1955–1958, livestock producers increased their income in 1959 more than other rural entrepreneurs and property owners, as the domestic prices of their products showed larger real improvements than agriculture as a group because of the lower export retentions levied on most livestock exports, the freeing of beef prices from all forms of control, and more favorable foreign prices for beef.[29] Land-owning cattle raisers and farmers benefitted not only from higher output prices but from soaring property values as well.

As pointed out previously, within the industrial sector those branches coming closest to the importable good producing category seem to have fared better in their real-nonwage income than other industrial sectors. The mining sector, primarily made up by the petroleum industry, showed during 1959 an increase in its real nonwages beyond the substantial increase in its output.

In spite of the removal of most export taxes and retentions during 1960 and 1961 and of other measures designed to preserve the rural income gains of 1959 in the face of the counteroffensive of the urban sector, real rural nonwages fell during those years, while most urban real wages and nonwages increased. It may be noted that manufacturing and construction real nonwages managed to increase by more than their corresponding output indices during 1960 and 1961.[30]

[28] In the model of Chapter 2, real nonwages or profits per unit of output would be expected to increase in the export and import-competing sectors of the economy, but not in the home-good sector. The increases in real profit rates that took place during 1959 in some home-good industries, however, appear to have been small and not very significant. Unfortunately, available data do not allow a neat differentiation within the manufacturing sector between truly import competing (in the sense of Chapter 2) and home-good industries.

[29] The wholesale-price index for livestock products rose by 195 per cent between 1958 and 1959, while that for agricultural products rose during those years by 119 per cent. This tendency was reversed to some extent during 1960 and 1961, when agricultural prices rose more than livestock prices.

[30] Fragmentary evidence suggests that there were significant increases in average labor productivity during 1960 and 1961, which on balance seem to have resulted in higher profit rates when comparing the period 1959–1961 as a

3. Monetary policy

Before examining the impact of the redistribution of income which took place in 1959 on the level and composition of absorption and output, it will be useful to analyze another major source of influence on these real variables, namely monetary policy. While for the sake of simplicity monetary factors were not taken into account explicitly in the model developed in Chapter 2, monetary policy plays in Argentina an important role in determining the level and composition of output and absorption.[31]

It seems best to judge the credit expansion during 1959, especially that directed toward the private sector, in relation to the minimum increase in the price level that could be said to follow inevitably from the devaluation of the exchange rate, assuming downward rigidity of prices. Taking into account other measures adopted by the stabilization program regarding import and export taxes and the removal of controls over foreign trade, it may be said that the domestic prices of importables and exportables could have been expected to rise, *ceteris paribus,* by about 190 per cent from the end of 1958 to the end of 1959. According to the discussion in Chapter 3 on the role of importables and exportables in the Argentine economy, such increase in the prices of these goods would have led to an increase of between 35 per cent and 45 per cent in the over-all price level of the economy, depending on what definition is used for such aggregate concept. If expansion of credit and the money supply failed to reach these figures, an autonomous depressing effect on real output would result, while increases above those figures could be said to have an autonomous expansionary effect.[32] The mechanism

---

whole with 1956–1958. A more rational use of the employed labor within each firm plus the higher relative growth of high productivity branches of production account for most of the productivity growth. In late 1960 and in 1961 an increase in the capital-labor ratio also played a part in increasing productivity in several industries. The wage and labor policy of the government during these years was naturally very important in channeling these increases of productivity into higher profits.

[31] Fiscal policy has had a smaller role and will be considered later. The financing of the government deficit by bank credit is considered here to fall in the province of monetary rather than fiscal policy, although obviously both monetary and fiscal policy are closely linked in this respect.

[32] These calculations are so rough that they do not warrant the inclusion of a "normal" real output growth in them; such real figure would be dwarfed by the change in the price level. It should also be noticed that as the devaluation is expected to result in a net decrease in the demand for home goods, due to the redistributive effect, no allowance is made for an increase in these prices as an inevitable result of devaluation. See A. C. Harberger, "Some Notes on Inflation,"

through which the relative ease or tightness in the money market will influence real output is mainly its influence on investment decisions, including changes in stocks of finished products and work in process, and on expenditures on durable consumer goods.

Tables 6.8 and 6.9 summarize the main *ex post* results of the monetary policy followed during 1959–1961. The increase in the money supply that took place during 1959 was much smaller than the increases registered in the over-all price level, but falls within the "neutral" target discussed in the previous paragraph. Other considerations, however, suggest that on balance monetary policy tended to be an autonomous depressing influence on output during 1959. First of all, the large money-wage increases that took place during the second semester of 1958 were not fully absorbed during that year, and their influence on costs and prices continued until 1959. Secondly, the new monetary policy had a rather discriminatory incidence during 1959; the private sector in general, and the mortgage market in particular, fared much worse than the public sector in the distribution of increases of banking credit. In a country where money markets are not well integrated, such discriminatory policies can produce severe distress in a particular sector even when over-all credit conditions are not unduly tight. It will be seen that the private housing construction industry, very much a home-good producer, represents an example of such distress during 1959–1961. It is also likely that small producers suffered greater hardships than the larger companies, which in most cases had a higher priority in the distribution of bank credit.

The credit expansion during 1959 actually resulted not so much from deliberate monetary policy as from unforeseen events and unavoidable past commitments, especially during the first half of the year. Thus, the Central Bank incurred heavy losses on exchange-rate guarantees issued before January 1959, which resulted in effect in an expansion of the money supply, while a lengthy strike of bank clerks during the second quarter of 1959 resulted in a substantial reduction in commercial bank reserves below their legal limits. During the second half of 1959, when these two special circum-

---

in *Inflation and Growth in Latin America*, W. Baer and I. Kerstenetsky, eds. (Homewood, Ill.: R. D. Irwin, Inc., 1964), for a model incorporating possible price increases of home goods as an inevitable result of devaluation, assuming, as it is done in Chapter 2, that the monetary authorities ". . . do not themselves ignite the fire, but neither do they operate in such a way as to deprive it of oxygen."

stances ceased to operate, the rate of growth of credit dropped sharply and the money market became rather tight.[33]

Credit availability to the nonmortgage private sector improved during 1960 and 1961, as the Central Bank relaxed legal reserve requirements, but without reversing the trend started in 1956 toward "harder" monetary policy. Net additions to outstanding mortgage credit were practically zero; the *real* value of the outstanding mortgage credit of course fell substantially. Perhaps under the influence of a more stable price level, time deposits and other items in quasi

TABLE 6.8
PERCENTAGE CHANGES IN MONETARY VARIABLES
IN ARGENTINA, 1958–1961

	December 1958 to December 1959	December 1959 to December 1960	December 1960 to December 1961
Money Supply	43.8	25.7	15.0
Quasi Money and Other Banking Liabilities	28.6	44.8	26.5
Net Banking Credit to the Public Sector	45.5	4.7	18.1
Total Banking Credit to the Private Sector	21.4	36.5	31.4

Sources and method: Sources as in Table 5.5. Net banking credit to the public sector refers to total banking credit to the public sector minus government deposits in the banking system.

money rose substantially during 1960 and 1961, thus helping to reduce the rate of growth in the money supply proper. The income velocity of circulation of the money supply, which had risen from 5.12 to 6.24 from 1958 to 1959, remained at about the same level during the following two years (6.22 in 1960 and 6.30 in 1961).

The sources of expansion in the money supply changed significantly during the intermediate stages of the stabilization plan, especially during 1960 and early 1961. Fresh credits to the public sector dwindled, while those to nonmortgage private sector increased, as shown in Table 6.9. Net increases in banking credit to the public

---

[33] Although the interest rates of the banking system remained under official control, sharp increases in interest rates in the Buenos Aires money market were reported. During the third quarter of 1959 short-term interest rates ranging upwards of 3 per cent per month were observed. See *The Review of the River Plate*, September 11, 1959, and *Argentina* by The Economist Intelligence Unit Ltd., October 11, 1959.

sector, which in 1959 still represented 3.1 per cent of the gross national product at current prices of that year, fell to 0.4 per cent during 1960, but rose again to 1.2 per cent of the gross national product in 1961. During both 1959 and 1960, a considerable part of the expansion in means of payments arose from increases in net foreign-exchange holdings of the Central Bank, a situation which had not occurred in such magnitudes for many years. However, the year 1961, especially during its second semester, witnessed again

TABLE 6.9
STRUCTURE OF SOURCES OF MONETARY EXPANSION
IN ARGENTINA, 1958–1961
(*In percentages of total expansion of money plus quasi money*)

	December 1958 to December 1959	December 1959 to December 1960	December 1960 to December 1961
Increase in Money Supply plus Quasi Money	100.0	100.0	100.0
Net change in gold and foreign-exchange reserves	23.2	27.4	— 25.4
Net change in banking credit to the public sector	38.6	5.0	25.3
Net change in banking credit to the private sector	38.2	67.6	100.1
Change in mortgage loans	(2.8)	(0.8)	(1.7)
Change in other loans and credit	(35.4)	(66.8)	(98.4)

Sources and method: Same as in Table 6.8.

rather substantial increases in credit to both the public and the private sector, under pressure from the industrial sector and the more "development-minded" members of the Frondizi administration, while foreign-exchange reserves fell.

Even during the second half of 1959 the conditions of credit stringency were to some extent offset by the increased efficiency and vigor of the domestic capital market. The free market for foreign exchange, both for spot and future transactions, facilitated foreign borrowing by Argentine entrepreneurs.[34] The Buenos Aires stock

---

[34] During the middle of 1960, a loan at an interest of 14 per cent per annum from foreign lenders was considered to be both "sensible and possible." Many Argentine firms, however, appear to have exceeded prudent limits in their increase of short and medium foreign indebtedness during 1961, much of which took the form of supplier credits. The devaluation of April 1962 hit these firms with special force due to their large short-term dollar debts, as they had not

market, although showing sporadic nervousness regarding political events, underwent a remarkable expansion of activity during 1959–1961, which allowed many firms to obtain long-term capital at fairly attractive terms. The Argentine Treasury also made a modest start in September 1959 in promoting a free market for government securities, especially treasury bills, while official mortgage institutions began to float mortgage certificates in the capital market in December 1960, after depending for fourteen years primarily on Central Bank credit to finance private housing. Nonbank finance companies mushroomed during 1960 and 1961, mainly in relation to the financing purchases of consumer durable goods, such as automobiles, television sets, and so on.[35]

In summary, it appears that monetary policy during 1959, and to a lesser extent during 1960 and 1961, tended to have a mildly depressing influence on the level of real absorption, especially on the level of real investment in housing. However, substantial increases during 1959–1961 in the cash flow or gross nonwage income of entrepreneurs and the improved efficiency of the money markets tended to offset the depressing features of monetary policy.

4. Fiscal Policy

Another potentially autonomous influence on absorption and output following a devaluation, not taken explicitly into account in the model of Chapter 2, is the fiscal policy of the public sector. As pointed out in the previous section, while public sector net borrowing from the banking system remained at a rather high level during 1959, it fell from the extraordinary figure of 1958, suggesting a drop in the deficit of the public sector. Table 6.10 confirms this inference, showing that a cut in expenditure, rather than an increase in real tax collections, was responsible for the improved fiscal position dur-

---

hedged against devaluation. In the same article it is remarked that the Treasury did not have to pay in the free money market more than 12 per cent for one-year money. See *The Review of the River Plate*, June 10, 1960.

[35] These companies were able to attract substantial amounts of liquid funds, as they were not subject to the interest-rate ceilings of around 10 per cent fixed by the Central Bank for commercial banks. During 1961 their influence on the money market became very strong; it was estimated at the time that the volume of funds attracted to these companies reached at least 10 per cent of the money supply. It is also said that a considerable share of these funds came from the rural sector.

TABLE 6.10
Revenues and Expenditures of the Public Sector in Argentina, 1958–1961
(In percentages of the gross national product at market prices)

	1958	1959	1960	1961
1. Current Revenues of the General Government	16.2	15.3	18.3	19.7
Tax revenues	11.0	10.9	13.4	14.5
(indirect taxes)	(8.3)	(8.6)	(10.3)	(11.2)
(direct taxes)	(2.7)	(2.3)	(3.1)	(3.3)
Social security revenues	5.0	4.2	4.6	5.1
Other current revenues	0.2	0.2	0.3	0.1
2. Expenditures of the General Government and Real Investment of Public Enterprises	21.6	17.8	18.9	20.5
Consumption expenditures of general government	9.6	8.5	8.7	9.6
Interest on the public debt	0.2	0.2	0.2	0.2
Net subsidies, primarily for operating deficits of public enterprises	2.5	1.1	0.8	0.7
Transfer payments to families, primarily social security	3.9	3.9	4.1	4.8
Public sector real-fixed investment (general government plus public enterprises)	5.4	4.2	5.1	5.1
3. (2) minus (1)	5.4	2.5	0.7	0.8
4. Net Public Sector Borrowing from the Banking Sector	5.8	3.1	0.4	1.2

Sources and method: Basic data for Sections 1 and 2 obtained from *Cuentas Nacionales de la República Argentina, op. cit.,* except for the net savings of public enterprises, which was obtained from the worksheets of the Consejo Nacional de Desarrollo. Those net savings were subtracted from subsidies to producers by the general government. Section 4 obtained as in Table 5.5. Tables 6.10 does not present a complete picture of public-sector revenues and expenditures, as it was not possible to obtain a detailed breakdown of revenues and expenditures on capital account other than real-fixed investment and the net borrowing from the banking system. Thus, borrowing from the nonbanking public and foreign sources, changes in Treasury cash balances (other than deposits with the banking system), changes in unpaid obligations of the Treasury, purchases of existing assets, and so on, are not taken into account. However, these items were relatively unimportant during these years, as implied by the comparison of Sections 3 and 4.

ing 1959.[36] As a matter of fact, in spite of the higher revenues arising from the new import and export taxes, real current revenues fell during 1959. When the rapid pace of inflation during 1959 and the rather archaic budgetary practices of the Argentine central and provincial governments is considered, it becomes hard to state whether the drop that took place in real expenditures during 1959 was intended or induced by the inflation. It is likely that some real cut was intended, but especially with regard to the real value of the wages and salaries payed to civil servants, a considerable part of the cut was induced by the increase in the price level, in a way not too different from the mechanism discussed in Chapter 2.[37] A cut in expenditure which can be placed in the voluntary category is the decrease in real net subsidies from the general government to cover the operating deficits of state enterprises, primarily railways, but also including urban transportation, an international and national airline, and many other minor enterprises. It will be remembered that an announced intention of the stabilization plan was to raise the fees and prices charged by public utilities and enterprises to reduce their operating deficits, which for several years have plagued the finances of the public sector.

On balance, the fiscal policy followed during 1959, when contrasted with that followed in 1958, reinforced the output depressing features of the redistributive effect and of the monetary policy of that year. However, with a deficit of nearly 3 per cent of the gross national product (the second highest deficit of the period 1950–1961), it is difficult to consider the fiscal policy followed during 1959 deflationary.

The recovery years of 1960 and 1961 witnessed a further contraction of the fiscal deficit as a proportion of the gross national product, as tax revenues rose sharply because of the import and export

[36] As explained in the notes to Table 6.10, the figures on which this table is based are incomplete, as they do not include expenditures on capital account other than real fixed investment. However, they give the main features of fiscal developments during these years, as confirmed by a comparison of rows 3 and 4, which were obtained from independent sources. It should be noticed that real gross national product fell between 1958 and 1959.

[37] Two concepts of the real expenditures and participation of the public sector in the gross national product may be distinguished. As will be seen below, if public sector expenditures are measured at constant prices of a given year, the drop in public consumption from 1958 to 1959 becomes much smaller than that suggested by the decrease in the share of this consumption in the gross national product. This is due to the change in the "terms of trade" of the consumption of the public sector (mainly wages) vis-à-vis the rest of the economy. Similar considerations apply to public investment.

taxes and other tax and administrative reforms tackled by the government, and as net subsidies to public enterprises continued to diminish, at least until the second half of 1961, following further increases in their fees and prices and to minor improvements in their efficiency. A modest attempt was made by the national government to finance part of the remaining deficit by floating public securities with the general public. Some foreign aid was also used to cover the shrinking deficit.[38] Progress was made during these years in reducing and rationalizing governmental and public enterprise bureaucracy, although the reduction in the number of civil servants was not immediately reflected in a decrease in expenditures, due to the heavy indemnity payments associated with dismissals.[39] During the latter part of 1961, however, the fiscal deficit started to expand once again, mainly as a result of wage increases granted to civil servants and to a deteriorating financial situation in the state railways.

Several small government owned industrial enterprises were liquidated during 1960 and 1961, and steps were taken to reorganize the public oil, coal, and steel corporations, which continued to lose influence vis-à-vis private capital in their respective fields. The government warned these public corporations to raise capital on their own and not to expect as in the past to be provided with capital funds from the Treasury. The government also reorganized the institutional arrangements in the field of electricity, creating an autonomous public corporation for the Buenos Aires area, which with the financial help of the World Bank launched a large investment program. However, in this flurry of fiscal activity nothing was done to decrease the budget of the Armed Forces, which amounted to about 40 per cent of the consumption expenditures of the national government during these years.

Another important feature of fiscal policy during 1959–1961 (and

---

[38] On the other hand, the practice of reducing the cash deficit by failing to meet Treasury obligations to civil servants and contractors was also resorted to, to some extent, although not reaching the extremes witnessed during 1962–1963.

[39] Employment in general government, which had grown by a total of 11 per cent between 1955 and 1958, grew by only 3 per cent between 1958 to 1961. During this latter period the personnel of the central administration was cut, but that of local governments seems to have increased. Employment in public enterprises appears to have been reduced between 1958 and 1961, but the thorny problem of excess manpower in the state railways (estimated at about 30 per cent of its labor force in 1961) was not tackled until late in 1961. At that time the government efforts to rationalize the railways met with stiff opposition from railway workers, who in effect emerged victorious after a prolonged strike.

in later years) was tax concessions to investments undertaken in areas considered especially important by the government. As most of these areas fell into the export and import substituting sectors, these incentives in general reinforced those arising from the devaluation. Foreign capital and the rural sector were especially favored in these tax concessions.[40] The greater reliance of the government during these years on indirect taxes, such as the sales tax and import surcharges, plus the special tax concessions that primarily benefitted high-income groups appear to have reinforced the regressive redistributive effect that followed devaluation.[41]

5. The Level and Composition of Real Absorption and Output

The redistribution of income from wage earners to non-wage earners was noted in Chapter 5 to tend to increase net hoarding in the short run, thus leading to a decline in absorption. A restrictive monetary and fiscal policy would of course reinforce such a tendency.

Between 1958 and 1959, *ex post* private family savings rose from 13.3 per cent of the gross national product to 14.0 per cent, while all net private savings rose from 14.4 per cent in 1958 to 15.2 per cent in 1959. If the private savings in 1959 are compared with the averages for 1957/1958 the increase is more marked; for 1957/1958 private family savings averaged only 10.1 per cent of the gross national product, while all net private savings averaged 11.1 per cent. All gross private savings rose from 15.5 per cent during 1957/1958 to 18.7 per cent during 1959, although the increase is much smaller if only 1958 and 1959 are compared. Table 5.1 compares the

[40] The concessions were attacked as leading to abuses which often hurt other import-competing firms. Thus, the exemption from import surcharges and customs duties of imports of machinery made by foreign and other companies was said to have damaged the domestic capital-good-producing branches of manufacturing. The large number of automobiles purchased by the rural sector under the heading of tax deductible investment also caused criticism. On the other hand, it should be remembered that the rural sector lost part of the devaluation benefits through the export taxes. For the view that tax concessions have a very minor stimulus effect on investment in Argentina see Consejo Federal de Inversiones, *Política Fiscal en la Argentina*, Tomo II, Buenos Aires, 1963, p. 606.

[41] During 1959–1961 import surcharges and export retentions accounted for about one third of the total tax receipts of the national government. Import surcharges represented around 60 per cent of that third. It was originally intended that the import surcharges were to be replaced as soon as possible by a new tariff, but the surcharges remained in force throughout the period 1959–1961.

saving rates of 1959–1961 with 1956–1958. These data taken as a whole support the presumption that the redistributive effect led during 1959 to an increase in the share of private savings and a maintenance of their real level, in spite of the fall in the real gross national product. As will be seen, real private investment declined

TABLE 6.11
PERCENTAGE CHANGES IN REAL DOMESTIC ABSORPTION IN ARGENTINA, 1958–1961

	1958 to 1959	1959 to 1960	1960 to 1961
Total Real Absorption	— 6.4	8.4	8.8
Private Consumption	— 7.9	2.0	11.1
Rural products and manufactured foodstuffs	— 8.8	3.2	6.4
Other goods and services	— 5.0	6.9	5.3
Public Consumption	— 0.3	7.5	2.1
Private Gross Fixed Investment	— 4.9	36.3	10.9
Construction	— 5.0	— 2.5	5.3
Equipment	— 4.7	65.4	13.4
Public Gross Fixed Investment	—22.1	39.9	2.9
Construction	—14.9	33.4	8.9
Equipment	—35.0	55.0	— 9.1

Sources and methods: Total real absorption includes changes in inventories (not shown) besides consumption and fixed investment. The total for private consumption is the one obtained in the national accounts as a residual, while the subtotals for rural products and manufactured foodstuffs (which also include drink and tobacco products) and for other goods and services are taken from the direct consumption estimates; the two series diverge slightly, giving rise to the discrepancy between the percentage change for the total and the ones for the two subtotals. Gross public and private investment in equipment at constant prices were obtained by applying the same proportions which public and private investment have in the investment figures for all equipment at current prices to the total investment in equipment expressed at constant prices. This procedure may overestimate the drop in public investment in equipment between 1958 to 1959. Basic data, expressed in current and 1960 prices, were obtained from *Cuentas Nacionales de la República Argentina, op. cit.*

during 1959, so that it seems quite plausible to suppose that a net voluntary increase in private hoarding took place during 1959, especially in the rural sector.

Table 6.11 shows that during 1959 total real absorption fell by more than 6 per cent, while private consumption decreased by nearly 8 per cent. Within the category of private consumption, those products that are primarily wage goods appear to have decreased the most; real meat consumption, for example, fell by more than 22 per cent from 1958 to 1959. The recovery of private consumption during 1960 and 1961 was rather slow, and seems to have been concentrated mainly in durable consumer goods purchased by relatively high-income groups. While in 1961 the real expenditure on durable consumer goods was more than 20 per cent above 1958 levels, real expenditures on nonmanufactured rural products plus manufactured foodstuffs, tobacco, textiles, leather, and rubber were nearly 3 per cent below 1958 levels.[42]

Private fixed investment declined by about 5 per cent during 1959, or by considerably less than private consumption. Besides the tighter monetary policy, another basic factor accounted for this decline. The sectors which as a result of devaluation received incentives, as well as funds, to expand their output were slower in drawing up and implementing their investment plans than those other sectors (home-good industries) which received the opposite signals from the devaluation and the stabilization policies. Thus, private investment in housing shrank at a faster rate than investment in the rural sector or on most import-competing industries expanded; the decrease in real gross private investment in housing is estimated in nearly 12 per cent between 1958 and 1959, while real gross fixed investment in the rural sector remained during 1959 at roughly the same level of 1958,[43] and fresh investments in import-substituting sectors outside oil only began to get under way in late 1959. It is also possible that many entrepreneurs held up their investment expenditures involving imported equipment during 1959 pending the re-

[42] Undoubtedly this change in the pattern of private consumption reflected, besides the change in income distribution, such factors as the increased availability during 1960/1961 (and/or lower real prices) of such durable goods as automobiles and the operation of Engel's law. But the sharp divergence in the evolution of the real consumption of wage and nonwage goods cannot be explained without reference to the redistribution of income. Data obtained from *Cuentas Nacionales de la República Argentina, op. cit.*

[43] The estimate for private housing investment is based on rough data made available by the Consejo Nacional de Desarrollo. According to these data, the annual percentage changes in private housing and nonhousing construction were as follows:

	1958 to 1959	1959 to 1960	1960 to 1961
Private housing	—11.7	—13.2	3.8
Other private construction	7.6	14.1	7.2

Data on gross fixed investment in the rural sector were obtained from A. Ferrer and A. Fracchia, *La Producción, Ingresos y Capitalización del Sector Agropecuario en el Período* 1950–1960, typewritten, Buenos Aires, 1961. Since during 1959, the slaughtering of cattle herds came to an end and a gradual rebuilding of cattle stocks took place, total gross rural investment, including changes in stocks, showed an increase in 1959 over 1958.

moval, partial or total, of the special import surcharges and deposits decreed in December 1958, which were gradually relaxed during late 1959 and 1960/1961.

Private nonhousing investment boomed during 1960 and 1961, especially in the import-competing sector of the economy, although substantial increases in fixed investment seem also to have taken place in the rural sector. The increase in real nonwage income that took place during 1959 and the price incentives created by devaluation appear to have been only one among many factors that led to this development. In the import-competing sector, other government policies had a greater influence on the investment boom than the devaluation and the redistributive effect. Besides the oil policy, special arrangements including tax concessions and other special benefits were made with foreign and domestic firms to expand the chemical, motor vehicle, metal, and other key "dynamic" industries. Private direct foreign capital poured into these industries, while foreign suppliers' credits, portfolio investments, and patent and licensing agreements helped to finance and support other private Argentine undertakings. The expansion in absorption that this boom generated during 1960 and 1961 was almost automatically matched during most of this period by the increase in the foreign private capital inflow; it was not until late in 1961 when the balance-of-payments situation began to show signs of serious trouble.

The drop in public-sector investment that took place during 1959 contributed to the general decrease in absorption; total public-sector absorption (consumption plus investment) measured in constant prices fell by about 8 per cent in that year. During 1960 and 1961, real public investment surpassed the 1958 levels. Public foreign capital played some role in this expansion, as foreign funds were channeled into long-neglected social overhead sectors, such as electricity. Public-sector real absorption rose by 18 per cent in 1960 and by an additional 2 per cent in 1961.[44]

[44] Because of the drop in the relative prices of investment in construction and in the real wages of civil servants during 1958–1961 the share of public-sector absorption in the gross national product, both measured at current prices, remained during 1959–1961 below the level of 1958. See Table 6.10. The relative prices of investment in both private and public construction have shown a downward trend since reaching a peak during 1949–1951. On the other hand, the relative prices of durable producers' equipment for both public and private investment were raised further by the devaluations and import surcharges levied during 1955–1961. The evolution and importance of the relative prices for capital goods in Argentina since 1935 cannot be fully discussed in this study and will be analyzed elsewhere.

Real output also fell following the devaluation, although by a smaller percentage than the decrease in total absorption. The real gross domestic product fell by nearly 5 per cent during 1959, as shown in Table 6.12. Among major industries producing exportables and importables the only one showing a sharp increase in output in 1959 is the petroleum sector, whose performance arose primarily from an ad hoc policy and not from devaluation. Rural output re-

TABLE 6.12
PERCENTAGE CHANGES IN TOTAL AND SECTORIAL
OUTPUT IN ARGENTINA, 1958–1961

	1958 to 1959	1959 to 1960	1960 to 1961
Gross Domestic Product	— 4.6	5.9	5.9
Rural, including fisheries	— 0.7	—0.4	— 1.7
(Agriculture)	(— 2.8)	(1.0)	(— 5.0)
(Livestock)	(2.5)	(— 3.4)	(0.7)
Mining	16.8	41.0	32.4
(Petroleum)	(25.7)	(57.5)	(39.8)
Manufacturing	— 7.4	5.8	7.5
("Vegetative")	(— 9.4)	(0.2)	(0.1)
("Dynamic")	(— 6.4)	(12.9)	(15.7)
Construction	— 8.6	8.1	7.1
Commerce and transport	— 8.3	12.7	9.9
Communications and electricity	— 2.0	7.1	15.5
General government	— 0.3	0.6	0.9
Other service sectors	1.6	2.3	2.1

Sources and methods: Basic data obtained from *Cuentas Nacionales de la República Argentina, op. cit.* "Dynamic" branches of manufacturing include paper and pulp, chemical products, rubber and metal products, vehicles and machinery (electrical and nonelectrical), stone and glass products, and petroleum derivatives.

mained roughly at the 1958 levels; an increase in livestock production (including increases in cattle stocks) was more than offset by a drop in agricultural output. Manufacturing branches most closely associated with the production of home- or wage-goods ("vegetative" industries) suffered the sharpest drop in output, while construction and most tertiary activities also fell.

The year 1959 witnessed an unusual number of strikes in the urban centers, but it does not appear that such strikes had an autonomous influence on the level of output. Indeed, it is alleged that in many cases employers arranged with cooperative trade-union leaders for strikes in the plants, as a way to work off excessive inventories while avoiding the payment of wages.[45] The fact that inventories of most industrial products grew in an involuntary fashion during 1959 provides a clear indication that the drop of industrial production of home goods in that year was caused by a corresponding decline in real purchasing power among wage earners. At a time of tight credit conditions and when the removal of capricious controls over foreign trade eliminated the need for large stocks of imported materials, an increase in inventories such as the one which took place during 1959 could only be unintended.[46]

Total gross domestic product recovered during 1960 and expanded further during 1961, but in 1961 it had reached a level only 7 per cent above 1958. Most disappointingly, rural output continued to stagnate during these years. Weather conditions appear to have had part of the blame for the failure of the rural sector to respond after a one-year lag to the incentives generated by the devaluation; the index of rainfall developed in Chapter 4 stood during 1959/1960 more than 10 per cent below the level of 1957/1958. According to Equation 4.2, for example, the output of cereals and linseed during 1960/1961 could have been expected on this basis alone to be 9 per cent below its 1958/1959 levels; in fact output of cereals and linseed fell by nearly 11 per cent between 1958/1959 and 1960/1961. It should also be remembered that the gains obtained by the rural sector, especially livestock producers, in 1959 were eroded during 1960 and 1961 by increases in industrial prices. Finally, during these years the rural sector continued to be plagued by steadily deteriorating social overhead capital, such as railroads, harbors, and stor-

---

[45] Discussing the increase in strikes in Argentina during 1959 the World Trade Information Service of the United States Department of Commerce commented: "As the year ended, however, a less intransigent labor attitude developed, a condition stemming in part at least from a willingness by some industrial sectors to welcome strikes as a means of reducing excessive inventories." United States Department of Commerce, *Economic Developments in the Western Hemisphere*, 1959. p. 7. On January 21, 1960, *The Review of the River Plate*, p. 17, stated: "There are many sectors of industry and trade today where, because of declining sales and large inventories, the employers' interests are probably better served than their workers' by the implementation of a threatened strike."

[46] Inventories of imported products were reported to have been drawn down during 1959 as importers waited for the removal or relaxation of the heavy surcharges and deposits levied since January 1959. For further evidence that inventories of domestic industrial products grew during 1959, see the memorandum presented to the government by the Unión Industrial Argentina, an association of industrial producers, on October 1959, where references are made to a growing accumulation of stocks of construction materials and other products. See *The Review of the River Plate*, October 20, 1959, p. 17.

age facilities. Yet even after taking these considerations into account, we find that rural performance during 1959–1961 showed a rather inelastic response to the 1959 incentives. The increase in capital formation and mechanization which took place in the rural sector during 1960–1961 showed in the output figures only as an offset to poorer weather conditions, perhaps due to the nature of these investments, which were primarily aimed at substituting machine power for manpower, rather than accomplishing substantial changes in rural technology.[47]

The recovery and expansion of output during 1960/1961 was led by oil and the import-substituting "dynamic" branches of manufacturing producing consumer durables, intermediate and capital goods. These industries plus oil were favored by direct foreign investors, often as a result of ad hoc arrangements with the government. Impressive output gains were registered between 1958 and 1961 by vehicles and machinery (61 per cent), rubber manufactures (51 per cent), and electrical machinery and appliances (34 per cent). Output of automobiles soared, in spite of prices two and three times those in the United States and Western Europe for comparable models. On the other hand, the output of branches of manufacturing producing mainly wage goods remained during 1960/1961 at depressed levels, often below 1958 output. Private investment in the "dynamic" industries plus public investment helped the construction industry to recover and expand in 1960–1961.

The evolution of absorption and output during 1959/1961 shows that while the short-run impact of devaluation in 1959 followed the outlines of the model of Chapter 2, 1960/1961 failed to bring the relative reallocation of resources needed to consolidate the balance-of-payment gains of 1959/1960 in a context of rapid economic growth. Some progress was made with the help of foreign funds in the fields of import substitution, social-overhead capital, and government organization; but it was not enough to offset the negative influence of the stagnant rural sector on the balance of payments, which again got into serious trouble late in 1961 and early 1962.

[47] During 1963–1965 it appeared that the efforts of earlier years were beginning to pay off, albeit with a considerable lag. Large crops were obtained in those years, but under very favorable weather conditions. It remains to be seen whether such expansions in rural output will prove to be permanent. It may also be noticed that the national accounts figures for the rural sector may have a slight downward bias, as they exclude some crops (for instance, sorghum) which expanded very rapidly during the last decade.

6. The balance of payments

As a result of the greater fall in absorption than in output during 1959 and of a slight improvement in the external terms of trade, the balance on current account improved by $270 million dollars between 1958 and 1959 as shown in Table 6.13. Net holdings of gold and foreign exchange by the monetary authorities rose, resulting primarily from the capital inflow in 1959.

TABLE 6.13
THE ARGENTINE BALANCE OF PAYMENTS, 1958–1961
(*In million United States dollars at current prices*)

	1958	1959	1960	1961
Balance on Current Account	— 256	14	— 197	— 572
Merchandise exports	994	1,009	1,079	964
Merchandise imports	—1,233	— 993	—1,249	—1,460
Net profit and interests	— 31	— 40	— 57	— 102
Net other services	14	38	30	27
"Autonomous" Capital Flows	32	63	457	349
Net private capital and unilateral transfers	— 17	75	318	272
Net official long term capital	49	— 12	139	77
Official and Banking Short-Term Capital and Monetary Gold	239	— 76	— 257	226
Errors and Omissions	— 16	— 1	— 3	— 2

Sources and method: Same as in Table 3.1. A negative sign indicates a debit entry.

It may be seen that the improvement in the balance of trade during 1959 was due almost exclusively to a drop in the dollar value of merchandise imports of nearly 20 per cent with respect to 1958 and 24 per cent with respect to 1957. A decrease from 1958 to 1959 in foreign prices for imports of around 6 per cent contributed significantly to this development. According to the import classification used in Chapter 3, the import quantum of capital goods actually rose during 1959, while the volume of imports of consumer and intermediate goods and raw materials fell sharply (by nearly 21 per cent).[48] It seems clear that the main cause for the drop of between

[48] The main increase in imports of capital goods (at constant prices) came in industrial machinery. See United Nations, Economic Commission for Latin America, *Statistical Bulletin for Latin America*, Vol. I., No. 1, mimeographed,

12 and 14 per cent in the over-all import quantum was the decrease of more than 6 per cent in domestic absorption in that year. However, other influences contributed to this result. As mentioned previously, scattered evidence suggests that many producers allowed their inventories of imported raw materials and intermediate products to run down during 1959 in anticipation of a relaxation of the import surcharges and deposits in effect since January 1959; all prior deposits were abolished and most of the surcharges on imports of capital goods not produced domestically were removed during the third and fourth quarters of 1959. The ratio of the wholesale price index of manufactured imported goods to the price index of domestically produced manufactured goods rose by more than 25 per cent between 1958 and 1959; although the price elasticity of demand for imports is very low in Argentina, as noted in Chapter 3, such sharp change was bound to have some effect on the import quantum, if for no other reason than the expectation of entrepreneurs that the relative prices of imported goods were bound to come down again in later years, as indeed they did in 1960 and 1961. On the other hand, the elimination of quantitative restrictions over imports and the increased vigor of the capital inflow tended to limit the extent of the decrease in imports during 1959. As a matter of fact, several domestic industries complained that the net result of the elimination of quantitative import restrictions, devaluation, and import surcharges had been a lower level of effective protection against foreign competition, especially during late 1959 and 1960–1961 when many import surcharges were eliminated or lowered.[49]

New York, March 1964. It should be observed that the classification followed in Chapter 3, which corresponds to that used by the Economic Commission for Latin America, differs from the import classification of the Dirección Nacional de Estadística y Censos in Buenos Aires. According to the latter, the quantum of all eleven import categories fell between 1958 and 1959 with the exception of textiles. Argentine official statistics record imports when these go through customs, rather than when they arrive to Argentine soil, causing further difficulties in the interpretation of very short-run events, as the stock of imported goods in harbor warehouses has shown considerable fluctuations from time to time. For example, the drop in the import quantum during the first quarter of 1959 reflects primarily the refusal of many importers to take their goods out of the harbor warehouses because of a bitter disagreement with the government regarding the application of the new import surcharges.

[49] Domestic producers of capital goods were the ones that complained the most, especially about the exemption from import surcharges and duties granted to foreign investors who brought into Argentina their own capital equipment. However, the share of domestically produced new equipment and machinery (excluding motor vehicles and tractors) in the total investment in new machinery and equipment, excluding tractors and motor vehicles, rose from 44 per

The redistribution of income during 1959 also tended to limit the fall in the import quantum, due to the observed higher marginal propensity to import of non-wage earners than wage earners. However, the higher level of imports of capital goods and disguised luxury goods (that is, parts of automobiles, television sets, and so on) which such redistribution helped produce did not begin to have much influence on imports until late in 1959. In other words, the depressing influence on output of the redistributive effect and of monetary and fiscal policy more than offset the tendency of the redistributive effect to raise the *average* propensity to import.

The dollar value of merchandise exports rose by less than 2 per cent between 1958 and 1959 and by less than 4 per cent between 1957 and 1959, reflecting primarily an increase in the quantum index. As in the case of the 1955 devaluation, we have the paradoxical situation where a sector relatively more favored by the devaluation, in this case, meat, decreases its contribution to total exports, while a less-favored sector, that is, grains, still manages to maintain and expand its contribution, keeping the over-all export quantum roughly unchanged, or with a minor increase. The larger grain exports of 1959[50] were due primarily to the favorable 1958/1959 crop, for which the measures announced late in December 1958 came too late to have much impact on its economic decisions. However, the larger exports of grains (and wool) during 1959 were also influenced by the lower level of real domestic absorption during 1959, which freed a greater share of the production of exportables for foreign consumption.[51]

The swing from cattle into grains which took place during 1956–

---

cent during 1956–1958 to 47 per cent during 1959–1961. These complaints seem more justified for the following two years, 1962/1963, when the domestic share fell to 36 per cent, in spite of considerable balance-of-payments difficulties and existing excess capacity in the domestic industry. Data obtained from worksheets of the Consejo Nacional de Desarrollo.

[50] Between 1958 and 1959 the export quantum for wheat rose by 13 per cent, that for corn by 60 per cent and that for linseed oil by 34 per cent. Wool exports also rose substantially (by 27 per cent) between 1958 and 1959. Data obtained from the International Monetary Fund, *International Financial Statistics*.

[51] Other special circumstances were also present. Thus, the large increase in corn exports can also be attributed in part to the greater domestic use of sorghum as animal feed, which liberated the corn previously used for that purpose for foreign consumption. As mentioned previously, sorghum output has grown very rapidly during the last decade. In the case of wool, part of the large increase in exports was generated by drawing down wool stocks which were at a high level during 1958. Wool output rose by only 1 per cent between 1958 and 1959, but by a larger percentage with respect to 1957.

1958 was reversed starting in 1959 as a result of the shift of grain and beef prices in favor of the latter. While a shift from cattle into grains may give in the short run a misleading impression of large increases in exportable rural output, as during 1956/1957, the reverse shift creates a more delicate short-run situation, for it does not yield an immediate increase in the availability of beef (as cattle producers will reduce their slaughter and will build up their herds, a process that will take one or two years). From 1958 to 1959, the weight of slaughtered beef cattle fell by nearly 24 per cent, decreasing by a further 3 per cent between 1959 and 1960, but the drop of cattle herds that began in 1956 was reversed starting in 1959. The impact of this decrease in current availabilities of beef on the beef-export quantum was dampened by a decrease of nearly 25 per cent in the domestic consumption of beef between 1958 and 1959, which however increased slightly, by 5 per cent, between 1959 and 1960. As a result of these trends in the domestic production and consumption of beef, the quantum of meat exports (mostly beef) fell by 21 per cent between 1958 and 1959 and by a further 18 per cent from 1959 to 1960. The drastic fall in the per capita consumption of beef during 1959, perhaps the most unpopular feature of the stabilization program, was a direct result of the fall of 18 per cent in real wages per worker and of the increase by 64 per cent in the retail price of beef deflated by the cost-of-living index. The income and price elasticities of the domestic demand for beef need not be very large, given the magnitude of the changes in real wages and relative prices, to yield the observed drop in per capita consumption. The recovery of real wages and the drop in the relative retail beef prices during 1960 and 1961 resulted in higher levels of domestic consumption during those years.

The paper-thin positive balance on current account achieved in 1959 disappeared during 1960 and 1961, as imports rose sharply following the recovery of domestic absorption, and exports showed only minor gains.[52] An increase in profits and interests sent abroad, the price paid for the capital inflow, also contributed to the negative balance, especially during 1961. However, during 1960 the current account deficit was more than offset by the private and long-term public capital inflow, so that net foreign exchange reserves continued to increase. By 1961 the current-account deficit soared be-

[52] If merchandise exports and imports for 1959–1961 are valued at 1958 dollar prices, the precariously achieved surplus of 1959 in current account would become a small deficit.

yond the "autonomous" capital inflow, again causing balance-of-payment difficulties, which became more acute toward the end of 1961, reaching a climax in the first half of 1962.

Merchandise imports during 1960/1961 reflected not only the recovery of domestic absorption but also the change in its composition. The high short-run marginal propensity to import of the Argentine economy was also very much in evidence. The dollar value of imports rose by nearly 26 per cent during 1960 and by an additional 17 per cent in 1961; such increases reflected primarily an increase in the quantum indices, as dollar-import prices rose only slightly during these years. The change in the structure of domestic absorption

TABLE 6.14

STRUCTURE OF MERCHANDISE IMPORTS OF ARGENTINA, 1957–1961
(*In percentages of total merchandise imports, c.i.f., measured in constant 1955 dollar prices*)

	1957/ 1958	1959	1960/ 1961
Nondurable Consumer Goods and Miscellaneous	5.4	4.7	6.9
Durable Consumer Goods	7.1	5.3	8.9
Fuels	19.2	20.2	10.9
Other Intermediate Products and Raw Materials	45.2	41.9	40.0
Capital Goods	23.2	27.9	33.3

Sources and method: As in Table 3.3. Automobile parts and parts for other durable consumer goods are placed under the durable-consumer-goods category. Vehicles for commercial or public use, however, are included under capital goods, which also include construction materials.

in favor of fixed investment and the consumption of durable and luxury goods, which reflected the shift in income distribution, influenced a similar change in the pattern of imports, as may be partially seen in Table 6.14, which also shows the impact of the oil policy adopted in 1958 on the import bill.[53] It would have been more elegant as well as more efficient if the increase in the level of investment implied by the expanded imports of capital goods had taken place *pari passu* with the drop of real consumption in 1959, but with the high balance-of-payments deficit in 1958, such a neat path be-

[53] A complete assessment of the oil policy from the point of view of the balance of payments would of course have to take into account the profit remittances, imports of capital goods, and so on, which it generated. In a similar vein, a full analysis of the impact of the change in income distribution on the import bill would have to undertake a minute examination of the imports of raw materials, intermediate and capital goods according to the types of industries (wage- or nonwage-goods producing) which purchase them.

came rather difficult for the authorities to follow. At any rate, the heavy imports of capital goods during 1960/1961 allowed many import-substituting industries and some export industries to expand, thus providing a base for a long-run improvement in the trade balance.

The value of merchandise exports during 1960/1961 was nearly 4 per cent higher than the corresponding figures for 1957/1958, and part of this slight improvement resulted from an improvement in dollar prices for exports.[54] Considering the nature of the swing from grains into cattle and the stagnation of rural output during 1959–1961, we must attribute the slight improvements in the quantum of exports primarily to a reduction in the domestic absorption of exportables and of domestic inventories of such goods. This fall in the domestic demand for exportables, however, was much smaller than the 1959 fall in the domestic demand for importables. Even in the case of wool, the only major exportable for which significant output gains were registered during 1959–1961, the export gains surpassed the increases in output, as may be seen in Table 6.15.[55] It seems that the main reason for the drop in the domestic absorption of exportables during 1959–1961 was the lower level of real wages of this period, although in the case of beef higher relative prices also discouraged consumption in a significant way. Had it not been for the decrease in domestic absorption and the exogenous factor of the favorable 1958/1959 crops, the 1959 devaluation may very well have been followed by a drop in the volume of exports, due to the precarious nature of the shift from grains into beef. Furthermore, as shown in Table 3.2, the period 1959–1961 benefitted from an improvement in the external terms of trade relative to 1956–1958.

While respectable increases took place during 1959–1961 among

[54] The extent of the increase in export dollar prices between 1957/1958 and 1960–1961 is not clear from available data; according to the statistics of the Dirección Nacional de Estadística y Censos, average export prices rose by less than 2 per cent, while the *International Financial Statistics* (International Monetary Fund) registered an increase of 5 per cent. While the latter source also shows an increase of 1 per cent in export prices between 1957–1958, and 1959, the former yields a decline of nearly 4 per cent between those dates.

[55] Dollar prices for wool during 1959–1961 remained below the levels of 1957/1958. At first sight, the evolution of dollar prices for the major Argentine exports during 1959–1961 suggests that Argentina has *some* influence on the international prices of these commodities, especially beef. In 1960/1961 dollar prices for meat exports were about 16 per cent higher than in 1957/1958, according to the unit-value index of the Dirección Nacional de Estadística y Censos. For most major export commodities, foreign prices rose as the export quantum decreased and foreign prices fell as the export quantum increased.

exports of miscellaneous livestock and agricultural products, there were few tangible results in attempts to increase the level of exports of nontraditional manufactures (manufactures other than slightly processed agricultural and livestock products) in spite of the devaluation and other incentives, such as exemptions from export taxes and retentions and a system of "drawbacks" which returns to the exporter of manufactured goods any import taxes paid on raw ma-

TABLE 6.15
EXPORT PERFORMANCE RELATIVE TO OUTPUT
OF EXPORTABLES, 1957–1961
(*Merchandise exports in million dollars at current prices;
all output indices 1958 = 100*)

	1957–1958	1959	1960–1961
Total Merchandise Exports	984	1,009	1,022
Meat	277	259	218
Hides	59	70	75
Wool	108	121	144
Other livestock products	60	71	81
Cereals and linseed	266	293	260
Other agricultural products	156	152	189
Industrial and other products	58	44	56
All Rural Output	100	101	100
All meat slaughtering	100	79	83
Wool	100	103	108
Dairy products	100	99	98
Cereals and linseed	100	107	93
All agricultural output	100	101	100

Sources and method: Value of merchandise exports obtained from *Comercio Exterior*, Dirección Nacional de Estadística y Censos, several issues. Output indices obtained from *Cuentas Nacionales de la República Argentina*, op. cit., and *Estadísticas Básicas*, op. cit.

terials and intermediate products used in the manufacture of such goods. However, it appears that in later years (1962/1963), a further devaluation coupled with a severe domestic depression induced a significant increase in exports of nontraditional manufactures, including such sophisticated items as machine tools and motorcycles.[56]

[56] For an interesting analysis of this experience, see a study by Dr. Simón Teitel for the United Nations Conference on Trade and Development, *Argentina-Exports of Manufactures and Semi-Manufactures*, mimeographed, E/CONF. 46/78, March 1964.

The large capital inflow during 1959–1961 substantiated the efforts of the Frondizi administration to attract foreign capital into Argentina; such efforts included, besides the change in oil policy, the settlement of a long feud between the Argentine government and the American and Foreign Power Company regarding assets of the latter expropriated in 1943, and a new law of December 1958 allowing unlimited repatriation of capital and profits. A large share of the capital inflow was in private direct investments, mainly for crude petroleum production and refining, electric power production, the petrochemical and chemical industries, the motor-vehicle and tractor industries, and metal-working industries. Foreign governments and international financial institutions also contributed to the capital inflow, mainly to finance social overhead projects. An unknown fraction of the private capital inflow was of a short- or medium-term nature; the substantial outflow of private capital during 1962–1963 implies that the share of these "hot funds" and suppliers' credits in the 1959–1961 capital inflow was significant.

Besides supplying additional real resources and technical knowledge in key import-competing and social-overhead sectors, the capital inflow of 1959–1961 in general smoothed the path for the readjustment of the Argentine economy during these years. However, the external debt of the public and private sectors grew sharply. By the end of 1961, it was clear that Argentina faced a heavy repayment schedule to service not only the new debt accumulated since 1959 but also earlier debts the repayment of which had in many cases been postponed during 1959–1961 as part of the foreign cooperation in the stabilization plan.

7. *The free peso*

When Argentina adopted a unified and freely fluctuating exchange rate in January 1959, it could have been hoped that this would shed some light on the several issues surrounding the discussion of freely fluctuating versus pegged exchange rates. As pointed out previously, however, the peso became pegged by the Central Bank for all practical purposes after the first semester of 1959, and the thin and nervous exchange market during the first semester provided information of only limited value. Table 6.16 shows the performance of the peso during 1959; it can be seen that a considerable deal of fluctuation took place before the Central Bank started to enter the market in August to keep the peso around the rates of 82 and 83 per dollar.

During the latter part of 1959 and throughout 1960, the Central Bank entered the exchange market mainly as a buyer, except during brief periods when political crisis sparked raids on the peso. Thus, for that period it may be said that the Central Bank kept the peso both from fluctuating in the instable political atmosphere and from appreciating.[57] Since the main cause for the excess supply of foreign exchange at the rate of 82/83 was the capital inflow, this policy of the Central Bank for those years seems wise. Low resource mobility and the uncertainties surrounding the capital inflow indicate that it

TABLE 6.16
MONTHLY AVERAGES AND RANGE OF DAILY CLOSING OF SELLING SPOT EXCHANGE RATES IN BUENOS AIRES, 1959
(*Pesos per United States dollar*)

Month	Average	Range
January	65.9	4.0
February	66.0	1.8
March	68.3	2.6
April	73.8	11.9
May	85.4	9.0
June	90.3	11.5
July	85.1	7.5
August	84.0	2.4
September	83.4	0.9
October	82.1	1.5
November	82.8	0.7
December	83.4	0.7

Sources and method: Average and range obtained from the *Memoria Anual, 1959*, of the Central Bank. Range refers only to closing quotations.

would have been foolish to allow a temporary appreciation of the peso to damage the export and import-competing industries. The downward stickiness of domestic prices and costs and the low level of net foreign-exchange reserves during 1959 also justify the policy of keeping the peso from appreciating as a result of the capital inflow. Given the high marginal propensity to import and the history

[57] Although it can never be known what would have happened if the Central Bank had stuck to its early policy of not intervening at all in the exchange market, it is doubtful that private speculators could or would have stabilized the rate to the extent that the Central Bank did in the face of political uncertainties. This presumption is strengthened by the wild June 1959 activity in the exchange market. On June 2, the spot peso was quoted at 107 to the dollar; six days later it reached a quotation of 75. It may be pointed out that the Argentine exchange market is far from perfectly competitive, as relatively few export firms account for a high share of exchange sales.

of trade deficits of Argentina, the Central Bank did not have to worry that its policy would interfere seriously with the accomplishment of the real transfer corresponding to the capital inflow.

During the second half of 1961, but especially in the last quarter, the Central Bank began to enter the market as a systematic seller of foreign exchange.[58] The drain of reserves accelerated during the first quarter of 1962, as the Central Bank continued to peg the peso at the old 82/83 level, perhaps with an eye to the elections of March 1962. In April 1962, a new administration once again freed the peso, allowing it to fluctuate freely. These events, however, are so influenced by the profound political crisis which led to the overthrow of President Frondizi in April 1962 that any attempt to judge the policies followed during the late quarter of 1961 and the first half of 1962 on purely economic grounds would be extremely difficult.

Epilogue to the 1959–1961 Cycle

The next chapter will present several final remarks and conclusions regarding the stabilization efforts of 1959–1961. It seems desirable, however, to sketch very briefly here the main economic events that followed the 1959–1961 cycle during 1962/1963.

The new increase in the dollar price of the peso in the first and second quarters of 1962, amounting to more than 60 per cent, was accompanied by a very deflationary monetary policy and a substantial capital flight, sparked by the most severe political crisis in many years. While real output fell sharply during both 1962 and 1963, leading to open urban unemployment, the price level once again increased rapidly; between the first quarter of 1962 and the first quarter of 1963 the over-all wholesale-price index rose by 44 per cent, while wholesale rural and imported prices rose by 57 per cent. During the same period, hourly industrial money-wage rates rose by only 29 per cent, while the cost of living rose by about 33 per cent. In spite of these trends in prices and costs, the money supply was allowed to increase by only 8 per cent between the first quarters of 1962 and 1963.

In general, it appears that these events were influenced much more by political circumstances and a highly restrictive monetary policy than the early stages of the 1959 stabilization plan. While the

---

[58] In April 1961, the Bank had faced a short-lived raid on the peso, triggered by the resignation of Ingeniero Carlos Alsogaray from the cabinet.

redistributive effect seems to have also played a part in the 1962/1963 events, its influence was weaker than during 1959–1961, perhaps because of the already relatively low level of real wages in 1961.[59]

[59] Both real public expenditures and tax receipts fell during 1962/1963, the latter more than the former, resulting in an increase in the public deficit. During these years, both the public and the private sector defaulted in their financial obligations to each other; tax evasion soared while the public sector delayed its payments to civil servants and contractors. The liquidity shortage of these years resulted in a mushrooming of special private means of payments, including I.O.U.'s, checks with endless endorsements, and so on. In contrast with 1959, after the 1962 devaluation net official foreign-exchange reserves continued to drop, primarily as a result of repayments by the public sector of its external debt. The peso value of the substantial private foreign debt, mostly short and medium term, of course increased proportionally with the devaluation of April 1962, causing severe hardships to many firms in the industrial sector, whose volume of sales was declining and whose output prices moved up less than the devaluation. Apparently, few of these firms had bothered to hedge against the threat of devaluation.

7

Conclusions

The conclusions that can be derived from this study may be divided into two categories: (*a*) those regarding the usefulness of the model developed in Chapter 2 in analyzing the impact of devaluation and (*b*) those regarding the implementation of the stabilization plan of December 1958, and more generally, the stabilization policies adopted during 1955–1963.

On the Fruitfulness of the Model of Chapter 2

The model in Chapter 2 sought to work out in some detail the implications of one aspect of the impact of devaluation on the trade balance of a semi-industrialized country which had received very little attention in the theoretical literature on exchange rates. By reducing the level of domestic absorption by more than the expected drop in output, the redistributive effect was found to be a potentially powerful weapon in bringing about a short-run improvement in the balance of trade, presumably more powerful than the short-run pure-substitution effects in production and consumption. In contrast to the traditional devaluation theory, which states that domestic output and absorption will reflect and move in the same direction as changes in the trade balance, Chapter 2 suggested that at least in the short run the balance of trade improves *pari passu* with a fall in both absorption and output. Chapter 2 did not deal explicitly with the rather straightforward effects that changes in fiscal and monetary policy could have on the trade balance because of the exhaustive attention they have received in the literature.

The post-1955 Argentine experience, especially that of 1959–1961, indicates that the redistributive effect has been a key factor in the balance-of-payments mechanism of adjustment and that it has operated along the lines presented in Chapter 2. Naturally, it has not been the only factor in such mechanism, but its importance has been greater than that of short-run relative price effects (or strictly speaking pure-substitution effects), which seem to be rather low in Argentina, primarily because of a lack of resource mobility. The quantitative importance of the redistributive effect appears to be roughly at par with that of changes in fiscal and monetary policies; on some occasions, the latter loomed greater in importance, as during 1962/1963, while in others the reverse was true, as during 1959.

The abstract and simplified scheme of Chapter 2 left out many variables which in the real world determine the precise magnitude and impact of the redistributive effect in any one specific circumstance. Thus, such other factors as the timing of devaluation within the price-wage inflationary spiral, price and income slippages due to the existence of goods other than pure F goods (both importable and exportable) and pure home goods, the existence or removal of price controls, asymmetries, and lags in the reactions of the expenditures of income-gainers and income-losers to income redistribution have to be taken into account when discussing the Argentine experience of 1955–1961. Yet these qualifications could be easily fitted into the framework provided by the abstract model of Chapter 2, thus proving its usefulness in guiding the analysis, rather than destroying its validity.

The Argentine experience also supports the choice of a short run of about a year as the critical period of analysis following a devaluation. Indeed, due to the more or less relentless upward movement of industrial prices and the pegging of the exchange rate following major devaluations, after one or two years most of the changes in relative prices brought about by devaluation had been wiped out, leaving little room for long-run pure substitution effects to operate. The model of Chapter 2 (turned upside down) has also been useful for analyzing the process of erosion of the short-run impact of devaluation, which can be interpreted as a mirror image of that early impact. The key variables in the one-year short run also have been seen to play the important roles in the three- or four-year stop-go politicoeconomic cycles that have characterized Argentine economic life in the last fifteen years. Thus, the conflicts between wage earners and non-wage earners, rural and urban producers, home consumption and exports, all of which are closely interrelated, are important not only in determining the level of absorption relative to output in the short run, but also in determining the composition of absorption, which has important implications for the long run. Furthermore, by introducing explicitly income-redistribution considerations into devaluation theory, it has been possible to view devaluation as just another weapon in the struggle of different sectors of the economy for larger shares in the national income.

Finally, even though a precise and exhaustive identification of importable, exportable, and home goods does not appear possible in the real world, a rough classification of that type seems indispensable for the analysis of devaluation, as the important relative changes that can be expected to occur following a devaluation will be those between home goods and both F goods, rather than those between importables and exportables.

Observations on the 1959–1961 Stabilization Efforts

It is clear that late in 1958 the deterioration of the Argentine balance of payments had reached such a point that corrective measures were required. The objectives of the plan announced in December 1958, which fitted neatly in the world-wide trend toward the elimination of controls over trade and capital flows, were to stop the inflation and to achieve both balance-of-payments equilibrium and a high rate of growth in total output. The key weapons in achieving these goals were to be a return to more or less orthodox fiscal and monetary policies, a reliance on the price mechanism, and the cooperation of foreign capital. During 1959–1961 balance-of-payments equilibrium was achieved in 1959 and 1960, and a reasonable degree of price stability existed from the last quarter of 1959 to the first quarter of 1961; but in 1961 the real per capita gross national product was only between 2 and 3 per cent above the 1958 level. On the other hand, nonhousing gross fixed investment rose sharply during 1960/1961 expanding capacity in several key import-competing and social-overhead sectors of the economy and thus providing a base for future output growth. Per capita real fixed gross investment, excluding housing, was in 1961 more than 40 per cent higher than it had been during 1958. While the foreign capital inflow accounts for a substantial part of this increase, the reduction of the real consumption of wage earners also helped make possible the upsurge of investment.

Perhaps the key failure of the 1959–1961 policies was in stimulating an increase in the output of exportable goods, primarily those of rural origin. The import-intensive nature of the process of import substitution plus unavoidable gestation periods kept the efforts made during 1960/1961 in the field of importable goods from showing quick results in improving the foreign-exchange position of Argentina.[1] Although real investment seems to have also risen in the rural sector during 1960/1961, its impact on output was not noticeable. Bad weather, the continued outflow of rural laborers into urban zones, and other exogenous factors may account for such a disappointing result; but it also seems that rural investment was not in the quantity and of the quality needed to raise agricultural productivity rapidly.

Even the modest achievements of 1959/1960, that is, balance-of-payments equilibrium and price stability in 1960, as well as other minor ones,[2] began to crumble during 1961 and collapsed dramatically during 1962/1963. It does not appear warranted to consider the events of 1962/1963 as a logical result of the continuation of the policies of 1959–1961. One may speculate that a new (but relatively minor) devaluation was inevitable during 1962 if the unified free-exchange market was to be maintained, and that such an event was likely to result in a drop in output. Furthermore, it is true that the cycle 1959–1961 had left behind it a very high level of foreign indebtedness with an unfavorable repayment schedule, which created additional pressure on the balance of payments, and that the output of the rural sector remained stagnant or even declined during 1962/1963 in spite of new incentives,[3] thus continuing to limit the extent of any potential over-all growth consistent with balance-of-payments equilibrium. On the other hand, the 1959–1961 cycle also

[1] The oil policy may be an exception, although even in this case the higher profit remittances and substantial direct and indirect import requirements decreased considerably the net savings of foreign exchange.

[2] Among other achievements of the 1959–1961 policies the following may be listed: a slight improvement in the efficiency and financial position of several public enterprises (but not in railways), a rebirth of an effective domestic financial market and gains in labor productivity in several branches of production and in general government because of more rational working rules. However, these gains in average labor productivity were offset from the point of view of the economy as a whole by a growing amount of open and disguised urban unemployment of labor and excess capacity in many industries, especially during 1959/1960 and 1962/1963. The oil policy, at least from the point of view of output and merchandise imports, continued to yield substantial dividends throughout 1962/1963.

[3] Serious droughts adversely affected the rural sector, especially livestock, during these years. The rainfall index of Chapter 4 was during 1961/1962 more than 33 per cent below the level of 1957/1958. The fact that rural output did not fall by a greater magnitude seems to indicate that the larger investments of earlier years began to yield a modest return. Rural output has increased substantially during 1964/1965.

left behind it very large increases in productive capacity in key sectors of the economy, most of which should have begun to yield their fruits by 1961–1963. In other words, while a new three- or four-year devaluation-recession-recovery cycle was due to begin in 1962, considering the policies followed in 1959–1961, there is no reason why by late 1963 or early 1964 the economy could not have recovered the per capita levels reached in 1961. The fact that in 1963 the actual per capita gross national product was about 12 per cent below 1961 can only be explained by the disastrous combination of a most restrictive monetary policy with a political situation verging on civil war, which also accounts for the exaggerated fall in the value of the peso in 1962.

With regard to the short-run impact of devaluation in 1959 and early 1960, it appears that a closer coordination between the drop in real consumption and residential construction and increases in real investment in key sectors of the economy, with the help of foreign capital, would have been desirable. Such a policy would have yielded a smaller improvement in the balance of payments during 1959/1960, but it would have also advanced the day when investment in export and import-competing industries, as well as in social-overhead capital, would have yielded its fruits. Furthermore, this policy would have helped to make the stabilization program more palatable to the public by showing that the sacrifices made in one sector of the economy were being rewarded by expansions in other sectors. During 1959, however, both consumption and investment fell, and with the exception of the oil sector, all sectors of production either stagnated or suffered a drop in output. The government during 1959 and early 1960 put too much emphasis on the first aspect of devaluation, that is, the deflationary and redistributive effect, and not enough on encouraging the long-run effect: a reallocation of resources. Part of the increase in net foreign-exchange reserves that took place during 1959 and 1960, so painfully obtained and so wastefully employed late in 1961 and early 1962 to defend the overvalued peso, could have been used to finance higher imports associated with a more vigorous expansion of key sectors of the economy in 1959/1960.

The understandable reaction against unfortunate past experiences with government intervention in the economy led the Argentine economic authorities to a rather extreme faith in laissez-faire and its short-run effectiveness. A more careful planning of the stabilization efforts, especially of their short-run impact, and the simultaneous adoption of direct measures in the fields of rural and urban investments above and beyond those signalled by the price mechanism, as well as of other nonprice policies, would have resulted in a smoother transfer of resources toward the bottleneck areas of the economy and a greater increase in their productivity. Such policies would also have tended to reduce the social and political conflicts of these years; a greater preoccupation with the short run in December 1958 could have had a handsome social as well as economic payoff during the following years.

The Price Mechanism, Devaluation, and Stabilization: Some Final Comments

The Argentine experience of 1955–1961 illustrates the case of an economy that after dispensing with or at least neglecting the price mechanism as a guide for resource allocation for several years, suddenly turns to it with the hope of solving severe structural imbalances. These imbalances, generated as a result of years of neglecting necessary marginal changes in the structure of production, caused the high short-run marginal propensity to import and the stagnation in production of exportables that have plagued Argentina during the last 15 years. This situation has made it extremely difficult to achieve equilibrium in the international accounts together with a high overall rate of growth, as well as to expand investment at the expense of consumption. Under these circumstances the price mechanism, a delicate instrument most effective in inducing small changes in the structure of production and consumption, loses a great part of its usefulness. Thus, it does not follow that the remedy for imbalances caused by years of neglect of market signals (as well as by the failure to devise a system of rational planning) is a return to a complete reliance on the price mechanism as the sole guide for resource allocation. To expect that a reintroduction of free prices will significantly improve the structure and level of production in the short run requires great optimism plus an enormous faith in the entrepreneurs of the country where this experiment takes place.

In Argentina the return to a freer price system coupled with an inflationary situation and pegged exchange rates yielded violent fluctuations in relative prices. Thus, besides structural imbalances the uncertainties regarding the length of time which a given level of relative prices would be maintained further reduced the response of entrepreneurs to the price signals. The fluctuations in relative prices became more of an instrument to redistribute income than a mechanism to trigger off a desired reallocation of resources. As a matter of fact, with some prices going up in an irregular fashion by 40 per cent and others by 30 or 50 per cent a year, it was not always clear to many entrepreneurs caught in the inflationary spiral which relative prices were increasing or decreasing, much less which would fall or rise in the immediate future.

Even if the fluctuations in relative prices achieved only in the short run a redistribution of income, at least it could be said that the sectors which should be growing the most obtained the largest income gains. Such gains provided them with liquid funds that could be used to increase their productive capacity and to expand their output in the long run. Where capital markets are very imperfect, such availability of liquid funds can be of great importance in stimulating capital formation. However, if the sectors benefiting on the average from the income redistribution invest in their own sectors only a small share of those additional funds, either because of pessimism regarding the long-run prospects or because of social and institutional reasons, even this effect of the changes in relative prices will bring small social benefits. Thus, in Argentina a further factor hindering the long-run effectiveness of the stabilization plans was the apparently lower reinvestment coefficient of gross earnings of the rural sector as compared with most urban sectors.[4]

The stabilization efforts in Argentina may be criticized for not having mobilized fiscal, credit, and other direct policies more quickly and effectively to increase productivity and expand output in strategic sectors of the economy. Thus, in the field of agriculture and livestock perhaps more attention should have been given, for instance, to schemes promoting improvements in rural productivity by the subsidization of key inputs and improvement of the efficiency

[4] On the other hand, such propensity to hoard of the rural sector reinforced the output-depressing features of the redistributive effect. According to the Central Bank, the growth of domestically financed investment in 1960 was due to an increase in profits rather than a change in the plough-back coefficients of firms. It was estimated that while in manufacturing 78 per cent of profits of incorporate firms were ploughed back in rural enterprises only 50 per cent of profits were reinvested. These figures refer to a sample of only incorporated firms; see *Memoria Anual, 1960,* Banco Central de la República Argentina (Buenos Aires, 1961), p. 41. The conclusion that the rural sector as a whole has a lower than average plough-back ratio is also reached in the study of Aldo Ferrer and Alberto Fracchia, *La Producción, Ingresos y Capitalización del Sector Agropecuario en el Período 1950–1960,* typewritten, Buenos Aires, 1961.

of social-overhead facilities than to higher prices for rural outputs. While the latter benefit all rural producers, whether or not they plan to expand output and increase productivity, the former could have a more discriminating beneficial effect, which from the point of view of the rest of society is likely to be less costly. In all likelihood both types of policies are needed; the criticism is simply that the stabilization efforts did not pay enough attention to policies other than those involving a rather simple-minded yet incomplete reliance on the price mechanism, with the result that the workings of the latter influenced primarily income distribution and to a lesser extent the consumption pattern of each social group, leaving the structure of production largely unchanged.

Previous paragraphs have criticized the stabilization plan of December 1958 for an excessive reliance on the free market. Yet, as it has been pointed out, exchange-rate policy did not follow, strictly speaking, a path of laissez faire. The policy of sharp devaluations followed by a pegging of the peso tended to yield alternating periods of under- and overvaluation of the peso. Such policy aggravated the erratic gyrations of relative prices. The similarities of the circumstances under which the devaluations of November 1955, January 1959, and April 1962 were undertaken are striking. All of them took place with gold and foreign-exchange reserves nearing a vanishing point, in the midst of a frenzy of speculation and severe social and political disturbances. They were also undertaken under inflationary conditions, closely following large increases in money wages and the money supply; tighter fiscal and monetary policies tended to follow rather than precede devaluations.

Two alternative criticisms present themselves to the policy of maintaining a pegged exchange rate in a single free and unified exchange market following each major devaluation. The first, consistent with the emphasis on the price mechanism as the basic tool to allocate resources, would be to advocate exchange rates that really fluctuate freely and move *pari passu* with inflation, perhaps tending to accelerate such inflation. The key advantage of this policy is that it would avoid the erratic fluctuations in relative prices, giving a consistent encouragement to the production of importables and exportables, and could eliminate or dampen the stop-go cycles associated with massive devaluations. The opposite suggestion is to give up the unified free-exchange market and to return to an overvalued peso maintained by exchange controls. The choice between these two policies very much depends on whether one feels that long-run supply responses would improve significantly if relative prices show greater stability than in the past.

In the light of Argentine experience, it seems doubtful that a policy of complete exchange control could induce the necessary allocation of resources to obtain balance-of-payments equilibrium in the context of rapid growth, even if coupled with other direct policies aimed at raising productivity in the import-competing and export sectors. There is, of course, no reason why conceptually one could not devise exchange control and other policies which could obtain these goals; but in light of past experiences, such a possibility seems remote in practice.

The key goal should be to divorce exchange rates and other relative prices as much as possible from the determination of income distribution. If ways can be devised to tax away quasi rents brought about by changes in relative prices, a basic objection to a scheme where the exchange rate moves up more or less *pari passu* with inflation would be removed, leaving the signaling role of the price mechanism unharmed. In general, the use of fiscal instruments to tackle any features of income redistribution that may be deemed undesirable, coupled with relative prices which reflected opportunity costs in a steady fashion appears as the best policy to follow. Other direct measures would also certainly be called for in efforts to raise production of importables and exportables; a country having the twin goals of rapid growth and equilibrium in international accounts cannot afford to neglect any available mechanism that may help in such endeavor. Sole reliance on the price system is as shortsighted as a neglect of this mechanism in economic planning.

The evidence of the last twenty years regarding the long-run supply responses of producers of importables and exportables is so ambiguous that one cannot rule out the possibility that some significant long-run supply response will be forthcoming from these sectors, especially from rural producers, if relative prices are maintained at reasonably remunerative and stable levels. Tax policy can be used together with credit policy and subsidization of certain strategic inputs to discriminate against producers in these sectors whose output and productivity remain stagnant, while showering dynamic producers with facilities and rewards.[5]

---

[5] An example of a tax that would discriminate against inefficient rural producers is one based on the potential productivity of the land. The inefficiencies that would undoubtedly be present in administering such a tax are

While maintaining relative prices that reflect opportunity costs implies an exchange-rate policy which keeps devaluing the peso *pari passu* with inflation, such a policy does not necessarily imply a freely fluctuating exchange rate. Indeed, in the light of past experience it seems that while a relative freedom in export- and import-merchandise transactions should be maintained, either open or latent controls over capital flows should exist. The danger, of course, is that the authorities would be tempted to use these controls more and more as the exchange rate becomes overvalued. But this danger and the inefficiencies in the enforcement of controls over capital flows seem less important than the inefficiencies brought about by the instability likely to result if the exchange rate fluctuates freely[6] or the peso is cyclically over- and undervalued. If the exchange authorities become convinced of the desirability of allowing the rate of exchange to drift (within fairly wide "gold points") along with domestic inflation, the traumatic shocks of massive devaluations could be avoided, making the exchange controls over capital flows mainly a preventive measure.

It remains true that "equilibrium" exchange rates would tend to imply lower real wages and a lower wage share than overvalued exchange rates, at least during the early stages of this policy. Yet if such a policy is accompanied with fiscal and other direct measures that eliminate unemployment and the enjoyment of higher incomes for producers not expanding their output, the net result would be not only a higher rate of over-all output but also an amelioration of the most obnoxious features of income inequality. Workers would benefit from the elimination of the recessions which in the past have followed massive devaluations and from the steadier (and presumably higher) growth rates which would result. At any rate, it seems extremely shortsighted to use the price mechanism, including exchange-rate policy, to bring about desired changes in income distribution.

It is quite likely that a policy of more or less steady devaluation would tend to accelerate inflation. Trying to stop inflation by con-

---

likely to be more than compensated by its favorable impact on rural productivity.

[6] The far from perfectly competitive nature of the domestic exchange market and the danger of fluctuations arising from political instability indicate that private domestic speculators are unlikely to smooth out exchange-rate fluctuations. Foreign speculators could conceivably do the task, but such assertion is not self-evident in a world where information, especially about future political events, is far from perfect.

trolling a few key prices in the economy, for instance, money-wage rates or the exchange rate, would no doubt slow down the inflation, at least in the short run, but at the expense of distorting relative prices. In the light of past Argentine experience, it appears that the costs implied by a policy of "homogeneous" inflation[7] are less than the costs implied by wildly fluctuating relative prices. Furthermore, it is more likely that a social consensus on the desirability of stopping inflation will be reached when it becomes obvious that even in the short run no one gains from its existence. The issue of income distribution is at the root of the inflationary pressures, and only when an implicit agreement is reached among the several social groups will it be stopped; a "homogeneous" inflation would keep these groups from avoiding such basic issues.

The policy recommendations implicit or explicit in the previous paragraphs are rather eclectic. They advocate the use of the price mechanism, but with discriminating fiscal, credit, and other direct measures in the context of long- and short-term planning to aid it in breaking bottleneck situations and also to correct the income distribution it produces, so that its incentive value is obtained at the least possible social cost. Furthermore, they suggest a greater preoccupation with making inflation a neutral influence on relative prices rather than with trying to stop inflation all of a sudden.

Few good things can be said for the Argentine inflation of the last twenty years and even less for its continuation. Yet it would be a non sequitor to advocate on the basis of these statements a policy of trying to stop it suddenly, especially if this involves concentrating the stabilization efforts on a few prices and sectors of the economy. A gradual deceleration that maintains the relative position of different sectors at levels desired for the long run appears to be the more reasonable solution. Neither inflationary countries nor governments can be compared with alcoholics who face all or nothing alternatives for their cure. If the "shock" treatment could yield the desired results in the short run, a case could be made for it; unfortunately, the dynamics of inflation are such that even after the authorities of the country return to the most orthodox fiscal and monetary policies, the price level is likely to continue moving up for several quarters,

[7] For an interesting discussion of the dangers and advantages of a "homogeneous" inflation, see Felipe Pazos, "Notas para un estudio de la espiral inflacionaria," *El Trimestre Económico,* Vol. XXX(4), No. 120 (October–December 1963), pp. 601–619.

as a result of lags in the system,[8] while real output may suffer substantially during the transition period. The social pressures these events generate are likely to destroy the false heroics of the first stages of the stabilization plans unless, of course, a repressive and quasi-dictatorial regime pushes on with its austere policies until the fruits of the new stability begin to show. Less dramatic efforts to slow down the pace of inflation over a period of several years may or may not fail depending on the will and resolution of the government, but it is doubtful that a "shock" treatment could succeed where the "soft" treatment fails, while the unfortunate side effects on output are likely to be much greater in the case of the former than the latter. While both 1958 and 1961 were years of balance-of-payments disequilibrium and inflationary pressure, real gross domestic product was in 1958 13 per cent above 1955, while in 1961 it was only 7 per cent above the level of 1958.

Regardless of how well the stabilization efforts are planned, however, they will normally require that some groups suffer a short-run cut in their absorption. A further weakness in the "shock" theory of returning an economy to price stability and reliance on the market as practically the only guide to resource allocation is that, by its very nature, it will be adopted with a minimum of public discussion. Under the "shock" treatment, the burdens of stabilization are likely to be haphazardly distributed[9] and those bearing the greatest losses in real income are not going to be easily mollified by *ex post* appeals and meretricious references to foreign "miracles" and obsolete economic dogmas. It seems foolish as well as unfair in democratic societies not to consult in advance those groups likely to be most affected by the stabilization programs. In the long run, the success or failure of these stabilization efforts will depend more on the ability of governments to obtain a national consensus on the goals and means of economic policy than on the approval and help they may receive from foreign investors, governments, and international financial organizations.

[8] This point was stressed by A. C. Harberger in "The Dynamics of Inflation in Chile," in *Measurement in Economics: Studies in Mathematical Economics and Econometrics in Memory of Yehuda Grunfeld*, Carl Christ, et. al., eds. (Stanford: Stanford University Press, 1963), and "Some Notes on Inflation," in *Inflation and Growth in Latin America*, W. Baer and I. Kerstenetsky, eds. (Homewood, Ill.: R. D. Irwin, Inc., 1964).

[9] Although some important sectors, such as the Armed Forces, manage to escape cuts in absorption as a matter of course.

Selected Bibliography

Books

Consejo Federal de Inversiones, *Política Fiscal en la Argentina* (Buenos Aires: Consejo Federal de Inversiones, 1963), two volumes.

Ferrer, A., *La Economía Argentina* (México: Fondo de Cultura Económica, 1963).

Ford, A. G., *The Gold Standard, 1880–1914, Britain and Argentina* (Oxford: Clarendon Press, 1962).

Friedman, M., *Essays in Positive Economics* (Chicago: University of Chicago Press, 1953), "The Case for Flexible Exchange Rates," pp. 157–203.

Harberger, A. C., "The Dynamics of Inflation in Chile" in Carl Christ, *et al.*, eds., *Measurement in Economics: Studies in Mathematical Economics and Econometrics in Memory of Yehuda Grunfeld* (Stanford: Stanford University Press, 1963), pp. 219–250.

———, "Some Notes on Inflation" in W. Baer and I. Kerstenetzky, eds., *Inflation and Growth in Latin America* (Homewood, Ill.: R. D. Irwin, Inc., 1964), pp. 319–361.

Hicks, J. R., *Value and Capital* (2nd ed., London: Oxford University Press, 1946).

Johnson, H. G., *International Trade and Economic Growth* (Cambridge, Mass.: Harvard University Press, 1958), "Towards a General Theory of the Balance of Payments," pp. 153–169.

———, *Money, Trade, and Economic Growth* (London: George Allen and Unwin Ltd., 1962), "The Balance of Payments," pp. 153–168.

Kindleberger, C. P., *International Economics* (rev. ed., Homewood, Ill.: R. D. Irwin, Inc., 1958).

———, "Flexible Exchange Rates" in Commission on Money and Credit, *Monetary Management* (Englewood Cliffs, N.J.: Prentice-Hall, Inc., 1963), pp. 403–425.

Lerner, A. P., *The Economics of Control* (New York: Macmillan, 1944).

Marshall, A., *Money, Credit and Commerce* (London: Macmillan, 1924).

Meade, J. E., *The Balance of Payments and Mathematical Supplement* (London: Oxford University Press, 1951).
Metzler, L. A., "The Theory of International Trade" in H. S. Ellis, ed., *A Survey of Contemporary Economics* (Philadelphia: Blakiston, 1949), pp. 210–254.
Oficina de Estudios para la Colaboración Económica Internacional, *Economía Agropecuaria Argentina, Problemas y Soluciones* (Buenos Aires, 1964).
Pascale, A. J., and E. A. Damario, *Agroclimatología dol cultivo de trigo en la República Argentina* (Buenos Aires: Imprenta de la Universidad de Buenos Aires, 1961).
Salera, V., *Exchange Control and the Argentine Market* (New York: Columbia University Press, 1941).
Samuelson, P. A., "Disparity in Postwar Exchange Rates" in S. E. Harris, ed., *Foreign Economic Policy for the United States* (Cambridge, Mass.: Harvard University Press, 1948).
Sohmen, E., *Flexible Exchange Rates* (Chicago: The University of Chicago Press, 1961).
Robinson, J., *Essays in the Theory of Employment* (2nd ed., Oxford: Blackwell, 1947), "The Foreign Exchanges."
Tinbergen, J., *On the Theory of Economic Policy* (Amsterdam: North Holland Publishing Co., 1952).
United Nations Economic Commission for Latin America, *Análisis y Proyecciones del Desarrollo Económico: V. El Desarrollo Económico de la Argentina* (Mexico, 1959).
Williams, J. H., *Argentine International Trade under Inconvertible Paper Money 1880–1900* (Cambridge, Mass.: Harvard University Press, 1920).

Articles

Alemann, R. T., "Monetary Stabilization in Latin America," *The Journal of Finance*, Vol. XVI, No. 2 (May 1961), pp. 167–174.
Alexander, S. S., "Devaluation versus Import Restriction as an Instrument for Improving Foreign Balance," International Monetary Fund *Staff Papers*, Vol. I, No. 3 (April 1951), pp. 379–396.
———, "Effects of a Devaluation: A Simplified Synthesis of Elasticities and Absorption Approaches," *American Economic Review*, Vol. XLIX, No. 1 (March 1959), pp. 22–42.
———, "Effects of a Devaluation on a Trade Balance," International Monetary Fund *Staff Papers*, Vol. II, No. 2 (April 1952), pp. 263–278.
Beckerman, W., "Price Changes and the Stability of the Balance of Trade," *Economica*, Vol. XIX, No. 76 (November 1952), pp. 408–414.
Bernstein, E. M., "Strategic Factors in Balance of Payments Adjustment,"

International Monetary Fund *Staff Papers*, Vol. V (1956–1957). Also in the *Review of Economics and Statistics*, Vol. XL, No. 1 (February 1958), Part 2, pp. 133–142.

Bhagwati, J., and H. G. Johnson, "Notes on Some Controversies in the Theory of International Trade," *Economic Journal*, Vol. LXX, No. 277 (March 1960), pp. 74–93.

Bickerdike, C. F., "The Instability of Foreign Exchange," *Economic Journal*, 1920.

Black, J., "A Savings and Investment Approach to Devaluation," *Economic Journal*, Vol. LXIX, No. 274 (June 1959), pp. 267–274.

Brems, H., "Devaluation: A Marriage of the Elasticity and Absorption Approaches," *Economic Journal*, Vol. LXVII, No. 265 (March 1957), pp. 49–64.

———, "Foreign Exchange Rates and Monopolistic Competition," *Economic Journal*, Vol. LXIII (1953), pp. 289–298.

Bronfenbrenner, H., "Exchange Rates and Exchange Stability: Mathematical Supplement," *Review of Economics and Statistics*, Vol. XXXII, No. 1 (February 1950), pp. 12–20.

Brown, A. J., "Trade Balance and Exchange Stability," *Oxford Economic Papers*, Vol. 6 (1942).

Cheng, H. S. "Statistical Estimates of Elasticities and Propensities in International Trade: A Survey of Published Studies," International Monetary Fund *Staff Papers*, Vol. VII, No. 1 (April 1958), pp. 107–158.

Corden, W. M., "The Geometric Representation of Policies to Attain Internal and External Balance," *The Review of Economic Studies*, Vol. XXVIII(1), No. 75 (October 1960), pp. 1–23.

Díaz Alejandro, C. F., "A Note on the Impact of Devaluation and the Redistributive Effect," *The Journal of Political Economy*, Vol. LXXI, No. 6 (December 1963), pp. 577–580.

Dorrance, G. S., "The Effect of Inflation on Economic Development," International Monetary Fund *Staff Papers*, Vol. X, No. 1 (March 1963), pp. 1–47.

Ellsworth, P. T., "Exchange Rates and Exchange Stability," *Review of Economics and Statistics*, Vol. XXII, No. 1 (February 1950), pp. 1–12.

Eshag, E., and R. Thorp, "Economic and Social Consequences of Orthodox Economic Policies in Argentina in the Post-War Years," *Bulletin of the Oxford University Institute of Economics and Statistics*, Vol. 27, No. 1 (February 1965), pp. 3–44.

Ferrer, A., "Devaluación, Redistribución de Ingresos y el Proceso de Desarticulación Industrial en la Argentina," *Desarrollo Económico* (Buenos Aires), Vol. 2, No. 4 (January–March 1963), pp. 5–18.

———, "Reflexiones acerca de la política de estabilización en la Argentina," *El Trimestre Económico*, Vol. XXX(4), No. 120 (October–December 1963), pp. 5–18.

Fleming, J. M., "Exchange Depreciation, Financial Policy and the Domestic Price Level," *International Monetary Fund Staff Papers*, Vol. VI, No. 2 (April 1958), pp. 289–322.

———, "On Making the Best of Balance of Payments Restrictions on Imports," *Economic Journal*, Vol. LXI, No. 241 (March 1951), pp. 48–71.

Gerakis, A. S., "Recession in the Initial Phase of a Stabilization Program. The Experience of Finland," *International Monetary Fund Staff Papers*, Vol. XI, No. 1 (March 1964), pp. 125–149.

Graham, F. D., "The Theory of International Values Re-examined," *Quarterly Journal of Economics*, November 1923.

Haberler, G., "The Market of Foreign Exchange and Stability of the Balance of Payments," *Kyklos*, Vol. 3 (1949), pp. 193–218.

Harberger, A. C., "Currency Depreciation, Income, and the Balance of Trade," *Journal of Political Economy*, Vol. LVIII, No. 1 (February 1950), pp. 47–60.

Harrod, R. F., "Currency Depreciation as an Anti-Inflationary Device: Comment," *Quarterly Journal of Economics*, Vol. LXVI (1952), pp. 102–116.

Hemming, M. F. W., and W. M. Corden, "Import Restriction as an Instrument of Balance of Payments Policy," *Economic Journal*, Vol. LXVIII, No. 271 (September 1958), pp. 483–510.

Hinshaw, R., "Currency Appreciation as an Anti-Inflationary Device," *Quarterly Journal of Economics*, Vol. LXV, No. 4 (November 1951), pp. 447–462.

———, "Further Comment," *Quarterly Journal of Economics*, Vol. LXXII, No. 4 (November 1958), pp. 616–625.

Hirschman, A. O., "Devaluation and the Trade Balance," *Review of Economics and Statistics*, Vol. XXXI, No. 1 (February 1949), pp. 50–53.

Johnson, H. G., "International Trade, Income Distribution and the Offer Curve," *The Manchester School of Economic and Social Studies*, Vol. XXVII, No. 5 (September 1959), pp. 241–260.

Jones, R. W., "Stability Conditions in International Trade: A General Equilibrium Analysis," *International Economic Review*, Vol. 2, No. 2 (May 1961), pp. 199–209.

Kemp, M. C., "Depreciation in Disequilibrium," *The Canadian Journal of Economics and Political Science*, Vol. 25, No. 4 (November 1959), pp. 431–438.

———, "Tariffs, Income and Distribution," *Quarterly Journal of Economics*, Vol. LXX, No. 1 (February 1956), pp. 139–155.

Kenen, P. B., "Distribution, Demand, and Equilibrium in International Trade: A Diagrammatic Analysis," *Kyklos*, Vol. 12 (1959).

Kennedy, C., "Devaluation and the Terms of Trade," *The Review of Economic Studies*, Vol. XVIII(1), No. 45 (1949–1950), pp. 1–27.

Laursen, S., and L. A. Metzler, "Flexible Exchange Rates and the Theory of Employment," *Review of Economics and Statistics*, Vol. XXXII, No. 4 (November 1950), pp. 281–299.

Machlup, F., "Elasticity Pessimism in International Trade," *Economia Internazionale*, Vol. III, No. 1 (February 1950), pp. 118–141.

———, "Relative Prices and Aggregate Spending in the Analysis of Devaluation," *American Economic Review*, Vol. XLV, No. 3 (June 1955), pp. 255–278.

———, "The Terms of Trade Effects of Devaluation Upon Real Income and the Balance of Trade," *Kyklos*, Vol. 9 (1956), pp. 417–452.

———, "The Theory of Foreign Exchanges," *Economica*, Vol. VI, No. 24 (November 1939), pp. 375–397.

McKinnon, R. I., "Optimum Currency Areas," *The American Economic Review*, Vol. LIII, No. 1 (March 1963), Part 1, pp. 717–725.

Metzler, L. A., "Tariffs, the Terms of Trade and the Distribution of the National Income," *Journal of Political Economy*, Vol. LXII, No. 1 (February 1949), pp. 1–29.

Morgan, E. V., "The Theory of Flexible Exchange Rates," *Amercian Economic Review*, Vol. XLV, No. 3 (June 1955), pp. 279–295.

Mundell, R. A., "A Theory of Optimum Currency Areas," *The American Economic Review*, Vol. LI, No. 4 (September 1961), pp. 657–665.

Nurske, R., "The Relation between Home Investment and External Balance in the Light of British Experience, 1945–1955," *Review of Economics and Statistics*, Vol. XXXII, No. 2 (May 1950), pp. 117–132.

Orcutt, G. H., "Measurement of Price Elasticities in International Trade," *Review of Economics and Statistics*, Vol. XXXII, No. 2 (May 1950), pp. 117–132.

Pazos, F., "Notas para un estudio de la espiral inflacionaria," *El Trimestre Económico*, Vol. XXX(4), No. 120 (October–December 1963), pp. 601–619.

Pearce, I. F., "A Note on Mr. Spraos' Paper," *Economica*, Vol. XXII, No. 86 (May 1955), pp. 147–151.

———, "The Problem of the Balance of Payments," *International Economic Review*, Vol. 2, No. 1 (January 1961), pp. 1–28.

Polak, J. J., and T. C. Chang, "Effect of Exchange Depreciation on a Country's Export Price Level," International Monetary Fund *Staff Papers*, Vol. I, No. 1 (February 1950), pp. 49–70.

Polak, J. J., and Ta-Chung Liu, "Stability of the Exchange Rate Mechanism in a Multi-Country System," *Econométrica*, Vol. 22 (1954), pp. 360–389.

Prebisch, R., "Economic Development or Monetary Stability: The False Dilemma," *Economic Bulletin for Latin America*, Vol. VI, No. 1 (March 1961), pp. 1–26.

Salter, W. E. G., "Internal and External Balance: The Role of Price and Expenditure Effects," *Economic Record*, Vol. XXXV, No. 70 (April 1959), pp. 47–66.

Samuelson, P. A., and R. M. Solow, "Analytical Aspects of Anti-Inflation Policy," *American Economic Review*, Vol. L, No. 2 (May 1960), pp. 177–222.

Seers, D., "A Theory of Inflation and Growth in Underdeveloped Economies Based on the Experience of Latin America," *Oxford Economic Papers*, Vol. 14, No. 2 (June 1962), pp. 173–195.

Smithies, A., "Devaluation with Imperfect Markets and Economic Controls," *Review of Economics and Statistics*, Vol. XXXII, No. 1 (February 1950), pp. 21–20.

Sohmen, E., "The Effect of Devaluation on the Price Level," *Quarterly Journal of Economics*, Vol. LXXIII, No. 2 (May 1958), pp. 273–283.

Spraos, J., "Consumers' Behavior and the Conditions for Exchange Stability," *Economica*, Vol. XXII, No. 86 (May 1955), pp. 137–151.

———, "Some Strange 'Marriages' between the Income Expenditure Lag and Variable Prices," *Economica*, Vol. XXIV, No. 94 (May 1957), pp. 154–159.

———, "Stability in a Closed Economy and in the Foreign Exchange Market, and the Redistributive Effect of Price Changes," *Review of Economic Studies*, Vol. XXIV(3), No. 65 (June 1957), pp. 161–176.

Stolper, W. F., "The Multiplier, Flexible Exchanges, and International Equilibrium," *Quarterly Journal of Economics*, Vol. LXIV, No. 4 (November 1950), pp. 559–582.

Streeten, P., "Elasticity Optimism and Pessimism in International Trade," *Economia Internazionale*, Vol. VII, No. 1 (February 1954), pp. 85–112.

Sunkel, O., "La Inflación Chilena; Un enfoque heterodoxo," *El Trimestre Económico*, Vol. XXV, No. 4 (October–December 1958). Also in *International Economic Papers*, No. 10.

Ta-Chung Liu, "The Elasticity of United States Imports Demand: A Theoretical and Empirical Reappraisal," International Monetary Fund *Staff Papers*, Vol. III, No. 3 (February 1954), pp. 416–441.

Tinbergen, J., "Some Measurements of Elasticities of Substitution," *Review of Economics and Statistics*, Vol. XXVIII, No. 3 (August 1946), pp. 109–116.

Tsiang, S. C., "The Role of Money in Trade-Balance Stability," *The American Economic Review*, Volume LI, No. 5 (December 1961), pp. 912–936.

de Vries, B. A., "Devaluation and the Price of Raw Materials," International Monetary Fund *Staff Papers*, Vol. 1, No. 2 (September 1950), pp. 238–253.

White, W. H., "The Employment Insulating Advantages of Flexible Exchanges: A Comment on Professors Laursen and Metzler," *Review of Economics and Statistics*, Vol. XXXVI, No. 2 (May 1954), pp. 225–228.

Official Publications and Periodicals

Banco Central de la República Argentina, *Balances de Pagos de la República Argentina, Años 1951–58*, Suplemento del *Boletín Estadístico*, No. 1, January 1960.

———, *Boletín Estadístico*, issues from 1956 to 1964.

———, *Estadísticas Monetarias y Bancarias, Años 1940–1960*, Suplemento del *Boletín Estadístico*, No. 6, June 1962.

———, *Memoria Anual*, issues from 1958 to 1963.

———, *Revista Económica*, issues from 1937 to 1940.

———, *Transacciones Intersectoriales de la Economía Argentina*, Suplemento del *Boletín Estadístico*, No. 6, June 1962.

Consejo Nacional de Desarrollo, Presidencia de la Nación, *Cuentas Nacionales de la República Argentina*, Buenos Aires, April 1964.

Dirección General (Nacional) de Estadística y Censos de la República Argentina, *Boletín Mensual de Estadística*, issues from 1956 to 1964.

———, *Comercio Exterior*, several issues.

———, *Costo del Nivel de Vida en la Capital Federal, Nueva Encuesta sobre Condiciones de Vida de Familias Obreras, Año 1960*, Buenos Aires, 1963.

———, *Síntesis Mensual de Estadística*, issues from 1948 to 1956.

The Economist Intelligence Unit, Ltd., *Economic Review of Argentina*, quarterly issues from 1958 to 1962.

International Monetary Fund, *Annual Report on Exchange Restrictions*, issues from 1956 to 1963.

———, *Annual Report of the Executive Directors*, issues from 1956 to 1963.

———, *Balance of Payments Yearbook*, issues from 1950 to 1963.

———, *International Financial Statistics*, issues from 1950 to 1964.

Junta Nacional de Carnes, *Estadísticas Básicas*, Buenos Aires, 1963.

Katz, R., *Economic Survey*, weekly bulletins from 1959 to 1964.

Kugler, W. F., *Ideas que Animarán la Acción de la Secretaría de Agricultura y Ganadería en el período 1963–69*, Buenos Aires, October 1963.

Moyano Llerena, C., *Panorama de la Economía Argentina*, quarterly issues from 1959 to 1964.

Prebisch, R., *Final Report and Economic Recovery Programme*, A report submitted to the Argentine government, January 20, 1956.

———, *Provisional Report*, A report submitted to the Argentine government, October 24, 1955.

———, *Sound Money or Uncontrolled Inflation*, A report submitted to the Argentine government, January 20, 1956.

The Review of the River Plate, weekly issues from 1955 to 1964.

Revista de la Bolsa de Cereales, several issues.

Secretaría de Asuntos Económicos, Poder Ejecutivo Nacional, *Producto e Ingreso de la República Argentina en el Período 1935–54*, Buenos Aires, 1955.

Teitel, S., *Argentina—Exports of Manufactures and Semi-Manufactures,* Document E/CONF. 46/78 in the United Nations Conference on Trade and Development, March 1964 (mimeographed).
Tornquist and Company, E., Ltd., *Business Conditions in Argentina,* quarterly issues from 1958 to 1961.
United Nations, *Yearbook of International Trade,* several issues.
United Nations Economic Commission for Latin America, *Economic Bulletin for Latin America* and *Statistical Supplement,* several issues.
———, *Economic Survey of Latin America,* issues from 1951 to 1958.
———, *Statistical Bulletin for Latin America,* New York, March 1964.
United Nations Food and Agricultural Organization, *Production Yearbook* and *Trade Yearbook,* several issues.
United States Department of Commerce, *Economic Developments in the Western Hemisphere,* several issues.
———, *World Trade in Machine Tools, 1955–58.*

Unpublished Materials

Dagnino Pastore, J. M., *Ingreso y Dinero; Argentina, 1933–60,* mimeographed, Centro de Investigaciones Económicas, Instituto Torcuato di Tella, Buenos Aires, 1964.
Di Tella, G., and M. Zymelman, *The Economic History of Argentina,* unpublished doctoral dissertation at the Massachusetts Institute of Technology, Cambridge, Mass., 1958.
Diz, A. C., *La Oferta de Dinero en la República Argentina (1935–1962),* mimeographed, Universidad de Tucumán, Tucumán, 1963.
Ferrer, A., and A. Fracchia, *La Producción, Ingresos y Capitalización del Sector Agropecuario en el Período 1950–60,* typewritten, Buenos Aires, 1961.
Olivera, J. H. G., "El Caso de la Argentina," in Economic Commission for Latin America, *Inflation and Growth,* mimeographed, Santiago, Chile, 1962.
Polak, J. J., "Depreciation to Meet a Situation of Overinvestment," International Monetary Fund Document, unpublished, 1948.
Villanueva, J., *El Proceso Inflacionario Argentino (1943–1962),* mimeographed, Buenos Aires, 1963.

Index

Absorption, changes in, 166–169
Absorption approach, 10–11, 18, 19
Agricultural sector, 72, 74, 142, 190–191
   output indices, 74
   and relative prices, 75, 151, 157
   structure of output, 72
Alexander, S. S., 9, 10, 11, 14, 17, 104
Alsogaray, Carlos, 146, 182
Aluminum, 50
American and Foreign Power Company, 180
Armed Forces of Argentina, 148, 154, 165, 195

Backward linkage, 35
Baer, Werner, 16, 46, 159, 195
Balance of payments of Argentina, 41 ff
   in 1958–1961, 173–180
Bananas, 49
Banco Central de la República Argentina, 41, 42, 51, 66, 75, 96, 117, 141, 147, 150, 159, 160, 161, 162, 180, 181, 190
Banking system, 133, 141
Barley, 73, 78
Beef, 68, 70, 73, 76, 88, 136, 141, 147, 157, 176
   in budgets of working-class families, 89–90
   data on prices, consumption, and output, 96–99

   domestic demand for, 92
   short-run supply of, 79ff
   see also Chilled beef; Meat
Bernstein, E. M., 10, 18
Bhagwati, J., 4
Bickerdike, C. F., 2
Black, J., 9
Bottlenecks, 37
Brazil, 52, 69
Bread, in budgets of working-class families, 89–90
Brems, H., 5
Brown, A. J., 3
Budget deficits, and the price level, 117
Bureaucracy, 148, 165

Canada, 148
Capital flight, 182
Capital formation, 37–38, 60, 172
   structure of, 103ff
   see also Investment
Capital goods, 49, 50–51, 60, 174, 177, 178
   imports of, time series, 67
   relative prices of, 105, 169
Capital markets, 103, 159, 187, 190
Capital movements, 21
   see also Foreign capital; Capital flight
Capitalists, 21, 22
Cash-balance effect, 8, 24
Cattle prices, data on, 96
Cattle raising, 78
Cattle stocks, 31, 81–83, 143, 170

206 INDEX

Central bank, *see* Banco Central de la República Argentina
Cereals and linseed, 69, 73, 84, 147, 171
    data on prices and output, 96
    supply responses of, 76ff
Chemicals, 49, 50, 55, 169, 180
Chile, 119
    inflation in, 116, 122
Chilled beef, 45, 69, 71
Cocoa, 49
Coffee, 49
Commerce sector, 153
Consejo Federal de Inversiones, 166
Consejo Nacional de Desarrollo, 45, 61, 65, 66, 72, 74, 85, 90, 101, 105, 139, 153, 155, 163, 168, 175
Construction activity, 133, 170
Consumption
    changes in, 167–168
    and demand for imports, 59ff
    of exportable goods, 143, 178
    time series, 64
Corden, W. M., 6, 13, 17, 34
Corn, 68, 69, 71, 73, 78, 86, 143, 175
Cost-of-living index, 122, 136, 152
Cotton, 90

Dagnino Pastore, J. M., 118
Damario, E. A., 79
Depreciation allowances, 103
Diminishing returns, 23
Dirección Nacional de Estadística y Censos, 43, 66, 69, 75, 89, 128, 135, 142, 174, 178, 179
Direct effects, 11, 14, 17
Diz, A. C., 118
Domike, Arthur L., 86
Dorrance, G. S., 104
Droughts, 113, 116, 187
Durable consumer goods, domestic demand for, 93, 168

Economist Intelligence Unit Ltd., The, 160

Elasticity optimism and pessimism, 3, 4, 10, 20
Electrical machinery and appliances, 172
Electricity, 148, 165, 169, 180
Ellsworth, P. T., 3
"End-of-frontier" thesis, 86
Energy, 134
Erhard, Ludwig, 146
Eshag, Eprime, 149
European Common Market, 71
Excess capacity, 19
Exchange control, 52, 53, 191–192
    and imports of capital goods, 62
Exchange rate
    annual rate of change, 119, 128
    changes in, 149ff, 182
    defined, 7
    devaluation of the, 1, 24
    and income shares, 114
Exchange surcharges, 45, 146
Export prices, indices of, 43
Exportable goods, 6–7, 14, 21, 32
    in Argentina, 44ff, 68ff
    data on, 97
    domestic demand for, 87ff
    domestic supply of, 72ff, 131
    prices of, 151
    share absorbed domestically, 88
    summary of supply responses, 85ff
Exports
    changes in, 143, 175–176, 178–179
    demand for, 21, 70
    of manufactured goods, 73, 87, 111, 179
    retentions on, 147
    share in world markets, 70
    structure of, 69
    supply of, 2, 6, 7, 19, 70–71, 131
External debt, 31, 137, 142, 180, 187

Ferrer, Aldo, 20, 72, 85, 149, 168, 190
First effect, *see* Initial effect
Fiscal policy, 13, 20, 141, 162–166
Ford, A. G., 20

Foreign capital, 38, 42, 136, 142, 148, 166, 172, 176, 180
Foreign debt, *see* External debt
Foreign-exchange reserves, 41, 43, 114, 133, 142
    and quantitative restrictions, 53ff
Foreign good, 11, 17, 21, 22, 34
Foreign-trade accelerator, 9, 104
Fracchia, Alberto, 72, 85, 168, 190
Freely fluctuating rates, 150, 180–182, 191–192, 193
Friedman, I. S., 17
Frondizi, Arturo, 145, 148, 161
Full capacity, 125
Full-employment conditions, 11–12, 19, 29
    and balance-of-payments equilibrium, 63

Gardner, W. R., 17
Gerakis, Andreas S., 149
Germany, 52, 69
    as an economic example, 146
Graham, F., 7
Grains, 44, 175–176
    see also Cereals and linseed
Great depression, 74
Gross domestic product, data on, 64
Gross fixed investment, data on, 65

Haberler, G., 3
Harberger, A. C., 8, 9, 11, 16, 46, 116, 119, 122, 158, 195
Hicks, J. R., 11
Hides, 68, 69, 90, 143, 147
Hinshaw, R., 7, 15
Hirschman, A. O., 2
Home goods, 6, 11, 17, 21, 32, 72
    prices of, 153
Housing, 105, 114, 168
    and monetary policy, 107, 159, 162

Illia, Arturo, 145
Implicit prices, 113, 152–153
Import-competing industries, 157, 169, 181
    index of value added, 66

Import functions, 52ff
Import prices
    in dollars, time series of, 43
    domestic wholesale time series of, 66, 174
Import substitution, 35, 134, 142, 144, 153, 168, 172
Importable goods, 6–7, 14, 19, 21, 32
    in Argentina, 44ff, 55
    data on, 97
    prices of, 151
Imports
    advanced deposits on, 146–147
    Argentine demand for, 47ff, 131
    changes, 142, 173–174
    data on, 66
    demand for, 2, 6
    and gross value of production, 51
    propensity, 10
    restrictions on, 133
    structure of, 48–49, 177
    supply of, 7, 21
Income distribution, 16, 17, 18, 59, 142, 192, 194
    according to factor shares, 112–113
    and inflation, 109ff
    during 1958–1961, 153ff
Income multiplier, 10
Income velocity, 106, 160
    data on, 127
Industrial crops, 72
Inflation, 13, 20, 29, 100, 109ff, 194
    and relative prices, 114–115
    dynamics of, 115ff
Initial effect, 2, 4, 14, 19, 20
Interamerican Development Bank, 61, 90
Interest rate, 14, 24, 106
Intermediate goods, 32, 44, 50
International Monetary Fund, 10, 143, 145, 148, 175, 178
Inventories, 171, 174
Investment, 100, 131, 168–169
    data on, 126–127
    and demand for imports, 59ff

INDEX

Investment (*continued*)
  factors influencing private, 107
  see also Capital formation
Iron and steel, 49, 50, 59
Italy, 68

Johnson, H. G., 4, 10, 17
Jones, R. W., 8
Junta Nacional de Carnes, 88, 143

Kenen, P. B., 17
Kerstenetsky, I., 16, 46, 159, 195
Kindleberger, C. P., 9, 80, 104
Kugler, Walter F., 86

Labor productivity, 136, 141–142, 157, 187
Land tenure, 85–86
Landowners, 21, 157
Laursen, S., 8
Lerner, A. P., 2
Linseed, 68, 71, 78, 86
Livestock sector, 72, 74, 142, 190–191
  output indices, 74, 147
  prices of, 157
  response to price changes, 73, 75
  structure of output, 72
Luxury imports, 59

Machine tools, 52, 179
Machinery, 56, 60, 172
Machlup, F., 13, 14
McKinnon, Ronald I., 47
Maize, *see* Corn
Manufacturing sector, 32, 45
  output of, 133, 170
Marquez, J., 17
Marshall, Alfred, 1, 2
Meade, J. E., 3, 8, 9
Meat, 44, 69, 71, 143, 166–167, 175
  see also Beef
Metals, 55, 60, 169, 180
Metzler, L. A., 2, 8
Mexico, 18
Mining sector, 45, 55, 157, 170
Monetary policy, 13, 14, 20, 24, 141, 158ff, 188

Money, 7
  changes in the supply of, 116–118, 127–128, 147, 159–160
  sources of expansion of, 160–162
Morgan, E. V., 4
Mortgage loans, 107, 147, 160
Motor vehicles, 50, 56, 60, 61, 169, 172, 180
Mundell, R. A., 14, 47
Mutton, 84

Netherlands, 68
Newsprint, 50
Non-wage earners, 17
  demand for exportable goods, 90, 91ff
  demand for imports of, 58, 61
  in total population, 66
Non-wage income
  and investment, 106
  during 1958–1961, 156ff
  savings out of, 102
  time series, 66, 98, 99, 126

Oats, 73, 78
Official capital flows, 43
Oficina de Estudios para la colaboración Económica Internacional, 88
Oil, 45, 50, 55, 148, 168, 169, 172, 177, 180, 187
  and foreign capital, 137, 145
Olivera, J. H. G., 109
Orcutt, G., 52
Organization of American States, 61, 90
Output, changes in global, 142, 166–173, 182, 195

Paper and cardboard, 49, 55
Pascale, A. J., 79
Pazos, Felipe, 18, 194
Pearce, I. F., 7
Perón, Juan D., 133, 149
Petroleum, *see* Oil
Polak, J., 10, 17–18
Prebisch, Raúl, 134, 135, 137, 139, 141, 145, 149

Price controls, 136, 147
Price elasticities, 2, 3, 5, 6, 21, 132
  in the demand for exportables, 87, 91–92
  in the demand for imports, 56ff
  in the supply of exportables, 77–85
Price level, 9, 14–16, 20, 29, 46, 149, 151ff, 158
  annual rate of change, 119, 129–130
Price mechanism, 189ff
Price stability, 134
Private foreign investment, see Foreign capital
Protection, 44, 45, 174
Public enterprises, 164–165, 187
Public opinion, 148, 195
Public sector
  construction expenditures, 133, 167–168
  consumption expenditures, 133, 167–168

Quantitative controls and restrictions, 14, 16, 45, 52, 53, 120, 135, 151, 174
  time series of index of, 66
Quebracho, 147

Railroads, 148, 164, 165, 171, 187
Rainfall index, 77, 79, 95, 171, 187
Reallocation of resources, 6–7, 13, 16, 19, 86, 134, 188
Redistributive effect, 17, 20–30, 184–185
Rentiers, and inflation, 110
Rents, 31, 136
Retentions, 166
Reversal effect, 2, 9, 19
Review of The River Plate, The, 81, 88, 96, 146, 148, 160, 162, 171
Robinson, Joan, 2, 8
Rubber, 49, 50, 52, 55, 59, 172
Rural producers, 20
Rural products
  output of, 134, 144, 171, 186
  wholesale prices, 75, 151

  see also Agricultural sector; Livestock sector
Rye, 78

Salera, Virgil, 20
Salter, W. E. G., 13
Samuelson, P. A., 3
Saving
  changes in, 166–167
  data on, 125–126
  propensity, 10, 22, 38, 100, 102ff, 131
  structure of domestic, 101
Secretaría de Asuntos Económicos, 74, 115
Second World War, 74, 76
Servicio Meteorológico Nacional, 95
Small country case, 5, 6, 7, 11, 21, 70
Smithies, A., 9
Sohmen, Egon, 4, 14, 15, 16, 136
Sorghum, 96, 172, 175
Spraos, J., 8, 18
Stabilization plans
  pre-1955, 133ff
  of December 1958, 145ff
  of October 1955, 134ff
Stock market 161–162
Streeten, P., 3
Strikes, 159, 170–171
Structural rigidities, 40, 189
Sugar cane, 73
Sunflower, 68, 73, 86
Supply functions, 7, 22–23, 76–85

Ta-Chung Liu, 52
Tariffs, 32, 114
Tax structure and policy, 102, 192
  and concessions, 166
Terms of trade, 5, 8, 9, 21, 43, 110–111, 142, 144, 178
Thorp, Rosemary, 149
Total effect, 9
Tradable goods, see Foreign goods
Trade unions, 21, 47, 114, 140
  see also Strikes
Transport costs, 21, 32, 44
Two-good models, 5, 6

Unemployment, 19, 21, 136, 182
United Kingdom, 52, 68, 71, 74
United Nations, 52, 179
United Nations Economic Commission for Latin America, 43, 48, 65, 70, 109, 134, 137, 142, 173, 174
United Nations Food and Agriculture Organization, 70
United States, 52, 69, 71, 133, 148
United States Department of Commerce, 52, 171

Venezuela, 52
Villanueva, Javier, 109

Wage earners, 17, 21, 22
   demand for exportable goods, 89, 91ff
   demand for imports of, 58, 61
   in total population, 66
Wage income, 22, 141
   savings out of, 102
   time series, 65, 98, 99, 126
Wage lag, 17, 21, 132, 137, 148, 154
Wage policy, 153ff
Wage rates, 20, 21, 23, 46, 133, 136, 151
   data on, 127–128
   in industry, 118
   and inflation, 109ff
   during 1958–1961, 153ff
   rural, 110
Walras' Law, 1, 2, 4, 7
Wealth effects, 30
Weather conditions, 171
   see also Droughts
Wheat, 68, 69, 71, 73, 78, 86, 143
   yields, 79
White, W. H., 8
Williams, J. H., 20
Wool, 44, 68, 69, 73, 84, 90, 143, 175
   data on prices and output, 96
   supply responses of, 76ff
World bank, 165